Critical Perspectives on Work and Employment

Series editors:
Irena Grugulis, Bradford University School of Management, UK
Caroline Lloyd, School of Social Sciences, Cardiff University, UK
Chris Smith, Royal Holloway University of London School of Management, UK
Chris Warhurst, University of Strathclyde Business School, UK

Critical Perspectives on Work and Employment combines the best empirical research with leading edge, critical debate on key issues and developments in the field of work and employment. Extremely well-regarded and popular, the series is linked to the highly successful *International Labour Process Conference*.

Formerly edited by David Knights, Hugh Willmott, Chris Smith, Paul Thompson, each volume in the series includes contributions from a range of disciplines, including the sociology of work and employment, business and management studies, human resource management, industrial relations and organisational analysis.

Further details of the *International Labour Process Conference* can be found at www.ilpc.org.uk.

Published:
Maeve Houlihan and Sharon Bolton
WORK MATTERS

Alan McKinlay and Chris Smith
CREATIVE LABOUR

Chris Warhurst, Doris Ruth Eikhof and Axel Haunschild
WORK LESS, LIVE MORE?

Bill Harley, Jeff Hyman and Paul Thompson
PARTICIPATION AND DEMOCRACY AT WORK

Chris Warhurst, Ewart Keep and Irena Grugulis
THE SKILLS THAT MATTER

Andrew Sturdy, Irena Grugulis and Hugh Willmott
CUSTOMER SERVICE

Craig Prichard, Richard Hull, Mike Chumer and Hugh Willmott
MANAGING KNOWLEDGE

Alan Felstead and Nick Jewson
GLOBAL TRENDS IN FLEXIBLE LABOUR

Paul Thompson and Chris Warhurst
WORKPLACES OF THE FUTURE

More details of the publications in this series can be found at http://www.palgrave.com/business/cpwe.asp

Critical Perspectives on Work and Organisations Series

Series Standing Order ISBN 978-0230-23017-0

You can receive future titles in this series as they are published by placing a standing order. Please contact your bookseller or, in case of difficulty, write to us at the address below with your name and address, the title of the series and the ISBN quoted above.

Customer Services Department, Macmillan Distribution Ltd, Houndmills, Basingstoke, Hampshire RG21 6XS, England

Creative Labour

Working in the Creative Industries

Edited by
**Alan McKinlay &
Chris Smith**

palgrave
macmillan

Published by
PALGRAVE MACMILLAN
Houndmills, Basingstoke, Hampshire RG21 6XS and
175 Fifth Avenue, New York, N.Y. 10010
Companies and representatives throughout the world

PALGRAVE MACMILLAN is the global academic imprint of the Palgrave
Macmillan division of St. Martin's Press, LLC and of Palgrave Macmillan Ltd.
Macmillan® is a registered trademark in the United States, United Kingdom
and other countries. Palgrave is a registered trademark in the European
Union and other countries.

ISBN-13: 978–0–230–22200–7   paperback
ISBN-10: 0–230–22200–5   paperback

This book is printed on paper suitable for recycling and made from fully
managed and sustained forest sources. Logging, pulping and manufacturing
processes are expected to conform to the environmental regulations of the
country of origin.

A catalogue record for this book is available from the British Library.

A catalog record for this book is available from the Library of Congress.

Printed and bound in Great Britain by
CPI Antony Rowe, Chippenham and Eastbourne

Contents

List of Tables

Notes on Contributors

Helen Blair completed her doctoral research into the labour markets of film crews at the University of Hertfordshire in 2001. She has since worked for the British Broadcasting Corporation as an employment adviser.

Susan Christopherson is the J. Thomas Clark Professor in City and Regional Planning, Cornell University. She has published widely on firms, production and labour markets in manufacturing, Hollywood and the new media. Her most recent book is *Re-making Regional Economies: Labor, Power and Firm Strategies in the Knowledge Economy* (2007).

Nigel Culkin is Head of Enterprise & Entrepreneurial Development at the University of Hertfordshire and Associate Dean of the Business School. He is Chair of the University's Film Industry Research Group (FiRG) and is a regular contributor to the media on film industry matters. Nigel was recently awarded a £2.5 m grant from the UK government to establish a Film & Digital Media Exchange (FDMX) for the film, TV and digital media industries.

Doris Ruth Eikhof is Lecturer in Organization Studies at the Stirling Management School, University of Stirling, and Research Associate at the Wirtschaftsuniversität Wien, Austria. Her research interests include creative industries, work-life boundaries, social theories in organisation studies and women's work. She has published in international and German academic journals and books, including *Journal of Organizational Behavior* and *Creativity and Innovation Management*, and is co-editor of 'Work Less, Live More? Critical Analysis of the Work-Life Boundary' (2008).

Irena Grugulis is the Professor of Employment Studies at Bradford University School of Management and an AIM Services Fellow. Her research focuses on skills including soft skills, organisational culture, national skill formation systems, fragmenting organisations, retail work and the creative industries. Her latest book is *Skills, Training and Human Resource Development* published by

Palgrave and her research has been funded by the ESRC, EPSRC and the ERDF. She is an associate member of SKOPE, an ESRC-funded research centre split between Oxford and Cardiff and sits on the expert panel of the UK's Commission for Employment and Skills.

Axel Haunschild is Professor of Work, Employment and Organisation at the University of Trier, Germany, and Visiting Professor at the School of Management, Royal Holloway, University of London. His research interests focus on changing forms of work and organisation, employment systems in the creative industries, the institutional embeddedness of work and employment, and the boundaries between work and life. He has published in journals such as *Human Relations, British Journal of Industrial Relations, International Journal of Human Resource Management*, and *Journal of Organizational Behavior*. He recently co-edited *Work Less, Live More? Critical Analyses of the Work-Life Relationship* (2008).

Mike Jones is course director for the MA in Music Industry Studies in the School of Music, University of Liverpool. He is currently working on a monograph – Management and Music Industry. Before taking up his position he was a member of the pop group Latin Quarter, best remembered for the hit record *Radio Africa* and the album *Modern Times*.

Nicole Mayer-Ahuja is Senior Researcher at the Sociological Research Institute (SOFI), University of Göttingen, Germany. Her work focuses on labour, employment and labour market policy, especially with respect to 'high skill' and 'low-skill' services. Selected publications: 'Everywhere is becoming the same?' 'Labour utilisation, regulation and the inherent tensions in transnational IT-production', in: *Work, Organisation, Labour, Globalisation 2008* (with P. Feuerstein); 'Female Labor between Public Employment and Domestic Service. The German Cleaning Trade as a Test for Current Labor Market Strategies', in: *Women's Policy Journal of Harvard*, Volume 3 (2006), 21–39; Normalarbeitsverhältnis in Internetfirmen? Zur schleichenden Entwertung eines Konzeptes, in: *WSI-Mitteilungen* 6/2006, 335–40.

Alan McKinlay is Professor of Management, University of St Andrews and an Associate of ICC, the ESRC-supported research centre for the creative industries (www.capitalisingoncreativity.ac.uk). He has published widely on business and labour history, most recently on British commercial television.

Fredrik Movitz (former Augustsson) is a researcher at the department of Sociology, Stockholm University. His research interests focus on work, organisation, labour market mobility and technology. He is currently involved in research projects aimed at studying unregulated working conditions, causes and effects of mobility among IT-consultants, as well as the formation and organisation of illegal markets for file-sharing.

Andy Pratt is a Reader in Urban Cultural Economy at the London School of Economics. He has researched and consulted the nature of the cultural economy: its location, operations, governance and policy. He is currently conducting research on the 'reputation economy of cultural clusters'.

Keith Randle received his PhD in 1999 from the University of Hertfordshire, UK, where he is currently Director of Research and Consultancy. He also leads the Creative Industries Research and Consultancy Unit [CIRCU] and has published widely on the employment and management of highly qualified 'knowledge workers'. Keith recently completed a major EU-funded study into barriers to diversity in the UK film and television industries and has previously worked on research projects around digitisation, computer games production and employment in both the US and UK film industries. He is a regular contributor to the International Labour Process Conference.

Åke Sandberg is a Professor at the Department of Sociology, Stockholm University. He is continuing the MITIOR research (Media, IT and innovation in organisation and work) that was built up at KTH The Royal Institute of Technology and at Arbetslivsinstitutet (closed down in 2007). His current research interests are in work organisation, and the impact of new forms of management and ICT, with a focus on restructuring of work and industry within IT, Internet and the media. An early book was *Technological Change and Co-determination in Sweden* (1992) and he is now finishing a volume in *English with Critical Scandinavian Perspectives on Management and Work* (2009).

Chris Smith is Professor of Organisation Studies and Head of School of Management, Royal Holloway, University of London. His research interests are in labour process theory, knowledge transfer through the transnational firm, and professional labour (especially engineers). He is currently research-ing tele-nursing in the UK and cross-nationally, and the organisation of the labour process in Chinese factories. He has been active the International Labour Process Conference for many years. Recent publications are: *Remaking Management: Between Global and Local* with Brendan McSweeney and Robert Fitzgerald (2008); *Assembling Work* with Tony Elger (2005).

Dimitrinka Stoyanova is a doctoral researcher at Bradford University School of Management. Her research interests include: creative industries; changing forms of work, organisation and employment; and skills development. Her doctoral thesis explores the influence of the new organisational and employ-ment arrangements on learning and skills development in the UK television industry.

Paul Thompson is Professor of Organisational Analysis in the Department of Human Resource Management at the University of Strathclyde. Amongst his recent publications are *A Handbook of Work and Organization* (co-edited with

Stephen Ackroyd, Pam Tolbert and Rose Batt, 2004) and a 4th Edition of *Work Organizations* (with David McHugh). His research interests focus on skill and work organisation, control and resistance, organisational restructuring and changing political economy. He is Research Notes, Debates and Controversies Editor of *Work, Employment and Society* and an Editor of the Palgrave Series – *Management, Work and Organization*.

Chris Warhurst is Professor of Labour Studies and Director of the Scottish Centre for Employment Research at the University of Strathclyde in Glasgow. He is also co-editor of the British Sociological Association journal *Work, Employment and Society*. His research and publications focus on labour process and labour market issues and developments. Current research examines aesthetic labour, knowledge work and union-led workplace learning. He has published numerous articles, including in *Administrative Science Quarterly, Economic and Industrial Democracy, Journal of Management Studies* and *Sociology*. He has also sole and co-authored and edited a number of books including *Work Less, Live More?* (2008), *The Skills that Matter* (2004), *Looking Good, Sounding Right* (2001) and *Workplaces of the Future* (1998).

Harald Wolf is a sociologist at the Sociological Research Institute (SOFI) at the University of Göttingen, Germany. He also teaches sociology at the University of Kassel. His research focuses on sociology of work and organisations, sociological theory, and French anti-structuralistic social theory. His publications include 'Work and Autonomy. An Essay on the Contradictions and the Metamorphosis of Capitalist Production' (*Arbeit und Autonomie. Ein Versuch über Widersprüche und Metamorphosen kapitalistischer Produktion*, 1999) and (co-edited with Nicole Mayer-Ahuja) 'Unleashed Labour – New Ties. Limits of De-limitation in Media and Cultural Industries' (*Entfesselte Arbeit – neue Bindungen. Grenzen der Entgrenzung in der Medien- und Kulturindustrie*, 2005). He is co-editor of the publication project Cornelius Castoriadis: 'Selected Writings' (*Ausgewählte Schriften*, 2006ff).

Part I
Theory and Overview

Creative Industries and Labour Process Analysis

1

Chris Smith and Alan McKinlay

Introduction

Definitional problems beset the field. What precisely are creative industries and who works in them; what do they produce and are these products commodities or goods with special social and national as well as private individual utility? How are creative goods distributed and how does the form of distribution affect the character of the product; how is a live concert or performance different from a recorded one, and what is the precise relationship between performance, audience and production? Is there a unified definition of the organisational field of creative industries and do those working in this field share common work organisation, employment relations, motivation and purpose?

Overarching terminology used to capture the entire field has shifted from the idea of the arts to cultural industries to creative industries. The concept of *the arts* is widely used as a sub-set for theatre, music and many branches of long-established creative expression with solo or ensemble production at its centre. An *art* also has the connotation of skill, talent or ability, thus drawing attention to the idea of an artist as a trained but also innovative person, with a gift or knack that might be innate, person-specific and hence not easily learnable; hence the centrality of individual expression, calling and aptitude in *the arts*. Asset or skill specificity is highly individualised, specific to the *person*, not occupation or company which is more typical of external and internal labour markets (Osterman, 1984: 174). This makes creative labour in the arts comparatively distinct. When generalised to sectors outside this tight list, such as advertising or new media, the term *the arts* loses purchase because the production system and skill structures in these sectors are different. There are also intense problems of ranking or stratification of taste, with notions of high and low brow, mass and elitist products, tastes and markets. But for reasons of narrowness, the concept of *the arts* is no longer used by those wishing to capture the entire field.

The idea of *cultural industries* raises the opposite problem of being too eclectic and broad. This is because the concept of culture is notoriously opaque, embracing as it does the role of tradition, identity, values and social belonging, with links into sub-cultures, multi-cultures and cultures as expressions of group identities, whether as national culture or youth cultures, counter-cultures or black and ethnic minority cultural identity. How these social manifestations of cultural identity are linked to notions of creativity or an industry or commercial production is a major problem, although culture has the advantage of placing social groups, society and broad definitions of producers and consumers of culture at the centre of the debate (O'Connor, 2007). *Cultural industries* as a term has the major disadvantage because of boundary problems – what to include and what to exclude in the term culture – and the relationship between social and unique or individual production, which is central to ideas of creativity. It also lacks a strong connection to a political economy, as commercialisation of life styles and youth cultures are within industries (fashion and clothing) with conventional mass or batch production labour processes, and are not usefully defined as creative.

Creative industries is the new dominant and politically fashionable term being more inclusive of new and old sectors, such as theatre and new media, but sufficiently discriminating so as to produce a relatively clear industry category. Nevertheless many insist that the term creative industry is too broad, as leading with the term 'creative' makes it difficult to discriminate between scientific/technical creativity and artistic creativity (Haunschild, 2008; Pratt, 2005). However we favour this term in this book to help explore the work of those working within traditional and new sectors that share certain features of innovation, risk, uncertainty, performativity and differentiation from repeat or mass production sectors.[1]

This book is not about definitional themes however, but will instead focus on the production of creative or artistic products, and the labour processes, employment relations and organisation of work that surround the different production processes. These labour processes vary across numerous components of the creative industries, and the book will explore the commonalities and differences between industry segments. Variation in work organisation and structure of the same branches also exists across various national contexts, and the theme of comparative difference is explored across several chapters. Comparative research is important for examining truth statements about 'an industry' or occupational group, as comparative research immediately reveals local prejudices and differentiation, thus testing the robustness of categorical statements about essential features of a particular field. An important part of a labour process account of creative labour in this book is to suggest that one cannot adequately or rigidly divide human labour power into creative and non-creative absolutes, as all human labour involves some creative elements, such that *envisioning* or imagining producing something prior to doing or execution is part of what it is to be human. We will pick this critique up in Chapter 2.

The purpose of the book is to look inside the production or work process of different creative industries, because how work is structured and what people do when they make creative products remains relatively under-researched. Authors within the book use a labour process perspective to different degrees, as what characterises this approach is a focus on production relations, and issues of control and authority, wage-effort exchanges, conflict and social or class relations between the owners of creative capital and those who work as employees or freelancers to help expand the value of this capital and their share of it. A labour process perspective, as we discuss below, looks inside the experience or actuality of production processes and reveals how inputs of human labour, machinery and 'raw materials' are transformed into finished products, which within a capitalist political economy, means creation for the purpose of profit or accumulating more capital, by producing use values which possess high value for both producers and consumers. Applying this framework to labour processes in film, television, theatre and new media will help interrogate some of the broader claims for the creative industries as unique or special sites of production compared with other branches of the economy.

Themes in the book include changes to the division of labour and job structures in key branches of creative industries; the expansion of jobs and reduction in wages as labour supply expands and capital moves around geographically to reduce production costs; the role of social networks for distributing information (especially job information) and people within the industry; the idea of craft or profession in some creative industries and its absence in others; the role of space as a type of social capital – for aggregating companies and people – and how spatial concentrations of creative capital and creative labour are undergoing important shifts as work is de-centred, globalised and distributed away from established locations (such as Hollywood) and the consequences this has for jobs, getting work and the intensity of work. Before examining in detail the structure of the book and the contents of the different chapters, we will briefly outline some of the different ways in which creative industries have been theorised and described.

The creative industries, labour and the state

The creative industries – film, theatre, television, radio, arts and new media – have become a distinctive and expanded sub-sector of the economies of many advanced capitalist countries. Some writers have even suggested a new *class* of employees – 'creative workers' – have emerged in cosmopolitan centres and cities, with their own identity, interests, employment structure, work ethic and networks of organisation and communication that are distinct from other occupational classes (Florida, 2002). The coherence of this 'class' has been questioned however. O'Connor (2007: 39) notes that Florida's creative class is an 'agglomeration' of creative professions' and the 'book is marked by an absence of any empirical investigation into what [the creative class] is (Healy, 2002; Peck, 2005; Montgomery, 2005).' At best this is 'occupational class'; in other words part of the internal differentiation within the waged population of workers; but there is also ambiguity as sellers of creative skills are also a class of petty-owners, and hence class in both a Weberian and Marxist sense can be applied to the category. It is an occupational structure stratified by levels of skills and expertise (which in Florida's case are the vague skills of 'intelligence, knowledge and creativity'), which produce distinctions between the owners of these skills and other waged workers, and not just between the sellers of these skills and those that buy and put them to work. We would suggest that whatever differentiations are opened up between skilled and less skilled workers (and skill hierarchies are normal in all labour markets) it is as *sellers* of labour power that they are united in having to enter labour processes to exchange these labour services for wages, and it is the exchange with owners that is the central economic and class relation, and not internal differentiation as waged workers.

Florida says that the skills or assets that the creative [occupational] class possess, is a *creative capacity* which is 'an intangible because it is literally in their heads' (Florida, 2002: 68). *Capacity* expresses precisely the commodity waged workers sell in the market place, but, as Warhurst and Thompson (2006) note, for 'that capacity to have any utility, it must be transferred from heads to balance sheets via forms of managing knowledge and creativity' and hence we need to explore the dominant relationship between sellers and buyers of 'creative capacity' and not assume that possession of this capacity itself has any economic or sociological novelty. The claim by Florida that the creative class 'are paid to create and have considerably more autonomy and flexibility ...to do so' than those 'primarily paid to execute or plan' raises the problem of not only the uniqueness of this activity to this field, but also the classificatory problem of abstracting creativity, as defined above, as an economic or social category. As Haunschild (2008: 253) has noted: 'since the creation of 'new ideas, new technology and/or new creative content' is not limited to arts, music and entertainment, but is also a core phenomenon of science and engineering, architecture and education, this perspective [a focus on the content of labour] further broadens the definition of creative industries.'

The complicating factor of labour power in the creative industries is the diversity of ownership of the means of production and problematic for the worker of selling or realising labour power through a production or labour process. Some occupational segments may own their means of production (instruments in the case of musicians, for example), and operate as jobbing producers moving from project to project, or venue to venue and hence share labour power features with many jobbing craft workers. They will also seek, as petty commodity producers, to control their intellectual product or property when this is commercialised, and there are major struggles between creative workers and employers over Intellectual Property (IP), especially in relationship to repeats or residuals – a significant issue in the 2007–2008 strike by the Writers Guild of America.[2] The degree of movement between self-employment, employee status and petty producer or owner positions seen in some segments is in contrast to creative occupations that are more typically wage labourers selling their skills or expertise as labour power – voice, looks, embodied and highly personal labour power as in the case of actors for example – through a collective production process and without a continued claim on the intellectual product or profit beyond the hours contracted to produce it. Often, this labour power is idle or not working to reproduce itself in a creative labour process. A typical actor is not usually acting but earning money through non-acting work, yet the individual will maintain a strong craft identity as an actor, and see not working, that is not being in a production process, as normal for the industry. Hence self definition and working practice are not always concurrent; and the under-utilisation of creative labour power is a major feature of segments of the sector, as there are always more people wishing to join the industry for the available demand, and the costs of maintaining this labour power is borne in other sectors, the family of the worker or through capital resources owned by the creative worker. These constraints often confine recruitment into certain segments of the creative industries to those with these other resources, and hence those from middle or upper middle class backgrounds have favoured entry. They also make the business of finding work – bringing labour power to the market – hugely problematic compared with most other labour processes. Hence much of the literature on working in the sector – and several chapters in this book – explore precisely this *problematic of realisation*, namely the difficulty of uniting labour power with labour processes, which strongly defines the experience of 'working' in the creative industries.

Returning to sector terminology, beyond looking at the *content* of creative labour, other approaches have preferred to focus on the special features of creative *industries*, arguing that there are a range of creative and non-creative occupations employed within this sector, which all share the features of the sector, most especially the precariousness of the market for creative products

(Caves, 2000). Success factors normal in mass industries are absent in the creative industries where a 'no-body knows anything' argument remains dominant, as in the film industry where despite massive attempts to reduce uncertainty through star systems, blockbusters, big budgets, ownership concentration and formulaic production – uncertainty remains and expensive flops are normal (De Vany, 2004). According to this perspective the risk and unpredictability of production and consumption shape the dynamic of the industry, and the sector is defined by *outputs*. Hence production for the supply of 'goods and services that we broadly define as cultural, artistic or simply entertainment value' (Caves, 2000: 1) are what constitutes creative industries and these 'products' are significantly different from mass production products because of the uncertainty surrounding their consumption or marketability. Caves' approach has the advantage of arguing that not all work in the creative industries is creative as defined by Florida, but consists of what he calls 'motley crews' of differentiated occupations. But to stress market uncertainty in the selling of creative products as unique, misses huge uncertainties in other areas of commodity production (even mass confectionery for example, Smith *et al*, 1990). More importantly it misses shifts in product markets everywhere to more turbulence, and hence suggestions of flexible specialisation or mass customisation, which despite being overblown, do highlight more rapid rates of product obsolescence, competitive pressures and increased uncertainty in more globalised markets.

Agents in the creative industries are not simply labour and capital; governments play a role because some of the goods produced in the sector are treated as *public goods*, for example those with educational value; others have national or cultural value, both for internal purposes of social or ideological control, and also for inter-country competition and prestige. Finally, state intervention might also be about supporting nascent industries which have innovative or strategic commercial power – as in the 1997 Labour Government championing of creative industries in the UK.[3]

O'Connor (2007: 5) suggested that 'Adorno's notion of the Culture Industry went in parallel with an emergent post-war cultural policy discourse which attempted to intervene against the market in order to secure culture from the miasma of commerciality.' But this public or national agenda for the state has moved towards narrower and more commercial objectives from the 1990s with the move 'from cultural to creative industries' and the discourse of partnership with the private sector being part of the policy strategy for integrating relations between employment in creative industries, production, the market and the state. Many research centres have been developed in universities to map the employment, size and industrial features of different segments of the industry, see for example, creative industries research centre at Copenhagen Business School[4] or the Film Business Academy at Cass

Business School, in the UK. There has also been the growth of new media, culture and arts courses within Universities to satisfy the demand of those seeking work within this emerging sector. There is increasing academic interest in the field. Witness a new *Creative Industries Journal* which has as its mission 'studying and practising activities which have their origin in individual creativity, skill and talent, and which have a potential for wealth creation.' Defining the field of study and practice as 'advertising, architecture, the art and antiques market, crafts, design, fashion, film, interactive leisure software, music, the performing arts, publishing, television and radio.'[5]

Establishing the idea of creative industries as national commercial champions has involved so called 'mapping exercises' which estimate employment and define the sub-sectors to be included within the field. These can distort or exaggerate numbers of 'creative workers', as within each sub-sector – film, video, software, design, publishing, advertising etc – there exists Caves (2000) 'motley crews', with many more routine than creative positions. We should therefore be very cautious of employment statistics. With this health warning, Warhurst and Thompson (2006) quote UK government sources that suggest: '...the creative industries in the UK generate revenues of around £112.5bn and employ some 1.3m people (DCMS 2001).'[6] These 'mapping exercises' are also about differentiating the field both economically and spatially, as O'Connor (2007: 30) has noted:

> First, that the different sub-sectors (music, performance, visual art, TV etc.) were highly networked at the local level and that they operated somehow as 'clusters'. Second, these clusters were generally centred on the larger metropolitan areas, acting as the locus for urban networks and as service hubs for more dispersed sectors (such as crafts or manufacture), suggesting that the City or urbanity itself offered something crucial to the cultural industries sector. Third, that the line between commercial and subsidised sectors, between primarily economic and primarily cultural activities, or indeed between motives of 'art' and motives of profit was by no means clear cut at this local level.

Warhurst and Thompson (2006) using the British case where the government has been active in policy formation, suggest there are three 'industry types' in the creative industries with 'quite different organisations, work and employment' features. The different institutional and organisational settings offer an important mediating relationship for different occupational groups, and add a layer of structural complexity to arguments based on pure ideas of creativity, skills or the content of people's jobs in the field. The three segments include: i. large organisations outside the formally designated creative industries 'with an in-house design, architectural, media facility' such as the public sector where employment conditions reflect those in the sector, and not the occupations at large; ii. large employers in the creative industries, such as major UK television companies, where 'employment practices tend to be more standard, but with higher numbers of freelancers and smaller firms used on a project (temporary) basis;' iii. SMEs in the creative industries 'with a mixture of permanent staffs and more use of freelancers and other small firms to meet variations in workflow or to create capacity to undertake large projects' (Warhurst and Thompson, 2006).

In all three types, 'work is essentially project-based, especially for firms in the second and third categories' and 'work levels vary considerably' and 'this variation contributes to the wider use of freelancers and alliances with other firms to complete projects' (Warhurst and Thompson, 2006). However, while firms in creative industries are typically small, some grow and mature and rationalise along conventional organisational lines, and therefore, one should not assume smallness as some kind of essential quality of the sector. There are, after all, huge corporations as well, such as public broadcasters, the UK BBC, or the 7 giant US media empires: Disney (market value: $72.8 billion); AOL-Time Warner (market value: $90.7 billion); Viacom (market value: $53.9 billion); General Electric (owner of NBC, market value: $390.6 billion); News Corporation (market value: $56.7 billion); Yahoo! (market value: $40.1 billion); Microsoft (market value: $306.8 billion); Google (market value: $154.6 billion) at 2006 values.[7]

Hence whether it is the rise of a new occupational class, a new industry or specific state policy to support a new employment field, there has been a growing interest in creative industries and creative labour.

Why a labour process perspective?

The strength of a labour process approach is that it reveals the dynamics of working in real situations and looks behind the hype and rhetorical claims that can surround new fields of work and employment. There is certainly a lot of excitable puff around the creative industries, whether in regard to the size and significance of the sector, the uniqueness of work and employment relations or the motivation of workers within the sector. As Warhurst and Thompson (2006) note: 'the use of creativity alone as a distinguishing feature tells us very little about the content of work, [or] how it is organised and managed.' Indeed there is considerable diversity between 'creatives'; some with a distinguished craft or professional collective tradition, as with actors; while others are more individualistic, writers for example, while others remain more embedded within a collective technical labour process, as with software writers. In other words, there is looseness about the term that means that detailed empirical research of the type presented in this book, is required to highlight the specificity of each particular case. There is also a neglect of research into the doing or producing side of creative labour, and a bias towards analysis of the consumption of cultural artefacts. While the complexity of consumption in this area is important, production processes and values require more attention as through production one can demystify some of the mystique of the field.

This book offers an insight into the real lives of those working in the sector, drawing on firsthand research, and covering key segments of the sector – film, television, theatre and new media.

The labour process approach centres on the actuality of work from the perspective and orientation of the direct producers, those who provide the service or make the product. The approach is especially concerned with the *control, resistance* and *consent* elements in work; the authority and structure of discipline that ensures that workers not only turn up to work, but are productively employed when there, and engaged in reproducing their own work discipline (Burawoy, 1979). The approach draws from the *indeterminacy* of labour power; the fact that although wages may be known in advance, how much work effort is required is open-ended or left to be determined by workers and managers, as labour product is not given over without some measure of external determination, constraint or structure. The selling of labour power is the selling of a *capacity* that needs to be set within a labour process – with purpose, raw materials and technology – to become transformed into a product, which within capitalism means commodities (goods, products or services) for the market. The approach offers insights into what is distinctive and common to work and worker's experiences in creative industries; in what ways work and labour replicate forms of labour process practice and management control in mass media, mass entertainment, mass publishing and the mass music industry, or conversely, how the creative labour process expresses work values that appear to have their own distinctiveness, such as innovation, self-motivation, individuality, personality, performance, emotional labour, aesthetic labour and self-promotion. We are able to explore how far these values and work practices are transferring into all service encounters.

Recent writing about labour process and labour power has suggested there are two uncertainties or indeterminacies in exchange and production relations between employers and workers: wage-effort bargaining or *effort power*, and mobility-effort bargaining or *mobility power* (Smith, 2006). In other words, how much effort is extracted from the commodity labour power is subject to consent-based bargaining between employers and owners of labour power, namely workers. There is uncertainty around the quantity and quality of effort because of the distinct interests of each party in the exchange, and due to competition between employers over trying to pin down performance standards – hence effort levels are not stable. There is also indeterminacy around mobility, as jobs are not secure and where the worker sells his or her labour power is their choice, and hence a potential source of uncertainty for the employer. There is a relationship between effort and mobility power, as increased intensity of work (effort power by employers) can push workers to exercise their mobility power and quit. There are similar equations between mobility power and effort power as threats of exit can change levels of work intensity.

Applying this language to the work in creative industries, we can say that the mobility power of workers can vary significantly depending on levels of talent and demand, but aside from 'star performers', workers mobility power is limited due to excessive labour supply and insufficient demand, and the difficulty for organised labour (uneven across the whole field) to close-off access to jobs. Hence employers have dominant mobility power over workers which affect effort power and this means employers can extract long hours or intensify work relatively easily. Therefore on the mobility account, workers are typically in deficit, except when they have established 'star status' which can increase an individual's (and possibly their chosen team or network) mobility power. But levels of work effort are also high, not only due to workers' mobility insecurity, but also because of the high occupational or craft value attached to work, this being an essential part of labour power in the field which places high value on intrinsic, person-specific talent.

Getting into creative industries is fiercely competitive, with performance or contest-based auditions for project-based short-term work contracts strong in many areas of the field. Labour power in this environment has to be maintained for the market in periods of idleness, and hence reserves of internal motivation or determination have to be strong, and external command control determination from employers concomitantly are weak and insignificant, as compared with other sectors. There can be exceptionally long periods of idleness for creative workers, when they have to maintain themselves and their labour power as their 'property' ready for the market, which requires, in the case of actors for example, keeping fit, investing in body and aesthetic maintenance, investing in networking and being connected or seen; doing free work to maintain contacts, sanity or collective identity. Getting training and maintaining investment in labour power without a formal hierarchy to train, requires a high degree of self-focused effort by the individual. The *contracting* of labour power in the sector reflects project-based work, absence of stable organisations in many sections of the field, cost-reduction and high labour supply which means that freelance or free-agents are more typical than permanent or secure employees. We have witnessed the hegemony of the self-employed contractor and critique of bureaucratic stability tied to dubious notions of innovation and insecurity, but this is sector specific and within the same occupational group, there can be different employment contracts, as Haunschild and Eikhof (Chapter 8) highlight in the case of theatre in Germany.[8]

In brief then, employers have objectively significant power reserves over effort and mobility in the sector, and workers have difficulty actualising effort and mobility power in their favour. But on the other side of the account, workers do have some key power resources. Firstly, the person-specific nature of much creative talent means it is sometimes non-substitutable, and hence the standard mobility power of the employer (to switch one troublesome worker for another potentially less troublesome one) is not always available. Secondly, excessive labour supply is also problematic for the costs of recruitment, and hence using tried and tested workers might be cheaper than recruiting new ones. Thirdly, because markets do not always function in all aspects of the sector (asset specificity of creative talent inhibits standardisation, for example) social networks or connections are endemic across the field, and these social networks can shelter workers from the pressures of excessive labour supply. Finally, the costs of production and the perishable nature of the product in certain creative industries means the threat of disruption from organised labour especially can be strong, and strategic effort bargaining can be effective – see McKinlay (chapter 9) for examples.

As O'Connor (2007: 52) notes while the neo-liberal hegemony of self-employment and the free agent dominates, this has mixed interpretations and may be ambiguous for the utilisation of labour power as mobility power for workers is expanded at the cost of organisational security:

> The new forms of (self) exploitation by 'creatives' raise another clear tension. Research looking at the nature of creative work involves a difficult set of working conditions, long hours for little or no money, or to the de-unionised, individualised responsibility for work, pensions, unemployment and health benefits; or the unequal power relations when it comes to negotiating IP rights on which they are supposed to thrive; or the constant struggle against de-skilling, usually in the face of new technologies (Ross, 2003; McRobbie, 2002; Bilton, 2007; Banks, 2007). Some see this supposed autonomy as a trick, the myth of free labour (Garnham, 1990; McRobbie, 2002). But others point to the pleasures and satisfactions of such work, as well as a commitment to the product and the process of creation. As Mark Banks makes clear, such creative satisfactions also come with ethical considerations; the 'moral economy' of creative work is one which – as with other areas of work – sets some real limits to economic logics of accumulation (Banks, 2007).

The book chapters

The book is divided into theory or overview chapters in Part I and detailed sector case studies in Part II. Chapters in Part I provide the reader with a coherent signposting of the sector, while the discrete and more specialist chapters in Part II illustrate some of the diversity and commonality within the field, especially cross-national differences and commonalities within the same sector. Hence the book acts as both an introduction to work in the sector using labour process theory and case study examples of different elements of the sector to illustrate the application of this theory.

Part II is split between chapters on core-established creative sectors – film, TV and theatre – and *new media* industries developed on the back of ICTs. The chapters compare differences in scale of production and labour process; they are comparative between forms of employment, although there is a strong emphasis on what is emerging as the 'dominant' model of the self-employed freelancer (against the employee with a stable attachment to a single organisation). Within this dominant employment model, social networks are important for distributing information about work and solidarity, and while 'life styles' of creative workers might be said to create social 'clubs' of shared tastes and normative orientations, it does not mean that being within a shared social milieu is sufficient to find work, and as such individual instrumentalism (what Blair, in Chapter 6 calls 'active networking') is necessary and strong. This breaks down boundaries between 'work and life' (inherent in the idea of 'art for art's sake' and artistic production) but in profoundly negative ways as Randle and Culkin (Chapter 5) demonstrate: 'leisure becomes work as 'seeing friends' means looking for job opportunities; the family becomes a source of continuing financial support, well beyond the years of higher education, as periods outside of paid employment mean falling back on parents; children become an unsupportable burden as periods in work mean long hours.' Christopherson (Chapter 4) also highlights the main problem of networks, as opposed to markets and open ability-based recruitment, namely the strong tendency for them to exclude.

The other critical factor explored in the case study chapters is the issue of space and the use of space as a force of production in creative industries. The theme of capital mobility to escape strongly embedded work organisation in which workers have institutionalised powers is discussed in several chapters, especially Chapter 5; the myth of virtual working, free of spatial constraints, is explored by Andy Pratt (Chapter 10); and the differences between marginal and metropolitan space is discussed by Irena Grugulis and Dimitrinka Stoyanova (Chapter 7). Finally, the role of national institutional differences for embedding creative industries in specific patterns of 'national' structures is explored in Chapter 11 and 12.

Moving to look at the individual chapters in more detail then, in Chapter 2 Chris Smith and Alan McKinlay discuss the nature of creative industries and 'creative labour' through three themes: the characteristics of the work *content* of creative workers, the types of employment *contracts* typical of the sector and finally the form of management *control* used in the sector. The *content* of labour – being creative – does not define the field, due to the envisioning quality of all human labour, and the authors warn against elitist rankings of labour through a creativity skill index. However person-specificity is a relatively unique aspect of work in the creative industries and this does have implications for specific forms of recruitment (agents, auditions, skill competitions for example); forms of labour power delivery (self-employment or free agents); and forms of work organisation – ensembles, bands, etc often with short life spans. As the authors note: ' the creative industries are distinctive in that competitive advantage and profitability are dependent not so much upon the routinisation of work but on harnessing individual and collective creativity.' This implies 'a distinctive managerial imperative that is likely to be extremely wary of deskilling strategies.' That is not to say that management in the creative industries is indifferent to controlling labour or cutting costs, but 'rather, we are more likely to see processes of marketisation that mesh with ideologies of 'releasing' worker creativity from bureaucracy.'

Contracting creative labour can come through long-term employment where continuous organisations exist, but this is harder for one-off projects, where small- and medium-sized enterprises and 'freelance' models of employment now dominate. The authors explore how this paradigm has infected stable areas (such as ITV companies and the BBC in the UK) as an ideological attachment to the supposed greater creativity of non-bureaucratic forms is elevated above stable work within a single organisation. Given the high level of self-motivation involved with getting work in the creative industries, the desire for performance and expression by creative workers, forms of management control typical of hierarchies is largely absent. Instead 'managerial authority turns on managers' ability to *demonstrate* their understanding and involvement in the creative process and to form administrative systems that impinge as lightly as possible on the labour process.'

The chapter looks at the value of labour process theory to the understanding work and employment relations in creative industries, stressing the importance of case study research in different occupations and sectors of the creative industries, as these are important for uncovering sources of difference as well as overlap within the field.

In Chapter 3, Paul Thompson, Michael Jones and Chris Warhurst argue that creative industries exist within two worlds – one of creativity of the artists, and another of the more routine and prosaic political economy of creative industries. They argue that two sets of claims can be identified across the literature on creative and cultural industries: the first, that creative work is the driving force of a 'new economy' (creative intensity); the second, that cultural industries have a special kind of creativity as an essential core characteristic – the aesthetic attributes of product and process (creative distinctiveness). After examining the literature and evidence the authors conclude that little explanatory power resides in expanded conceptions of either set of 'industries'. The central problem in such literature is that writers too frequently move from conception of artistic work to its consumption, without exploring through concrete analysis the activity of management, work, and employment relations. Whilst ultimately cultural industries possess their own logics and dynamics, given the nature of symbolic goods and the associated indeterminacy of outcomes, a narrower conception of creative distinctiveness in cultural industries has some analytical purchase. Hence the authors favour specificity of analysis, and to illustrate these boundary effects they analyse the popular music industry, where they outline a double articulation of creativity: musicians may self-manage their own creativity, but within a framework whereby record company personnel engage in multiple points of management, setting the terms of access to resources and influence, and ultimately to the market-place.

The concentration of media industries in specific cities and regions has meant that economic geographers have been the central discipline in developing our empirical and theoretical understanding of how they operate. Susan Christopherson's many fine-grained studies of the impact of corporate strategies on labour and labour markets in Hollywood and the US film industry have shaped debates for over two decades. In Chapter 4 she reminds us that labour has always adapted to shifts in corporate strategies. The danger, she warns, is that there is a slippage between the 'work' of developing and sustaining the personal ties that criss-cross the labour market and the 'networking' activities of corporate projects and managements. Nor is this slippage avoided by the use of neologisms such as 'heterarchy,' Grabher's (2001) influential, but fundamentally mistaken concept that depicts both local, 'village' sociality and corporate alliances as essentially similar in their capacity for organic self-regulation. While it is vital to register the social ties that ease job search, so it is no less important to acknowledge the unintended, structural effects these have for different types of workers. As Hollywood has shifted away from mid-range movies to global blockbusters, so the proportion of permanent employment has dropped as product portfolios have shrunk. Of course, since 1945 Hollywood studios have concentrated on genre and star vehicles to reduce market uncertainty: Christopherson is highlighting an acceleration of this long-established trend (Sedgwick, 2002).

Together with this move in production priorities, Christopherson points to the increase in young, college-trained labour ready to accept temporary, poorly-paid assignments to build their experience, contacts, and reputations.

The craft identities – and the union jurisdictions to which they were bound – are giving way to more amorphous job titles and roles. Such 'hybrid' labour has learnt to cope with depleted budgets and foreshortened deadlines, but at the cost of accepting a labour market immune to union regulation. Workers struggles to cope with this new, kaleidoscopic production system by intensifying its use of established worker networks to mediate this increasingly unfamiliar, uncertain, and balkanised labour market. One key fracture is gender: one man's inclusive network is another woman's almost impenetrable charmed circle. Gender disparities in job opportunities and salary levels have increased as Hollywood has concentrated on global blockbusters. Together with downsized in-house writing and production staffs, Hollywood has sub-contracted vital roles to *established* social networks to reduce risks as it saves cost. The uncertainty that has *always* been a characteristic of jobs in the media industries has increased in the last decade, yet we know little of how such risks are perceived, evaluated, and coped with by creative labour over time. Equally, there has been little detailed investigation of the formation of corporate strategies in the media industries, beyond issues of financial engineering and public policy concerns over, for example, the nature of political debate or retaining national distinct cinemas. Nor do we have any detailed appreciation of how work roles and labour market opportunities are reshaping social identities. We can see an abrupt move from what were clear craft loyalties based on tools, techniques and the labour process to, perhaps, less focused identities defined, in part, by an acceptance of risk and a *rejection* of 'outmoded' production-based identities. Just as broad categories such as 'knowledge work' threaten to usurp the defining prerogatives of the professions, so the easy use of the umbrella term 'creative labour' can mask significant – and sometimes deliberate – changes in job jurisdictions and contracts. Trade unions and producer associations, in Hollywood and beyond, cannot develop effective recruitment or representation strategies if they remain wedded to concepts of labour that fail to recognise these profound shifts in the identities and networking practices of contemporary media workers.

It has become commonplace to understand the dominant mode of organisation in the creative industries as the network, rather than the 'market' or 'hierarchy.' And this is true whether the subject is a global alliance between corporations, the intimate ties of knowledge, mutuality and trust that comprise collegiality, or the information screening and diffusion that increase the efficiency of labour markets. In all cases, however, network is a term that is almost always couched in wholly positive terms: the dynamic, flexible, social alternative to the impersonality of market forces or the dead-hand of corporate bureaucracy. Several chapters in this collection examine such phenomena. A particular strength of these chapters is their focus on networks in specific times and places: sector, project, or region.

Keith Randle and Nigel Culkin (Chapter 5) provide an account of working in the entertainment industries in southern California, and the sources of threats to film and television segments of the industry as work migrates to Canada and other production sites. Freelance working in the US entertainment industries provides a graphic picture of the insecurity and uncertainty of project-based employment in the creative industries. The chapter opens with a discussion of the Hollywood film industry and the sources of employment uncertainty in the audio visual media industries more generally. The chapter dove-tails with that of Christopherson, and provides empirical details of the coping strategies of workers in the new environment. The traditional strength of industrial relations institutions in Hollywood have reduced as market uncertainties, the increased mobility of film capital and greater competition have weakened these sources of labour support. Against this background the chapter, using informant interviews, aims to examine the nature of employee strategies in a climate of uncertainty. These include amongst others, working for free and increased reliance on family support. Thus the chapter provides evidence of changes to the spatial concentrations of production mentioned above. While detailing background to employment relations in film and television, the main thrust of the chapter examines 'the reality of freelance work' as described by a panel of respondents. This evidence shows how increasing competition has affected finding work, and how longer periods without work mean more 'free working' simply to maintain contacts and labour power; and how this throws workers back on the resources of family support. Hence the traditional ways in which individuals start and develop their careers are being disrupted, and the author's interviews comment on the personal impacts on work that have been introduced due to the structural shift of employment out of Los Angeles.

In Chapter 6 Helen Blair's study of the social networks of a UK film crew is embedded in a wider consideration of how we understand the formation, durability and purposes of social networks in, amongst other things, building a reputation and finding work. For all the categorical sophistication of four decades of research into social networks, there is little insight into how workers gain access to – or develop their own – resources or how agency operates in such complex, dynamic contexts. Agency, Blair suggests, is vital to the dynamism of social networks, yet there have been few empirical studies of how this plays out in practice. Part of the explanation, of course, is the enormity of the methodological and logistical difficulties confronting any long-run or comparative study of social networks.

Theoretically, network research is bedevilled by a false dichotomy between, on the one hand, a rational calculating agent and, on the other hand, agents who are little more than unconscious dupes of established routines and habits. Blair seeks to overcome these false alternatives by using the concept of 'active networking'. Active networking is employed to capture both formal, rational networking activities and the maintenance and use of informal communications to convey one's self-image of, perhaps, professional competence or creativity and to receive soft information about job prospects. Soft information could include not just the availability of a job and its technical demands but also important impressions about the social ordering of a long-established film crew. Sociability, a capacity to read and adapt to a social setting quickly, is no less important than technical competence in a project-based organisation, working as they do to tight deadlines. For the job-seeker, the aim, to amend Mark Granovetter's (1973, 1983, 1985) notion of the 'embeddedness' of social networks, is to be a *familiar stranger*, socially adept *and* technically competent. For the individual hiring through social networks, the task is to establish which recommendations can be endorsed without personal knowledge of the applicant. And for the sponsor, the calculation involves both an evaluation of their own reputation and whether the job-seekers performance will enhance or jeopardise this important source of social capital.

In Chapter 7 Irena Grugulis and Dimitrinka Stoyanova provide a sectoral study of skill formation in film and TV, and thus add new insights into the differences and overlaps between these processes in a regional and geographically marginal location compared with more metropolitan centres. Whereas the literature focuses (understandably) on the activity of 'hubs' or the centres of excellence, Grugulis and Stoyanova suggest professional work and occupational learning are not confined to these areas and regionally-based networks, with all the limitations that that these possess are also important. Skill acquisition and development occurs through the medium of a community of workers, where newcomers learn on the job through observation and discussion with their peers and their entry into a professional network (coupled with the effectiveness of that network) is central to the success or failure of skills development. Generalising beyond the specific study, the authors speculate that this pattern follows optimistic predictions of the way expert labour will function in the future. Their research certainly reveals how effective professional communities can be at supporting skills development across formal organisational boundaries (see, for example Finegold, 1999; Blair, 2001; Piore and Sabel, 1984).

Clearly this form of development encourages and supports rather different behaviours to those fostered by a skill formation system based on lifetime employment and strong internal labour markets and we might expect technical skills to be combined with strong social skills, impression management and self presentation as opposed to, perhaps, loyalty, independent judgement and rigorous professional standards. Such communities or 'learning networks' are still comparatively understudied so this group of workers are of interest. The chapter opens with a discussion of work and employment in the Film and TV industry in Britain, before moving to examine their distinctive contribution, namely a focus on 'community skill' formation within a regional setting. Evidence is gathered through fieldwork and the authors quote informants experiences of 'getting a foot in the door' and 'learning on the job'.

In Chapter 8 Axel Haunschild and Doris Eikhof examine the social character, life style and motivations of German actors and how these interact with their labour process practices. They apply new German theories of employment to discuss this specific sector and seek to make generalisations about project-focused creative production in general. This type of work requires a high level of flexibility and mobility by creative workers as this requires severe uncertainties for work planning for both organisations and individuals. Working in such contexts can be interpreted as 'self-employed employees' characterised by high degrees of self-control, self-marketing and economisation of life. The aim of the chapter is to explore the effects of working as self-employed employees in a specific creative industry: German theatre. Based on qualitative empirical research, the chapter analyses how self-control, self-marketing and economisation of life shape the labour process in theatres. Finally, the chapter deduces general consequences of working in project-focused work relations.

This chapter looks at labour market strategies of creative worker and how these strategies impact on the labour process. As such the chapter proposes to fill a gap in the existing literature by analysing project-focused work from a wider perspective of trans-organisational work of theatre artists at an individual level by using the concept of 'Arbeitskraftunternehmer' or 'self-employed employee'. The analysis is based on 45 in-depth interviews in three major German theatres and in selected inter-firm institutions. The concept of the 'self employed employee' is more familiar in Germany and does not describe a category of employment so much as a broader theoretical terrain to illustrate a highly market-oriented and individualised form of work supply. The term 'self-employed employment' was not coined to describe existing forms of work or employment and their specific underlying contractual arrangements and as such it is an '...analytical framework for analysing a mode of labour use which, at the individual level, is characterized by the following three features: (1) a high degree of self-control, (2) self-marketing, and (3) economization of life together with blurring boundaries between work and private life.'

The chapter shows how: 'Networking and the strategic accumulation and use of social capital are the main practices of self-marketing in theatre. For intrinsically motivated self-employed employees, working in trans-organizational projects leads to a seemingly paradoxical situation: Individuals understand themselves as creative, self-controlled and intrinsically motivated bohemians (for whom "art for art's sake" is a central professional value), but at the same time they have to be very clever as well as calculating managers of themselves as human resources.' Self-employed employees do not separate work and life with respect to, for instance, time, place or partners, but tend to mix or integrate both spheres. The authors suggest that lessons can be generalised from this sector and they argue that the sector's dynamics echo wide-ranging changes of the labour process beyond the creative industries.

The labour processes of the creative industries are – like any other industry – necessarily collective and involve issues of job controls, managerial authority, efficiency and coordination. Too often the object of academic study is defined in terms of empty abstractions, such as 'the organisation' or 'the project,' with little or no empirical grounding or sense of long-run change and continuity. Studies of the creative industries that simply assume that a loose, shifting labour process is a 'natural' response to the functional requirements of a project-based industry ignore the role of employers in *unmaking* regulated labour markets and *making* a deregulated market regime. Alan McKinlay's (Chapter 9) study of British commercial television locates contemporary work organisation as the result of a systematic assault on job controls and union contracts that stretched over two decades. From the foundation of the commercial sector in the late 1950s, union rules were codified in increasingly comprehensive national agreements. This national contract established a *de facto* pre-entry closed shop in which only union members could work. The national contract allowed the broadcast union to control local and national labour supply. Each task in a complex, time-sensitive labour process was the jurisdiction of a specific craft group. The television crafts developed strong identities and jealously guarded their job domain. Encroachments into neighbouring jurisdictions were rare and incurred heavy penalties, particularly for management. Accordingly, management and unions assumed mutual responsibility for a stable labour process that absorbed technical change into the *status quo*.

This regulated regime began to dissolve in the first half of the 1980s as key companies confronted the union. In turn, this coincided with a more assertive bargaining strategy by the national employers' federation. By 1988, the national agreement had been virtually abandoned. Over the next decade the main broadcasting union all but collapsed as controls of working time, contracts and work organisation evaporated. The broadcasting union rebuilt a presence in the commercial sector, but has lost all control over labour supply, has at most minimal control over role definitions, and the correspondence between work and union identity has virtually disappeared.

The main drivers of change in commercial television have been the penetration of accounting and performance measures into the fabric of the labour process. Nevertheless, McKinlay argues that the deregulated landscape of the contemporary television studio has opened up some paradoxical spaces for creativity. He portrays not so much a single television labour process as a spectrum that ranges from highly choreographed, high-budget network productions to local, 'live' programmes. Across the range, however, no programme form allows for the resurrection of craft controls or identities. Rather, echoing Christopherson's account of the emergence of new hybrid job titles in the US film industry, McKinlay hints at the ways in which television crews gain glimpses of how production *could* be organised differently, ways in which their collective skills are not just used but enhanced. Above all, crew members were required not just to use their craft skills but also to make aesthetic decisions about the look and feel of the programme. Of course, in commercial television, these are just that: paradoxical moments of collective, creative space that close down quickly as the crew disperse onto other projects. This rediscovery of the reciprocity and the language of mutual responsibility for a project is, suggests Banks (2006), the harbinger of a different sort of moral economy in the creative industries that is at odds with the realities of self-exploitation identified by many commentators (see Bilton, 2007; Ross, 2003). Further still, these individual experiences are collectively woven into an overarching narrative that provides a form of collective self-regulation that both limits *and* venerates entrepreneurialism, professionalism and a determination to complete projects to deadline and budgets, no matter how unrealistic (Wittel, 2001). The *craft* identity of broadcasting labour has virtually disappeared. Perhaps these fleeting moments of collective technical and aesthetic work will form the basis of 'new' identity of broadcast professionals, with no necessary connection to a shared craft heritage.

Human geographers, as noted above, have played a seminal role in charting the development of the creative industries, from the cluster to the city to the neighbourhood. Dense social networks based on intense face-to-face communication and concentrated in specific locales were identified by the geographers of culture. 'Place' itself became an essential *force of production*, especially where particular locations became identified not just with effective economic activity but also, and no less importantly, with specific cultural movements. This was as true for the 'Swinging London' of the 1960s as for 1980s Seattle and grunge, and the late 1990s dotcom boom of San Francisco. This interpenetration of cultural and business activities embedded in specific places has been empirically demonstrated by cultural geographers (see Scott, 2000). The inherent uncertainties of cultural products often results in a complex co-production process between client and provider, especially during the definition an innovative product or service (Wittel *et al*, 2002). Essentially, these networks operate as something between a collective factory and a collective entrepreneur.

Andy Pratt's (Chapter 10) study of the emergence of the new media industry of San Francisco demonstrates an acute sensitivity to time, place and process. This location of industrial development is especially important when considering new media which held the promise of a perfect virtuality that completely transcended place. On the contrary, just as there are geographies of distribution and consumption for new media, so also there are location-specific clusters of production. Indeed, Pratt offers something of a micro-geography of a global industry. He focuses on one small place, a scruffy park that became a focal point for San Francisco's emergent new media sector. The overblown hype that surrounded the dotcom boom was not just that this technology enabled a 'perfect' market for goods and services, but also a new form of enterprise organisation entirely based on specific projects. In practice, this rhetoric reflected much more chaotic processes on the ground. The life-cycle of firms was not perfectly synchronised with that of projects. Rather, firms, or at least a handful of core staff, would remain more or less intact while churning through technologies, staff and wildly different business models. New media workers did not just soak up the sun in this Bay area park, but used it to update their skills, awareness of new business plans, and to project their entrepreneurial/technical selves to their lunching peers. Nor was this voracious networking simply bounded by place. Very real temporal constraints were placed on new media entrepreneurs/workers who had to work and play in the firms, bars and restaurants with the most buzz; hence, far from being freed from 'old economy' restraints that tie production to specific times and places, the new media industries exhibited extreme locational and temporal specificity.

If geographies of physical and social spaces have been dominated by the neighbourhood and the city, the two final chapters in the books add to this by considerations of national employment systems. They explicitly consider the relationship between national employment systems and the new media industries. The management and organisation of knowledge and work in the German internet industry is considered by Nicole Mayer-Ahuja and Harald Wolf (Chapter 11); the Swedish case by Fredrik Movitz and Åke Sandberg (Chapter 12). Both cases are markedly different from the experience of San Francisco described by Andy Pratt (Chapter 10). Where the San Francisco labour market was unregulated and highly volatile, in Sweden and Germany employment was much more permanent, and organisations more conventional in terms of their internal hierarchies and reward systems. In Swedish interactive media companies, employment was relatively stable and contracts typically permanent, in sharp contrast to the American experience of chaotic churn. The Swedish employment contracts were peculiarly imprecise relative to the national norm, but were far from the freelance project-bounded contracts of America.

The German case sits somewhere between the American and the Swedish experiences. There is extensive freelance employment in the German internet industry, but this was regulated to some degree by organised labour pools. There were two areas in which all three cases had similar patterns of organisation. First, the main form of labour control strategy was 'self-organisation', a pervasive assumption that made for an uneven and uncomfortable development of employing bureaucracies. Second, in all three settings, this 'self-organisation' included workers search to maximise their individual autonomy and a willingness to sacrifice any reasonable notion of work-life balance. Again, as both the German and Swedish cases highlight, the danger is that we mistake the unsustainable expectations of a young workforce in an emerging industry with a permanent *status quo*. Only long-run panel data would allow us to track how the ethos of 'self-organisation' and internet career structures has actually developed or evolved.

The Swedish study also provides two important methodological correctives to short-run studies of particular places, companies or occupations. The Swedish methodology was replicated by the German study. Inevitably, such snap-shot studies are prone to being bedazzled by the shock of the new. Equally, by concentrating on the specificities of a single moment, snap-shots are necessarily atemporal and aprocessual, liable to generalise from – or rather conflate – the needs of a particular phase of a project. The first methodological development is their use of surveys and interviews over time. This allows the Swedish study both to capture the wider distribution of tasks undertaken by new media workers and something of how they relate their project-based experience to their career development. By focusing on a broader range of tasks, Movitz and Sandberg remind us that new media employees have responsibilities that are not unlike those in any organisation, large or small: reporting on project, negotiating, specifying targets, coordinating production. Nor are creative workers 'creative' all the time. Second, by categorising the labour process into three distinct elements – aesthetic, technical, and economic – we can compare project, firm, sector and national forms of organising interactive media production. This tripartite schema *does* allow for genuine comparative research.

Indeed, the Swedish study could be used as a template for how to study the creative industries more generally. Of course, in practice, these categories of task overlap. But, if Swedish employment contracts differ markedly from the 'natural' market assumptions that have shaped the Anglo-American experience, the production *is* organised around the project. Project management restricts – or directs – the 'creativity' of creative labour to specific phases, tasks and individuals. 'Creativity' is not, therefore, a necessary feature of all parts of the labour process. Again, this is an obvious, but important, theoretical counter to any futile search for the moment of 'pure' creativity. Much more important is the finding that production is characterised by a blurring of vertical hierarchies and complex, iterative exchanges across job roles as expertise is swapped and developed. The development of a wide range and unusually deep forms of tacit knowledge could be symptomatic of an emerging industry. It remains to be seen the extent to which industry standard modes of project management bureaucratise such tacit knowledge, and whether such administrative innovations target the technical and economic aspects of creative labour and remain frustrated by the elusiveness of 'creative' labour.

Notes

1 For an excellent overview of these issues and one which maintains a concern with arts/cultural production and not just consumption, see O'Connor (2007).

2 The Writers Guild of America 'demanded a greater share of residuals from DVD sales, new media revenues (digital downloads of movies and television shows), and jurisdiction over animation and reality television shows, which employ non-union writers. Before the final settlement was reached, the WGA removed their proposal on DVD residuals and concentrated instead on the issues involving new media and jurisdiction over reality shows and animation.' (Klowden and Chatterjee, 2008: 16) See: http://www.milkeninstitute.org/pdf/writers_strike.pdf writers.

3 See O'Connor (2007: 41–7) for an extensive discussion of the role of New Labour in shifting government towards 'creative industries' in the UK.

4 http://uk.cbs.dk/forskning_viden/institutter_centre/institutter/imagine/menu/publikationer

5 http://www.intellectbooks.co.uk/journals.appx.php?issn=17510694

6 **Table 1.1** Disaggregated employment in the UK creative industries for 2001

Industries	Employees
Software & Computer	555,000
Publishing	141,000
Music	122,000
Television & Radio	102,000
Advertising	93,000
Design	76,000
Performing Arts	74,000
Film & Video	45,000
Art & Antiques Market	37,000
Crafts	24,000
Architecture	21,000
Interactive Leisure Software	21,000
Designer Fashion	12,000
Estimated Total Employment	**1,322,000**

From Warhurst and Thompson (2005).

7 http://www.motherjones.com/news/feature/2007/03/and_then_there_were_eight.pdf

8 Previous centres of secure, bureaucratic waged labour forms, such as the BBC, have now undergone retrenchment, delaying and downsizing. This has effects of transforming former employees (who had salaries, access to internal training rights, job ladders, and pensions) into independent producers or small production companies. However as then Chairman of the BBC makes clear below, insecurity can have a negative impact of innovation, against assumptions that entrepreneurial insecurity keeps talent focused:

> Casualisation [of employment in broadcasting] is leading to derivative ideas. You give the commissioners what you think they want, not what you are passionately dying to make and believe in. Because you're desperate for the work. Somewhere in British broadcasting there has to be a bedrock of sustainable talent with time to think, to observe, to absorb what's going on in the world outside broadcasting and to turn that experience into programmes of challenge, ambition, quality and innovation. Innovation does not come from watching other channels. But in return for the huge privilege of secure funding [employment security] that this implies, the BBC has to be able to demonstrate it is spending the licence fee prudently in the public interest. And it has to be able to do that openly and transparently.

Sources: Michael Grade Speech 'Building Public Value' Tuesday 29 June 200[0]4 ref from Website [http://www.bbc.co.uk/print/pressoffice/speeches/ stories/bpv_grade]

REFERENCES

Banks, M. (2006) 'Moral economy and cultural work', *Sociology*, 40 (3): pp. 455–72.

Banks, M. (2007) *The Politics of Cultural Work*. London: Palgrave Macmillan.

Blair, H. (2001) 'You're only as good as your last job: the labour process and labour market in the British film industry'. *Work, Employment and Society*, 15: 149–69.

Bilton, C. (2007) *Management and Creativity: From Creative Industries to Creative Management*. Oxford: Blackwell.

Burawoy, M. (1979) *The Politics of Production*. London: Verso.

Caves, R.E. (2000) *Creative Industries: Contracts Between Art and Commerce*. Cambridge, Mass: Harvard University Press.

Klowden, K. and Chatterjee, A. (2008) *Writers' Strike of 2007–2008 The Economic Impact of Digital Distribution* Californs: Milken Institute – California Center, http://www.milkeninstitute.org/pdf/writers_strike.pdf

De Vany, A.S. (2004) *Hollywood Economics: How Extreme Uncertainty Shapes the Film Industry*. London: Routledge.

►

▶
Department for Culture, Media and Sport (DCMS) (2001) *Creative Industries, Mapping Document*. London: DCMS.

Finegold, D. (1999). 'Creating self-sustaining, high-skill ecosystems', *Oxford Review of Economic Policy*, 15: 60–81.

Florida, R. (2002) *The Rise of the Creative Class*. New York: Basic Books.

Garnham, N. (1990) *Capitalism and Communication: Global Culture and the Economics of Information*. London: Sage.

Grabher, G. (2001) 'Ecologies of Creativity: The Village, the Group and the Heterarchic Organisation of the British Advertising Industry', *Environment and Planning A*, Vol. 33 (2): 351–74.

Granovetter, M. (1973) 'The Strength of Weak Ties', *American Journal of Sociology*, 78 (6): 1360–80.

Granovetter, M. (1983) 'The Strength of Weak Ties: A Network Theory Revisited', *Sociological Theory*, 1: 201–33.

Granovetter, M. (1985) 'Economic Action and Social Structure: The Problem of Embeddedness', *American Journal of Sociology*, 91 (3): 485–510.

Haunschild, A. (2008) 'Challenges to the German Theatrical Employment System: How Long Established Institutions Respond to Globalisation Forces', in Smith, C., McSweeney, B. and Fitzgerald, R. (eds) *Remaking Management Between Global and Local*. Cambridge: Cambridge University Press.

Healy, K. (2002) 'What's new for culture in the new economy?', *Journal of Arts Management, Law and Society*, 32 (2): 86–103.

McRobbie, A. (2002) 'Clubs to companies: Notes on the decline of political culture in speeded up creative worlds', *Cultural Studies*, 16 (4): 516–31.

Montgomery, J. (2005) 'Beware "the Creative Class". Creativity and Wealth Creation Revisited', *Local Economy*, 20: 337–43.

O'Connor, J. (2007) *The Cultural and Creative Industries: A Review of The Literature*. London: Creative Partnerships, Arts Council of Great Britain.

Osterman, P. (1984) (ed.) *Internal Labor Markets*. MIT, Mass: The MIT Press.

Peck, J. (2005) 'Struggling with the Creative Class', *International Journal of Urban and Regional Research*, 29: 740–70.

Piore, M. and Sabel, C. (1984) *The Second Industrial Divide: Possibilities for Prosperity*. New York: Basic Books.

Pratt, A. (2005) 'Cultural Industries and Public Policy: An oxymoron?', *International Journal of Cultural Policy*, 11 (1): 31–44.

Ross, A. (2003), *No Collar: The Humane Workplace and its Hidden Costs*. New York, NY: Basic Books.

Scase, R. and Davis, H. (2001) *Managing Creativity*. Milton Keynes: Open University Press.

Scott, A. (2000) *The Cultural Economy of Cities*. London: Sage.

Sedgwick, J. (2002) 'Product Differentiation at the Movies: Hollywood, 1946 to 1965', *Journal of Economic History*, 62 (3): 676–705.

Smith, C., Child, J. and Rowlinson, M. (1990) *Reshaping Work, the Cadbury Experience*. Cambridge: Cambridge University Press.

▶

Smith, C. (2006) 'The double indeterminacy of labour power: labour effort and labour mobility', *Work, Employment and Society*, 20 (2): 401–14.

Warhurst, C. and Thompson, P. (2006) 'Assumptions and Evidence: Work and Organisation in the UK Creative Industries', mimeo *Scottish Centre for Employment Research,* Department of Human Resource Management, Business School, University of Strathclyde, Glasgow Scotland.

Wittel, A. (2001) 'Towards a Network Sociality', *Theory, Culture and Society,* 18: 51–76.

Wittel, A., Lury, C. and S. Lash (2002) in S. Woolgar (ed.) *Virtual Society? Technology, Cyberbole, Reality.* Oxford: Oxford University Press.

http://www.wipo.int/ip-development/en/creative_industry/bibliography.html

Creative Labour: Content, Contract and Control

2

Chris Smith and Alan McKinlay

Introduction

The 'creative industries' have emerged as a key metaphor for mainstream management and organisation: project-based organisations deploying flexible technologies used by labour in high-trust, but ephemeral, teams. If the dissolution of the Hollywood 'system' into flexible specialisation (Christopherson and Storper, 1989) is portrayed as emblematic of meso-level changes, then the improvisation of jazz musicians has become iconic for the qualities of intuition and spontaneity deemed necessary for effective work teams or said to characterise work where conception and execution, composition and performance occur 'in concert' (Kamoche *et al*, 2002: 101). Despite the growing attention to film, music, advertising and television, however, the nature of creative *labour*, the creative labour process, and the management of creative labour, have remained little examined.

This overview paper is organised in three sections. First, we examine the content – the *labour* – of work in the creative industries. Although all labour necessarily involves some degree of creativity, the creative industries are distinctive in that competitive advantage and profitability are dependent not so much upon the routinisation of work but on harnessing individual and collective creativity. This implies a distinctive managerial imperative that is likely to be extremely wary of deskilling strategies. That is not to say that management in the creative industries is indifferent to controlling labour or cutting costs. Rather, we are more likely to see processes of marketisation that mesh with ideologies of 'releasing' worker creativity from bureaucracy. Second, we consider the range of employment contracts used in the creative industries. Above all, the sector has experienced a profound shift from internal and regulated labour markets to labour as atomised independent contractors. The networks of friendship and shared experience that are precondition of the 'fast trust' essential to the viability of the sector's project-based organisation are also mechanisms that allow labour to cope with highly fragmented labour markets. Third, given the strong identification of creative labour with the production process and its output and the uncertain profitability of cultural products, the forms of labour control tend to rely on high degrees of self-motivation. While the management of self-motivated labour reduces fixed administrative costs, it does expose management to intense scrutiny in terms of its organisational, innovative and creative capabilities. In the creative industries, managerial authority turns on managers' ability to *demonstrate* their understanding and involvement in the creative process and to form administrative systems that impinge as lightly as possible on the labour process.

Between creative and mass industries

Analyses of creative industries have long drawn upon 'industrial' metaphors. Hollywood's 'studio system' is often portrayed as analogous to mass production: standardised 'safe' products, mass marketing and routinised production. The disintegration of the studio system has been depicted as a transition from mass production to 'flexible specialisation'. Similarly, Scott Lash has argued that the creative industries *practiced* the management and organisational techniques of 'post-Fordism' in *advance* of manufacturing and services. In both cases, however, the implicit assumption that the media and manufacturing industries have developed in parallel with little or no diffusion of personnel, practices, or ideologies. This seems an unrealistic assumption: it neglects, for instance, the inter-penetration of executive personnel; the increasing cross-ownership of media and consumer electronics; the power, reach and durability of mass production management practices; and the continuous interaction of mass production and flexible systems in all industries.

The importance of mass production as a regulative ideal for managers in the creative industries stretches beyond the 'studio system'. For over 40 years Disney's animation production was *explicitly* modelled on strictly hierarchical management and a tightly controlled, routinised labour process, closely modelled upon scientific management and Fordism (Bryman, 2000). Similarly, Berry Gordy, founder of Motown Records, claims he modelled the production of pop music on the assembly line principles learnt in Detroit. The backing tracks were laid down by the Funk Brothers and vocals were added by different artistes until one track was singled out by Motown's 'quality control department'.

> ...my own dream for a hit factory was quickly taking form, a concept that
> had been shaped by the principles I had learned on the Lincoln-Mercury

assembly line. At the plant the cars started out just as a frame, pulled along on conveyor belts until they emerged at the end of the line – brand spanking new cars rolling off the line. I wanted the same concept for my company, only with artists and songs and records (Gordy, 1994: 140).

If contemporary manufacturing is defined by the pursuit of a durable balance between efficiency and flexibility, between standardisation and differentiation, then similar competitive pressures are experienced by even the most elite sectors of the cultural industries. According to some commentators contemporary international opera has become a high-brow form of just-in-time labour process in which a standardised cultural product is differentiated by the addition of a name singer in much the same way as the global car makers combine shared components with distinctive carcasses and brands to cover a market spectrum.

...most European opera houses had dissolved their resident companies after World War II, and now these singers toured as international vocal consultants. Their training had become a matter of mastering a menu of ready-made parts to be marketed in auditions and assembled just-in-time. Artists flew in the morning, rehearsed during the afternoon, delivered their arias in the evening, and caught the last plane home the same night. An audience that did not know the story of the opera by heart and had not studied the score and libretto had no chance of understanding a complex plot like that of *The Marriage of Figaro* or *Cosi Fan Tutte* when it was produced in such an industrial way. Unschooled newcomers believed opera to be a competition to reach high C amid a demonstration of lovely arias interspersed with bits of incomprehensible knockabout. One might even wonder if all the singers themselves knew the details of the plot they so professionally delivered on stage. The strange logic of modern production technique had shortened rehearsal time and ignored recitatives; it had turned operatic art into show-biz entertainment (De Monthoux, 2004: 12–13).

Disentangling metaphor from substance, understanding the dynamics of management knowledge in and between sectors is essential if we are to go beyond broad allusions to a discredited Fordist 'past' and a bright flexible 'present'.

The labour of creative workers

In this section we are interested in comparing the *content* of work of the creative worker – artist, musician, actor or writer – with non-creative occupations in order to examine in what ways being innovative or original is divergent from other types of labour. In other words, how far do the *traits* of being a creative worker come together in a typology sufficiently distinctive to warrant different ways of understanding and classifying the economic and social qualities of the labour process of the creative worker? Or conversely, how this category of work shares general characteristics with other (or all) human labour.

There is a misconception connected with the idea of 'creative labour': that somehow the act of creativity, and occupations associated with creative work such as art, writing, music or film, are fundamentally different from the *labour* involved in other occupations, such as being a plumber, gardener or engineer. We will argue that *all* labour contains a creative element. That following Marx it is a characteristic of humans that their labour possesses a conceptual side, which involves the individual alone or in collective association, *envisioning* their work prior to its execution or enactment. However, the conceptual and imaginative side of labour in commodity production for mass or repeat market consumption is not under the direct control of the individual producer. Rather it is usually divorced, externalised or collectivised in a separate group (management and their allies) or embodied within the technology of production. Furthermore, in repeat work, especially volume production for mass markets, there is little room for imagination once the product and production process has been designed. What counts in these production areas is conformity to set protocols, following standard operating procedures and the ability to produce the same thing repeatedly on a continuous and extended scale. Of course, in every moment of production the commodities have to be created, but there is no originality, innovation or new thinking embodied in what will appear or the means by which it will appear, as both have already been defined.

Creative labour in the sense of work that is non-standard, non-repeatable, innovative or newly imagined is rare. Improvised jazz might be an exception, where conception and execution are united and sound is created spontaneously and instantaneously. While each product of the creative labour process is a one-off, the degree of variation and individuality of the product can be inhibited by it fitting within a style structure, genre or particular musical or artistic school, which has the effect of *institutionalising the unique*. Most labour, even that of an artist has a routine or familiar component. Routine comes from following training as an artist or musician, one that is acquired through the practice of being a musician or artist within a community of fellow artists or musicians. Routine comes from working within a particular *genre* or style that the individual does not create, but which is there as a template or recipe for the individual to 'follow' or work within. Style can be cultural, linked to a particular group, or situational – the vogue of the time which the artist absorbs and expresses in particular but recognisably 'stylised/structured' terms. In this sense, creative labour is *craft like*, it requires working within a tradition or established form, which acts as an externalised and institutionalised set of normative rules that the individual is required to learn and follow. But once the technique or style is mastered by the individual, there is then room for 'innovation' and interpretation that may be different from the received standard, and reflect the individual's unique talent, or a new 'school' of practice and technique that the individual shares with other originators or revolutionaries within the field.

Moreover in what could be called creative industries (Caves, 2000), the producer is more immediately involved in conceptual *and* operative elements of work. There is more *totality* in the productive process and therefore more control for the individual. And the product and possibly the way it is produced are not necessarily repeatable, but rather one of a kind. Further as Caves (2000) notes, for the capitalist in this sector, demand for creative products is not guaranteed. Therefore profit cannot be known in advance of the costs of production being committed and there is extreme uncertainty around how many people will buy the piece of music or view the film once it has been produced. Such uncertainty does not apply in mass or repeat market situations, where orders have already been taken and sales are highly predicable. But it may be increasing as a phenomenon in saturated consumer markets, as differentiation grows as a selling strategy.

We need to reiterate the problem of establishing a clear-cut distinction between occupations based on the content of work, and that routine and creative elements combine in all human labour. However, we also recognise that for certain sectors, where the market is volatile and unpredictable, the product is highly perishable, and where the act of creativity in production is difficult to standardise or routinise, the originality in creative labour is accentuated and may define a whole sector of work. When such labour encounters commercial or industrial capitalist forces, the creative purpose emphasised by the musician or artist – the 'art for arts sake principle', or the intrinsic/critical value – meets the economic purpose of making profit. Moreover, the possibility of earning money (and dreams of stardom and economic power) will animate the motivations of individuals as creative industries commercialise and production takes place along principles of profit maximisation, greater shareholder value and economic returns to owners. This may create what Caves (2000: 7) calls 'vertically differentiated skills', but it will also shape individual preferences and motivations, segment sectors and sub-sectors between more or less commercially oriented production – art house films and Hollywood, the *avant-garde* and mainstream. But in a world dominated by commoditisation, it is difficult to remain unaffected by the forces of monetised and mass capitalist production values. Moreover as O'Connor (2007: 20) has noted:

> There is thus an underlying tension between exchange and use value at the heart of the cultural commodity. Cultural commodities are expensive to produce but cheap to reproduce – the more copies sold the greater the return on the original investment. But there are limits on this reproduction; people are not content to consume the same, they want new and different products. For this reason cultural commodities are prone to a short shelf life, and income has to be maximised before it hits the sell-by date.

What the capitalist industrialisation of creative arts represents is an attempt to get more value from the creative labourer by applying industrial principles and practices to the production of creative artefacts. This usually means widening the *distribution* of creative products, by means of technological solutions by mass (repeat) producing or storing products in new ways (reprographic photography, film, video, vinyl, digital etc) that make them marketable to a global audience. Capitalist principles of production can be applied to production, distribution or circulation, but with the same purpose, to make more profit. This can mean bringing the creative labourer into a collective, industrial complex, where rules from factory production can be applied. Or it can mean simply bringing the product into a marketing machine that can then turn the artist and their artefacts into 'merchandise'. Often it is not possible to de-compose the artistic/creative labour process and bring the producer into industrial production. However, as the example of Motown Records illustrates, artistic creativity can be institutionalised if not industrialised. Popular music, for example, remains largely individualistic and tied to handicraft production. The same is true for art. However once created, *copies* of the 'product' can subsequently be industrially mass-produced, distributed and marketed. But new creative sectors, such as film and television, are industries, with an extensive division of labour, a more and less creative occupational hierarchy, formal employment relationship and many other rules taken from capitalist production which are applied to ensure continuous supply of usable products from a 'collective' creative labourer.

An essential part of the globalisation of the music industry over the last two decades has been the increasing interpenetration of music, media, and consumer electronics conglomerates (Scott, 2004: 184–6). The experience of the format wars during the introduction of consumer video technology had a double impact on corporate strategy. First, it underscored the vital importance of establishing global rather than rival standards both to establish the possibility of a mass market and to amortise the enormous costs of product development. The VCR format wars were echoed by the complex pattern of competition and cooperation between the global electronics companies in establishing standard formats for audio compact discs and DVDs. Irrespective of their technical capabilities, other multimedia technologies were squeezed out by increasingly formalised strategic alliances establishing global technical standards, underscored by the availability of high-end music and film content, and has emerged as a critical to competitiveness and to the nature of technological innovation (Dai, 2000: 221–40; Tassey, 2000). Second, global 'hardware' companies Sony, Matsushita and Philips, in turn, acquired major music and media businesses in order to ensure a reliable supply and back catalogue of 'software' (Sadler, 1997; Wasko, 1994).

Content: the labour of creative labourers

Borrowing from Marx we can say it is not the content or material aspect of a persons job that defines their social position in society, but rather their social relations to the means of production – whether or not they are owners of their labour power, their tools or means of production and their product, or rather simply sellers of labour time for producing a product which is appropriated by another. In other words, it is the social relations towards production that define a worker not job characteristics. Weberian writing is different, looking at the value of the skills a worker possesses, and implying that skills are *assets* with different marginal value, and therefore skill assets act as a kind of property that can differentiate workers into different occupational 'property classes'. Applied to creative labour we could say that these workers have particular skill assets, which give them more or less market value, more or less autonomy and perhaps more or less social status. Moreover, they may own their product, and be petty commodity producers, but they will not own the means of distributing the product, and capital in this sphere can be concentrated and control access to market for the distribution and sale of the product of creative labour. Alternatively, they can be 'jobbing workers' (actors for example) and move from project to project selling their labour time.

It is not possible to make definitive categorisation of creative labour by examining the content of people's work. This is because all human labour has both creative and non-creative elements, and no worker is wholly creative, as artists, musicians and writers etc. have routine elements to their work – in the form of styles, genres etc. If we explore other aspects of occupational sociology in which one group is defined against others, then the case of professions within Anglo-Saxon cultures is telling. Here, an early and influential approach is what is known as 'trait' theory. This involved listing the characteristics of professions that made them different from other occupations. The problem with such boundary or classificatory exercises is that traits are not stable, and other groups acquire what were considered 'exclusive' qualities, and we witness what one writer called the 'professionalization of everyone' (Wilensky, 1964). Critique of the limitations of trait theory looked at issues of power relations (Johnson, 1972; Freidson, 1994), the role of the state (Johnson, 1972); and the type of contracts and labour market position used in locating professionals (Abbott, 1988).

For Abbott, professional occupations establish spheres of influence over their task activities/work ('jurisdiction' in Abbott's terminology) through first addressing human problems through particular types of expert solutions; through legitimating their claim to jurisdiction in the social and public sphere, and then closing their labour market through a variety of legal and other mechanisms. (This chronology of professional formation, from work/ labour market → public support → legal sanction for jurisdiction, is questioned by Johnson (a 'power theorist'). For Johnson, the state often initiates the process of professionalisation and deprofessionalisation. However, Abbott is ambiguous about the direction of causation, and does not always suggest that the process moves from work through public legitimisation to legal control. Unlike the power perspective which emphasises the importance of knowledge monopoly, or statutory/legal monopoly of the professional over the client, problem or public, and hence a superior/subordinate relationship, Abbott stresses the '*negotiated* nature of the status of professions'. Jurisdictional settlements are *historical* and are therefore constant competition, and not once-and-for-all monopoly closure, best characterises the system of professional jurisdictional struggle over particular problems, tasks, knowledge or activities.

In creative industries there are groups that have professionalised along these lines, such as classically trained musicians, painters, actors and broadcast technicians, who have professional associations or trade unions representing their interests and attempting to build boundaries around their labour market niche.[1] However even for these groups, there might be competition from amateurs, there are multiple entry routes, and formalised training may not be a necessity in order to practise (Haunschild, 2003). Television and film are vehicles for actors without formal credentials, especially with the explosion of docu-drama, reality TV and various programmes that dispense with skilled labour and use increased participation of (cheaper) 'audience' labour as a means of lowing production costs. Although most actors in TV and film will have some 'drama school' credentials, such qualifications are not essential to practice – unlike say being a doctor. The boundary between qualified and non-qualified labour is policed by unions, and possession of an Equity card is a necessity in motion pictures, and British stage and TV acting.

But as Davenport (2005) suggest unions in the UK have reduced bargaining power with the fragmentation of the sector through contracting out of work from TV companies (see McKinlay Chapter 9). For other groups – writers, cinematographers, sound engineers, and lighting engineers – routes into the industry are more circumspect and less dependent on formalised training (see Blair, 2000). The ability of trade associations and trade unions to regulate the labour market or to sustain demarcation lines in the workplace has declined markedly in the last two decades. We shall return to this point later.

The blurred distinction between technical and aesthetic dimensions is a key characteristic of creative labour processes. Hollywood's 'studio system' relied upon the clear separation of aesthetic and technical dimensions of production. American technicians had clearly defined *technical* roles, strictly subordinated to the director's aesthetic decision-making powers. In Britain, by contrast, film crews expect to be involved in *aesthetic* decision-making, encroaching on the director's space, and in return would improvise to overcome technical or budgetary limits (Lassally, 1987: 36–7, 69; Petrie, 1996a: 56). However, others have argued that the British film industry is characterised by narrow specialist skill, low levels of flexibility and a reluctance to embrace change (Davenport, 2005). Yet certain groups within the industry are more adaptable. The British cinematographer observed Freddy Young 'is an artist and a technician. ...The cameraman stands at the natural confluence of the two main streams of activity in the production of a film – where the imaginative meets the reality of the film process' (Young and Petzold, 1972: 23). British film directors accepted that their relationship with the crew was necessarily negotiated, irrespective of formal distinctions between technical, commercial or aesthetic areas of responsibility:

> The relationship between director and other staff is so much a question of teamwork that it would be a very unhappy unit if the 'boss and employee' techniques were applied. No director with any sense at all would try to enforce that feeling. A director needs the friendship of the unit and although at times he might be rather bossy he finds in the long run that he gets much more out of the unit if he keeps them all happy (Young and Petzold, 1972: 34–6; Petrie, 1996b: 110–11).

Conversely, an inexperienced director who flouted the crew's expectation of involvement in all aspects of decision-making – operational and aesthetic – risked passive resistance and expensive over-runs (Young, 1999: 85–7). A consistent theme of European and British film-making has been that film crews are enduring groups of collaborators rather than complete strangers (Petrie, 1991: 184–94). Indeed, one Californian study suggests that moderate familiarity – neither friends nor strangers – inside crews, is positively correlated with higher levels of film success (DeFillippi and Arthur, 1998: 127). This familiarity with generic industry working practices and the specific skills of fellow crew mates is an essential part of the film and television labour processes. However, as we shall see in the following section, these 'thick' connections have been seriously eroded over the last two decades.

The temporary nature of the film labour process, the interaction of technicians with directors and chronic under-funding of film all combined to reduce formal collective bargaining and demarcation disputes to a minimum. By contrast, the rapid rise of television and the profitability of commercial companies meshed to produce a highly institutionalised and combustible form of industrial relations. Until the last decade, television studios were crowded, with heavy, often fragile equipment, snaking around the set. Camera and lighting crew had to work quickly, making fine adjustments to their cumbersome, temperamental equipment to compensate for manifold contingencies involved in shooting a scene (Jones, 1972). The depth of television technicians' job controls was matched only by the sheer vulnerability of management. Tight demarcation rules, a ferociously policed pre-entry closed shop, and an expensive, time-sensitive product combined to heighten union and informal bargaining power. As electro-mechanical equipment rapidly gave way to computer-assisted and then digital equipment, so the craft skills of television technicians were replaced by those of speed and selecting alternative shots to increase the variety available to the director and editor (McKinlay and Quinn, 1998). Paradoxically, then, the erosion of formal and informal collective bargaining has been paralleled by the emergence of a more cooperative set of relationships between the director and crew in television, much closer to the historic norm in film than before digitisation.

Contract: reproducing, recruiting and retaining creative labourers

We now turn to the types of employment *contract* that characterise work in the creative industries, and in what ways the short-term, one-off or temporary quality of the output from creative industries necessitates particular contract relations that do not depend on a continuous employment relationship with a single employer typical of most service and manufacturing employment situations. All labour contracts are open-ended, in the sense that the buyer of labour services offers up a wage in exchange for a definite amount of labour time from the seller, time in which the seller offers up their labour capacity. This capacity has to be realised or extracted by the buyer through the apparatus of work supervision in which notions of fair exchange, effort bargain and a 'going rate' for the job are implicit rules that guide seller and buyer in reaching agreement on the amount of effort required. Caves emphasises the open-ended nature of contracts within creative industries:

> Most contracts that we find in the creative industries have strong incomplete incentive provisions. The contracts are commonly simple, and they evade complete contracts needed to describe each input or action ex ante and monitor it ex post (Caves, 2000: 13).

A labour process and institutional perspective would suggest that this is typical of the capitalist employment relationship, not simply creative industries. For Williamson, like Marx, the employment contract is not a conventional legal contract, in that there is no effort to specify all obligations in advance, but rather employees concede to manage the authority to make them do particular tasks, within certain customary constraints. This is therefore more flexible; people can be moved, retrained, and made more adaptable within the terms of a direct employment contract. The *incomplete nature* of the employment contract gives employment relations a potential advantage over fixed types of contract – 'contingency claims'; or 'sequential spot contracts' and many other contract types Williamson outlines.

These types of contract do not fully overcome the problem of being unable to specify in advance all obligations between parties or the costs that arise due to unforeseen contingencies.

> In the context of the employment relation, the existence of uncertainty over the precise work task required to be performed during any particular period, when combined with bounded rationality, makes the negotiation of a complex contract covering all potential contingencies extremely costly, if not impossible. Hence, Williamson argues the contract between employers and workers will necessarily be incomplete (Marginson, 1993: 148–9).

Creative industries avoid the costs of having elaborate enforcement machinery – usually considered unnecessary in such simple contract forms, because to a large extent the *reputation* of the provider of creative services helps ensure that the work contracted for is actually delivered. Reputation functions in the industry as a substitute for hierarchy, there to ensure contract delivery chiefly due of the short-term nature of contract work, the competition to get into the market from competing groups, and the need to ensure that access to work flows through the networks of job distribution which are dependent on the performance of the individual in their last contract. A poor reputation for delivering work weakens access to future work, which with short-term contracts, means the individual can easily become all but unemployable.

The individual worker as well as being problematical or bothersome to the hirer, is also costly, and this increases the incentive to minimise, replace and cheapen this input, either through capital substitution, making workers work more productively or swapping expensive skilled labour for cheaper less skilled labour. In the creative industries these conventional strategies may not work, primarily because the skill or creativity of the individual is such an essential part of the creative product or commodity that can neither be replaced nor displaced. This only leaves finding ways of maximising the productivity of existing workers as the major method of increasing surpluses in these industries. Hence we have in these industries the following features:

- A surplus of skilled over unskilled labour
- A productivity dilemma that means raising output requires engaging with labour not replacing or displacing it
- A surplus of individuals wishing to join the creative industries relative to available places providing wages at levels that would support the living costs of the individual. This surplus army helps depress average wages, and create vertical segmentation in wages and not just skills

These features give rise to contracts between agents and principals that do not follow the typical employment contract. They also give rise to unique forms of recruitment and retention, as the surplus of workers to living-wage places, added to the uniqueness, rarity and premium wages of certain individuals means the labour market does not function normally to equalise wages and access to jobs. Rather the sector is segmented and networks are used to distribute work (Blair, 2000 – Chapter 6 this volume). Furthermore particular forms of management control, which also involves more personal, value dependent or attitudinal forms of engagement between buyer and seller, exist within the sector.

Capitalism converts independent producers into dependent workers whose only means of livelihood is selling their labour power for a wage through the labour market. Braverman (1974) devotes a large part of *Labor and Monopoly Capital* to exploring the spread of waged labour, and especially the change in the United States workforce from independent small farmers into waged workers, and then from working as an autonomous skilled craftsmen to working as a more dependent unskilled worker. Applied to creative industries, we can see two processes in operation: firstly, the retention of the independent producer 'class' within this sector, and the absence of the waged labour form as applied in mass production or mass service industries. Producers remain as independent contractors, who through managing agents and other networks have market forms of short-term exchanges with production companies, or purchasers of their services. In other words the waged labour form is weakly developed. Secondly, the 'de-bureaucratisation' and contractualisation of creative industry hierarchies that were previously centres of waged labour forms of contracting and have now undergone retrenchment, delaying and downsizing. This has the effect of transforming former employees – who had salaries, access to internal training rights, job ladders, pensions etc – into independent producers or small production companies. The *marketisation* of the BBC or ITV companies has involved this process. In the film industry it happened several decades before, as the studio system disintegrated (Caves, 2000: 87–102). In the music industry it began to collapse in the 1950s before re-establishing in the late 1960s (Perrow, 1986: 183–9). The change here is one of moving away from salaried or waged forms and exchange within an internal market, towards a network or external market of competing and numerous small companies or contractors.

One of the reasons for studying the creative industries is that they exemplify forms of labour contracting, management control and firm organisation that have broken free of sector constraints and entered more mainstream organisations as a viable way of putting the firm together. Hence in a simple sense there are lessons to be learnt from this sector for organisations in general and the management of the labour process in particular.

One striking example of the marketisation of a creative industry is British television broadcasting. The BBC signalled the shift to marketisation with the introduction of Producer Choice. Market rhetoric was paralleled by the introduction of more fine-grained management accounting systems in the mid-1990s that reached from Corporation's apex to the individual project. Historically, slack budgeting using broad categories was deployed at the level of the programme division rather than the individual production. More than this, despite a McKinsey inspired divisionalisation in the mid-1970s, producers had been able to exercise considerable autonomy in moving resources between different budget headings or even between projects (Burns, 1977; Lury, 1993). The tighter financial controls imported by the new accounting system clashed with the established 'redistributive, compensatory logics' of programme makers. It is almost impossible to exaggerate the depth of this marketisation of the BBC's cultural bureaucracy (Born, 2004: 115).

For more than a year, parallel processes of financial management coexisted. The accountants championed the new framing and planning procedures; the department managers and their teams continued to employ their redistributive, compensatory logics. The drama department heads, their executive producers and producers continued to work with the original teams, and successful efforts were made to isolate and freeze out the new accountants; while on their part, the management accountants and cost controllers tried determinedly to exert their authority and controls. The bizarre stand-off was manifest at lunchtimes in the cafeteria. One or two tables would be occupied by a group of unfashionably dressed people, among them a number of young British Asians. These were the outcasts from Drama Finance, invariably hunched together laughing, orderly but defiant. They were ignored by the rest of the lunchtime crowd, whose behaviour made it clear that the accountants lacked the cultural élan to become truly part of Drama Group.

Within a year, however, the new accounting system was sufficiently embedded in the BBC to withstand such local resistance. The budgetary – and ideological – revolution heralded by Producer Choice resulted in and partly legitimised departmental closures (Born, 2004: 107–9, 126). It is not that the language of competition and markets wholly displaced the Corporation's Reithian mission or staff allegiance to the ethos of public sector broadcasting. Rather, it is that public sector broadcasting was no longer sufficient justification on its own but had also to secure legitimacy in terms of efficiency and competitiveness.

The profound casualisation of British broadcasting has triggered – suggests Starkey *et al* (2000) – the emergence of 'the latent organization', a form of organisation that both transcends and incorporates 'hierarchy' and 'network' forms. While 'the latent organization' is a term that captures the rapid diffusion of technical and 'business' knowledge across the sector, it singularly fails to register that first generation production companies and contractors were drawing upon the shared repertoires they had developed while employed by the BBC and commercial broadcasters (McKinlay and Quinn, 1998; Dex *et al*, 1998; Ursell, 1998; Paterson, 2001; Wittel *et al*, 2002). While it is unclear how durable these repertoires have proven, some commercial broadcasters – faced with severe and chronic skill shortages and severe wage inflation – have cautiously reversed the powerful trend towards outsourcing by increasing their 'core' technical workforces precisely because of their need for (Tempest *et al*, 2004; Saundry, 1998). As in British film, the social networks that traverse the broadcasting labour markets are not just vital coping mechanisms but also important mechanisms for ensuring the continued viability of labour processes of the main broadcasters. Similar patterns of acute labour shortages and insecure employment are unfolding across Europe as broadcasters move for professional bureaucracies to 'lean' models (Sydow and Starber, 2002). But as McRobbie (2002: 519) cautions, in the speeded up world of the cultural sector, the demands of sustaining a constant performance of self-promotion, with few mechanisms for solidaristic organisation and no fixed workplace, informal networking is unlikely to generate any durable collective responses to profound employment insecurity.

Control: managing creative labourers

What forms of labour *control* characterise the creative industries? Superficially there is a strong identification between the worker (musician, writer or artist) and both their 'means of production' and the product of their labour, such that levels of self-motivation are extremely high, and the need for external supervision and work pacing may not exist or be marginal to the process of adding value in the industry. Interior or normative discipline seems most evident in the sector, but market forces, peer-pressure and performance targets are also apparent, and these kinds of control would seem common to other forms of employment, and therefore fashion bridges between creative and other industries.

Labour within a capitalist economy, regardless of the degree of intensity between creative and routine elements, exists to serve the purpose of producing a surplus for the hirer or capitalist. The purpose of labour power or services is to provide both utility *and* value, in order for money to be made. Within commodity production, and the employment relationship, labour is the creative component, but also the problematical element. While wages may be known (or are determinate), the performance of the particular individual for those wages cannot be known in advance, as labour is indeterminate, and exists as a mere capability that requires motivation (control, cajoling and commitment) to be productive. The individual cannot be manipulated in the same way as other non-human 'elements' of production, such as machinery, which can be bought and sold at the will of the owner. Human labour (time and capability) is hired, not bought outright, hence the purchaser is required to establish a *social relationship* with the hired worker in order for purposeful and productive work to be realised. In creative industries, labour may need to be 'controlled' or managed in different ways from mass production or repeat production settings. This is because the value of the individual worker may be higher as they are hard or impossible to replace (due to the function of individual asset specificity or unique individual skills), and therefore ownership relations are more complex.

Control is a central concept in labour process analysis. It is derived from the nature of labour as a productive resource, and what is referred to as the indeterminacy of labour power, that is as discussed above, the uncertainty of the return to the hirer of labour services of predictable revenue or product, and the requirement for management to ensure that hired labour is productively utilised. The control function is *one* part of management for classical theorists, but the *central* function for labour process writers, the *raison d'être* for management agency in the firm. This is evident in the hierarchical ordering of most work organisations, of the control invested in the design of jobs, through technology pacing of work for example. Supervisors or team leaders not only co-ordinate, but ensure that workers work with purpose during the working day.

The means of control in creative industries reflects the character of the sector so far described. Labour market pressures to access the industry ensures high self-motivation for those working, as the weight from the mass reserve army of unemployed (and under-employed) actors or musicians is acutely felt by the working individual. Self-motivation and control is also high due to the identification between the individual and the product or creative process, such that considerable pleasure and satisfaction is derived from working hard and productively. Normative or value control evident in other occupations is magnified in this sector. Finally, self identification and occupational identification are strong in the sector, and the prestige, status and glamour attached to many creative occupations in public perception and media interest reinforces the emotional and personal attachment between the individual and their work.

Perhaps the most striking features of the creative economy are the continuation of the deeply held attachment to a form of *gift economy*. It is not that workers in the digital economy are having their knowledge wrested from them and bitterly resent excessive hours and constant demands upon technical and aesthetic skills. Rather, as Terranova (2000: 37) argues:

> the end of the factory has spelled out the obsolescence of the old working class, but it has also produced generations of workers who have been repeatedly addressed as active consumers of meaningful commodities. Free labour is the moment where this knowledgeable consumption of culture is translated into productive activities are pleasurably embraced and at the same time shamelessly exploited.

We can contest the Italian autonomists notions of the 'social factory' and 'immaterial labour', but still acknowledge that 'creative labour' is not duped or coerced by management but typically *engages* with the production process and is profoundly attached to the integrity of the product (McRobbie, 1998, 2000; Ursell, 2000). The profundity of this attachment is signified by extraordinary displays of commitment and pleasure: extremely long working days combined with the acknowledgement of poor or no pay and uncertain career prospects. This contrast between an awareness of the precarious nature of employment and careers in the creative industries is used to underscore the depth of the individual's attachment to their aesthetic practice. For advertising practitioners, for example, uncertain employment combines with an equally uncertain professional status to produce an intense form of self-scrutiny, a critical evaluation of their work relationships, and a profound unease about their work identities (Alvesson, 1994: 545, 558; Cronin, 2004; Nixon and Crewe, 2004: 142–3).

Unlike manufacturing or routine service work, the moment of production is difficult to monitor, far less to evaluate or codify. This is clearest during live radio or television broadcasts. Organisational logics – structures, budgets and performance measures – are of no consequence to work in practice. Formally distinct roles – director, vision mixer, floor manager – overlap as tasks become less differentiated. Coordination is achieved not through the articulation of formal roles and responsibilities but via gestures, signals, looks and routines (see Glevarec, 1999: 287–90). Such production processes are coordinated by interpersonal exchanges rather than managerial direction. Indeed, the intimacy of such coordination renders it – temporarily – both *opaque* and *impervious* to formal management control. Similarly, through the mid-1990s, despite major investments in understanding the creative moment – driven by tight markets and margins – advertising agencies remain under-managed organisations. Several London agencies dissolved the relationship between status, function and space to maximise the frequency, diversity and rapidity of interaction between all types of staff (Nixon, 2003: 52–6).

Nor does the opacity of production depend upon the labour process being confined to a single space. The importance of place in the creative industries has been highlighted by the research of social geographers into the emergence of new media companies and their interaction with clients. Place remains vital not just in establishing pools of skilled labour but also permitted San Francisco's new media companies to develop the 'studio model' in which management overcomes the small-scale of the individual firm through building project teams (Pratt, 2002: 40–1). During the new media boom of the late 1990s the lack of standardised protocols for project management and the permanently unfinished product development was reflected in organisational practices:

> In the dizzyingly fluid environment in which new media evolve, organisational practices are driven by the imperatives of bricolage, improvisation, self-organisation, and adaptability. Problem definition and goal setting are shared and symptomatically involve constant negotiation and recalibration. Instead of a strictly sequential work process, with central subsystems defining the boundary conditions for the subsequent design of subordinate components, separate project teams subsystems concurrently (Grabher, 2002: 1911, 1913).

The technical and business uncertainty of the web products and services resulted in close, intense co-production by client and producer (Wittel *et al*,

2002). Inside new media firms, the inter-penetration of design and execution, relentless redesign, and the radical form of simultaneous engineering involved in product development and delivery resulted in constant re-negotiation as these parallel labour processes jostled for priority, without clear, directive organisational direction or structure. Longitudinal studies of London and New York new media firms have charted significant shifts in their competitive strategies, organisational structures, and internal management processes (Lash and Wittel, 2002; Girard and Stark, 2002). Successful survivors from the new media boom have moved from direct providers of new media products towards consultancy services and close relationships with relatively few clients. Organisationally, new media firms moved from heterarchy towards hierarchy and increasingly controlled, more linear labour processes.

Conclusion

Let us return to our three themes. A consistent feature of the labour of creative labour, narrowly defined, is its opaque nature. The process of creative labour is often difficult for management to monitor and observe, far less to codify and control. The dynamics of skill are also distinctive in two ways. First, skills are highly socialised in that they rely on the imaginative borrowing from other areas of life, not just other art forms, youth cultures, or historical genres. This is true for 'creatives' in advertising or in film or music. The idea of work as 'life style' rather than economic action rigidly divided from a non-work sphere is important here. Skills are also, secondly, highly socialised at the moment of production. Jazz improvisation, so often a motif used to capture the improvisational capability required of post-bureaucratic organisations, relies upon a prior and shared mastery of standard tunes. Only this collective control of a standard repertoire allows improvisation to break from these conventions. In film and television, similarly, technical crews' shared technical background allows them to work effectively in short-cycle project teams and to work at the interface of the technical and the aesthetic. In film, television and advertising the introduction of new technologies has not displaced these collective, highly tacit skills, although they have shifted the balance between preparation and the quick decision-making during the production and editing. The overlap between aesthetic, commercial and technical decision-making remains a distinctive feature of creative labour.

If continuity is a major theme of creative labour processes, then with few exceptions, the labour markets for creative labour have experienced major shifts as major cultural organisations have progressively marketised and outsourced their operations. Again, these changes are evident across the creative sectors. Chronic insecurity and limited controls on entry to creative labour markets have weakened trade unions and increased the vital importance of social networks in finding jobs and building reputations. There may be exceptions to this move to market, Haunschild's (2003) research on German repertory theatres reveals a stable 'employment system', underpinned by state funding, collective bargaining and functioning 'rules of the game' in which employment is more secure. But he acknowledges that this is exceptional, and the embracing of short-term and dynamic networks remains more typical of creative labour in theatre and film elsewhere. But his work does serve to underline the importance of the societal contexts for industries, including creative industries, and the institutional variations that can flow from the embedding of labour within different state and cultural contexts. Our paper has aimed at a broader argument, but would not wish to discount this layer of meaning and diversity.

Finally, the dominant strategy for management is that which allows the organisation to mobilise the deep attachment displayed by creative labour to the product. The paradox is that management cannot be content with simply assembling crews for different projects and setting broad parameters. In films, television, advertising and web production, firms have not just experimented with different organisational forms but also invested heavily – if sporadically – in attempting to monitor, cost, and control the creative labour process itself. It is not so much that the creative industries are impervious to deskilling, but that Taylorism would so severely damage the very creativity it was attempting to control.

Note

1 Indeed Hollywood writers and actors have been exercising the collective voice in 2007–8 with major industrial disputes, emphasising the 'worker' element of their position.

REFERENCES

Abbott, A. (1988) *The System of Professions: An Essay on the Division of Expert Labor*. Chicago: University of Chicago Press.

Alvesson, M. (1994) 'Talking in Organizations: Managing Identities and Impressions in an Advertising Agency', *Organization Studies*, 15/4: 535–63.

Blair, H. (2000) 'You're Only as Good as Your Last Job': The Relationship Between Labour Market and Labour Process in the British Film Industry', unpublished PhD thesis, University of Hertfordshire.

Born, G. (2004) *Uncertain Vision: Birt, Dyke and the Reinvention of the BBC*. London: Secker & Warburg.

▶

Braverman, H. (1974) *Labor and Monopoly Capital*. New York: Monthly Review Press.

Bryman, A. (2000) 'Telling Technological Tales', *Organization*, 7/3: 455–75.

Burns, T. (1977) *The BBC: Public Institution and Private World*. London: Macmillan.

Caves, R. (2000) *Creative Industries: Contracts between Art and Commerce*. Cambridge, Mass: Harvard University Press.

Christopherson, S. and Storper, M. (1989) 'The Effects of Flexible Specialisation on Industrial Politics and the Labor Market: The motion Picture Industry', *Industrial and Labor Relations Review*, 42 (3): 331–47.

Cronin, A. (2004) *Advertising Myths: The Strange Half-Lives of Images and Commodities*. London: Routledge.

Dai, X. (2000) *The Digital Revolution*. Aldershot: Ashgate.

Davenport, J. (2005) Project-Based Firms in the UK Film Industry: Theoretical and Political Implications, unpublished PhD thesis, University of Manchester.

DeFillippi, R. and Arthur, M. (1998) 'Paradox in Project-Based Enterprise: The Case of film-Making', *California Management Review*, 40/2: 125–39.

Dex, S., Willis, J. and Paterson, R. (1998) 'Freelance workers and contract uncertainty: The Effects of Contractual Changes in the Television industry', *Work, Employment and Society*, 14: 283–305.

Freidson, E. (1994) *Professionalism Reborn: Theory, Prophecy and Policy*. London: Polity Press.

Girard, M. and Stark, D. (2002) 'Distributing Intelligence and Organising Diversity in New Media Projects', *Environment and Planning A*, 34: 1927–49.

Glevarec, H. (1999) 'Le Travail a France Culture Comme Actione Situee: Sociology de la Production Radiophonique', *Sociologie du Travail*, 41: 275–93.

Gordy, B. (1994) *To Be Loved: The Music, the Magic, the Memories of Motown*. New York, NY: Headline.

Grabher, G. (2002) 'Fragile Sector, Robust Practice: Project Ecologies in New Media', *Environment and Planning A*, 34/11: 1911–26.

Haunschild, A. (2003) 'Managing Employment Relations in Flexible Labour Markets: The Case of German Repertory Theatres', *Human Relations*, 56 (8): 899–929.

Johnson, T. (1972) *Professions and Power*. London: Macmillan.

Jones, P. (1972) *The Techniques of the Television Cameraman*. London: Focal Press.

Kamoche, K.N., Cunha, M.P. and Cunha, J.V. (eds) (2002) *Organisational Improvisation*. London: Routledge.

Lash, S. and Wittel, A. (2002) 'Shifting New Media: From Content to Consultancy, from Heterarchy to Hierarchy', *Environment and Planning A*, 34: 1985–2001.

Lassally, W. (1987) *Itinerant Cameraman*. London: John Murray.

Lury, C. (1993) *Cultural Rights: Technology, Legality and Personality*. London: Routledge.

McKinlay, A. and Quinn, B. (1998) 'Management, Technology and Work in Commercial Broadcasting, c.1979–1998', *New Technology, Work & Employment*, 14/1: 2–17.

►

McRobbie, A. (1998) *British Fashion Design: Rag Trade or Image Industry*. London: Routledge.

McRobbie, A. (2000) 'From Clubs to Companies: Notes on the Decline of Political Culture', *Cultural Studies*, 20.

McRobbie, A. (2002) 'From Holloway to Hollywood: Happiness at Work in the New Cultural Economy', in P. DuGay and Pryke (eds) *Cultural Economy*. London: Sage.

Marginson, P. (1993) 'Coercion and Co-operation in the Employment Relationship: Efficiency and Power Theories of the Firm', in Joseph McCahery, Sol Picciotto and Colin Scott (eds) *Corporate Control and Accountability*. Oxford: Clarendon Press.

Monthoux, P. de (2004) *The Art Firm: Aesthetic Management and Metaphysical Marketing from Wagner to Wilson*. Stanford, CA.: Stanford University Press.

Nixon, S. and Crewe, B. (2004) 'Pleasure at Work? Gender, Consumption and Work-based Identities in the Creative Industries', *Consumption, Markets, Culture*, 7/2: 129–47.

Nixon, S. (2003) *Advertising Cultures: Gender, Commerce and Creativity*. London: Sage.

Nixon, S. and Crewe, B. (2004) 'Pleasure at Work? Gender, Consumption and Work-Based Identities in the Creative Industries', *Consumption, Markets and Culture*, 7/2: 129–47.

O'Connor, J. (2007) *The Cultural and Creative Industries: A Review of the Literature*. London: Creative Partnerships, Arts Council of Great Britain.

Paterson, R. (2001) 'Work Histories in Television', *Media, Culture & Society*, 23: 495–520.

Perrow, C. (1986) *Complex Organizations: A Critical Essay*. New York, NY: McGraw-Hill.

Petrie, D. (1991) *Creativity and Constraint in the British Film Industry*. London: Macmillan.

Petrie, D. (1996a) *The British Cinematographer*. London: BFI.

Petrie, D. (1996b) *British Film-Makers at Work*. London: BFI.

Pratt, A. (2002) 'Hot Jobs in Cool Places: The Material Cultures of New Media Product Spaces: The Case of South of the Market, San Francisco', *Information, Communication & Society*, 5/1: 27–50.

Sadler, D. (1997) 'The Global Music Business as an Information Industry: Reinterpreting Economies of Culture', *Environment and Planning A*, 29: 1919–36.

Saundry, R. (1998) 'The Limits of Flexibility: The Case of UK Television', *British Journal of Management*, 9: 151–62.

Scott, A. (2004) 'The Other Hollywood: The Organizational and Geographic Bases of Television-Program Production', *Media, Culture and Society*, 26/2: 183–205.

Starkey, K., Barnatt, C. and Tempest, S. (2000) 'Beyond Networks and Hierarchies: Latent Organizations in the UK Television Industry', *Organization Science*, 11: 299–305.

►

▶

Sydow, J. and Staber, U. (2002) 'The Institutional Embeddedness of Project Networks: The Case of Content Production in German Television', *Regional Studies*, 36/3: 215–27.

Tassey, G. (2000) 'Standardization in Technology-Based Markets', *Research Policy*, 29: 587–602.

Tempest, S., McKinlay, A. and Starkey, K. (2004) 'Careering Alone: Careers and social capital in the financial services and television industries', *Human Relations*, 57/12: 1–23.

Terranova, T. (2000) 'Producing Culture for the Digital Economy', *Social Text*, 18/2: 33–58.

Ursell, G. (1998) 'Labour Flexibility in the UK Commercial Television Sector', *Media, Culture & Society*, 20/1: 129–53.

Ursell, G. (2000) 'Television Production: Issues of Exploitation, Commodification and Subjectivity', *Media, Culture & Society*, 22/6: 805–27.

Wasko, J. (1994) *Hollywood in the Information Age: Beyond the Silver Screen*. Cambridge: Polity.

Wilensky, H.L. (1964) 'The professionalisation of everyone?' *American Journal of Sociology*, 70: 137–58.

Wittel, A., Lury. C. and Lash, S. (2002) 'Real and Virtual Connectivity: New Media in London', in S. Woolgar (ed.) *Virtual Society? Technology, Cyberbole, Reality*. Oxford: Oxford University Press.

Young, F. and Petzold, P. (1972) *The Work of the Motion Picture Cameraman*. London: Focal Press.

Young, F. (1999) *Seventy Light Years*. London: Faber & Faber.

From Conception to Consumption: Creativity and the Missing Managerial Link*

3

Paul Thompson, Mike Jones and Chris Warhurst

Introduction

The present advertising recession and its knock-on effects are forcing media firms to tighten their management control processes, imposing more rigorous performance targets and work schedules. Stress and long working hours are the result. The resentment of creative employees is likely to increase and the conflict between 'them' (the suits) and 'us' (the creatives) become more evident (Scase, 2002: 8).

Richard Scase, a leading writer in this field, refers to the persistence of 'inherent tensions' in the management of creativity. This could suggest that there is nothing much new in the eternal battle between creatives and suits, or whatever names we may have given them in the past. Yet Scase and many other writers also argue that something has decisively changed in the significance attached to creativity. The economy, and within it the nature of management, work and organisation, is said to be transforming. Two significant changes are seen to be at the heart of this transformation. First, that there is more creative work in general, requiring less or different types of management. Second, that specific creative and cultural industries are expanding their scale and influence: 'they are at the leading edge ...constitut[ing] a critical case' for current developments in the workplace (Davis and Scase, 2000: 23).

In theory and policy, the terms creative and cultural industries are often used interchangeably (Pratt, 2002). Both should be regarded as parallel framing devices used to organise and understand changes in and from the 'old' to the 'new' economy and organisations. The main question that we address in this chapter is: How new and different are the drivers and outcomes of creative work and its management?. In the literatures, two main arguments can be distin-

*This chapter was originally published in *Journal of Organizational Behaviour* 28.5, pp. 625–40, 2007 and is reprinted with permission from the publishers.

guished and disentangled. First, that creativity is now more important with creative work the driving force of a 'new economy' and cultural industries a lead exemplar of that process. We call this the *creative intensity* argument. Second, those cultural industries have a special kind of creativity at their core based on expression that makes its management and contribution to value creation different. This can be described as the *creative distinctiveness* argument. In this chapter, we examine the utility of each of these arguments and find them limited in crucial respects. We therefore address the above question through a critical examination of some of the key recent contributions to such literatures, followed by examination of a particular cultural industry – the music industry – as a way of exploring key themes of theory and practice in greater detail.

The chapter has two purposes. On the one hand we want to critique existing frameworks in order to open up more space for analysis of management, work, and employment relations. Ranging through different levels of analysis, we argue that that the conceptual and empirical foci on creativity and the cultural industries are characterised by a major hole in the middle: focusing on conception and consumption, expectations and assumptions largely fill the gap in between. If we accept that in a new economy, there is little or nothing between conception and consumption, the tensions in the management of creative work are in danger of disappearing from view.

On the other hand, we want to contribute to alternative analysis. Utilising the categories of creative intensity and distinctiveness, the chapter argues that cultural industries are significant and have some distinctive characteristics but argues that there is far greater continuity of conditions and concepts than allowed for in 'new economy' frameworks. In addition, we make a contingent argument that there is a dual distinctiveness, with particular cultural industries manifesting their own dynamics of organisation and management. This argument is explored through a discussion of the popular music industry, drawing on the work of the authors (Jones and Thompson, 2001). That industry is a useful test of ideas of new forms of management of creativity in that it is under-researched within organisation and management studies, and yet associated with the most romanticised notion of creative individuals whose talent is not susceptible to organisational discipline.

The characteristics of creativity: disentangling terms and territories

Instead of pulling coal out of the ground, potatoes out of the earth or fish from the sea, we are pulling art and creative ideas out of essentially nothing (Janice Kirkpatrick, founding partner of *Graven Images* design firm, quoted in *The Scotsman*, 2 March 2001).

This formulation follows Charles Leadbeater (1999) and his book *Living on Thin Air*. The idea that commodities are the combined outcome of creativity and entrepreneurship is a quintessential piece of post-modern myth-making in which the material structures of labour markets and labour processes count for nothing. Whilst this view may be an exaggerated one, it picks up on more general themes in the literature about a new creative intensity. A frequent starting point is an *a priori* assumption that creative workers' search for autonomy and the intangible nature of intellectual assets requires and results in an abandonment of the traditional, hierarchical structures and practices of industrial society – echoing a familiar theme of knowledge economy theories. Because firms need ideas to survive and these ideas are intangible, dependence on 'core' or 'elite' workers increases. Moreover for creativity to be nurtured and talent realised, workers require a degree of autonomy making 'creatives' difficult to manage. This heady mixture of flexibility, autonomy and intangibility results in a dramatic shift in the nature of work and employment. In *Managing Creativity*, Davis and Scase (2000) argue that such employees will not be told what to do and if they meet bureaucratic barriers, they will withdraw their creativity. Whereas the workers of the 20th century company were employees, those of the 21st century company are to be a mixture of employees and 'free agents' of various kinds (Pink, 2001).

Florida (2002: 106–7) draws back from the excesses of such claims. Nevertheless, the 'company as oppressor' view is equally rejected and the key management task becomes attracting, retaining, and motivating the best talent through enhanced terms and conditions of employment. With 'free workers' able to choose between the best employers, firms find themselves 'in a war for talent' according to one IBM executive (cited in Coy, 2000: 42). To win this war, firms need to provide these workers with 'creative space' where work and fun become blurred and old-style 'command and control' replaced.

To evaluate such views, let's begin by returning to the issue of definitions. The UK Government defines the creative industries as 'those industries that have their origin in individual creativity, skill, and talent, and which have a potential for wealth and job creation through the generation and exploitation of intellectual property' (DCMS, 2001: 5). Such definitions are consistent with well-known expositions of the creative economy (Florida, 2002; Howkins, 2001) in which creative ideas are the key asset in economic success – intellectual work creating intellectual value.

In one sense therefore, creative industries are being defined by their labour content. Yet, if economic development is being driven by creative *work*, what are its characteristics? It is a theme of this chapter that the literature has seldom generated detailed or credible accounts of the management of the labour process associated with creativity. Florida's *Rise of the Creative Class* is a prime example. It is a stimulating and wide-ranging book but despite a section on 'Work' containing five chapters, most of the evidence presented concerns orientations *to* work rather than *of* work. One of the problems is that management and creative labour are seen as antithetical. Organisation and creativity are in 'fundamental tension' (p. 41), backed up by a reference to Sun Microsystems, which claims that it just hires talented people and then leaves them alone. The best ways of harnessing and managing creativity, are apparently, 'still being worked out' (p. 132).

It is not clear that labour content can be a robust distinguishing feature. All human labour contains both creative and non-creative elements, though clearly the balance can be radically different. It is what is done with and to that labour that counts, and within the broader market and industrial context (Smith, 2002). Arguably, because creativity alone tells us very little about the content of work or how it is organised and managed, and in the absence of actual descriptions of that work, the need for an additional organising or defining characteristic becomes necessary in the Howkins, Florida and similar studies. Howkins utilises a *sector* approach as a means of classification. Fifteen sectors are identified ranging from R&D, through to software, film, video games, architecture and art, linked in part by their products falling within the framework of intellectual property law (copyright, patents, trademarks, and designs). Such a dividing line has its attractions but can only bring all the different (and often not very creative) jobs together under one heading by treating the products as the *de facto* responsibility of the collective labourer. It is hard for example, to see what the work of ticket collectors or cleaners in a theatre have in common with the artistic director or actors.

Florida (2002: 68), in contrast, defines a creative economy through commonality amongst a set of *occupations* in which people 'add economic value through their creativity'. The 'super-creative core' consists of scientists, engineers, university professors, poets, actors and architects, whilst the secondary group is based on creative professionals in knowledge-intensive industries such as financial services and healthcare, and who draw on complex bodies of knowledge to solve more particular problems. Nevertheless, many of the same categorisation problems re-appear. Standard Occupational Classification codes inevitably aggregate different types of work. Many jobs within categories such as computer, library or sports occupations would be very difficult to classify as creative – super or otherwise.

The logical conclusion of such observations is that whilst a sector or occupational approach has its advantages, it is important to have clearer and perhaps more restricted boundaries. One way that this dilemma is handled is by shifting to the idea of *cultural* industries that envelop the *creative* industries (see e.g. DCMS, 2002). However, the familiar problems recur of heterogeneous skills and knowledge amongst the component occupational groups (Healy, 2002). Whichever way one defines the boundary between cultural and creative industries, significant problems remain of distinguishing work that meets any creative intensity criteria. What about the second criteria of creative distinctiveness? To address this question, we have to turn to a different, though related, literature about the cultural industries.

A cultural economy?

Debates around cultural industries have been around a long time and arguably go back to the Frankfurt School. The forced re-location of its leading theoreticians to the US led to the formation of an extremely pessimistic account of the (lack of) value of popular culture and to the one-way and wholly negative impact of 'commerce' on 'art'. In this account (Adorno and Horkheimer, 1979), *industry* is firmly equated with standardised factory-like production and passive mass consumption.

Subsequent perspectives on industry/culture relations have understandably wanted to bend the stick back to a limited role for directive management in the cultural industries and to the persistence of creativity. There is a degree of consensus that culture is playing a more significant role in the management of organisations, though there is less agreement on its character and effects (du Gay and Pryke, 2002). But something much more substantial is also being claimed – a general, epochal shift to a cultural economy, a perspective most associated with Lash and Urry's (1994) *Economies of Signs and Space*. They point to a range of indicators such as the centrality of cultural hardware and software in contemporary economies, the growing aestheticisation of goods and services and the increased influence of occupations (e.g. design and marketing) whose function is 'cultural intermediary' between production and consumption.

Though there are exceptions (Jessop and Sum, 2006), 'cultural turn' arguments tend to direct our attention away from political economy and the influence of production on culture to an expanded realm of cultural production. Some of the implications for organisations and management are most evident in Lawrence and Philips (2002). They reinforce the argument that economic rationality has been displaced by a cultural one. Cultural products are valued for their meaning not their usefulness and are consumed in an act of interpretation. Two types of products are identified. Entertainment products – novels, theatre, music – are interpreted directly by the consumer, whilst fashion products – designer sunglasses and running shoes, are interpreted by others. Cultural industries are, in turn, defined by their mode of consumption not production, competing in the symbolic realm. In this context, 'Managing in cultural industries is therefore not about efficiently producing a product but about creating and maintaining an organisation that can produce and sell meaning' (p. 431). Even Shorthose and Strange

(2004), in the Marxist journal *Capital and Class*, claim that the fundamental distinction between creative artistic work and alienated 'managed creativity' is being eroded in the new cultural economy.

Unfortunately, such arguments and distinctions do not hold up to serious scrutiny. Whilst we accept that cultural industries deal in symbolic goods (Hesmondhalgh, 2002), there is no separate realm of cultural products valued solely for their meaning; all products have at least use-value, whether material or otherwise. The motor industry is a case in point. Cars are material objects par excellence, are still manufactured largely through mass production, and meaning was always central to their consumption – themes still recurrent today in the sales pitch for cars as lifestyle accessories. In addition, whether goods are consumed through (direct or indirect) interpretation, the literature fails to appreciate that these products still have to be produced. Lawrence and Philips (2002) use the example of Adidas running shoes that were once athletic products that were driven down market only to return as high priced, retro, cultural goods in the 1990s. During this periodic change in 'fashionability', the shoes still had to be made by real workers in real factories, and these workers had to be managed, presumably by methods not solely reliant on the manipulation of meaning. Or, as Pratt (2002: 6) puts it, 'what the advocates of the weightless economy seem to ignore is the material nature of immaterial goods. They still require manufacture either as items or for reproduction'.

When the evidence of Shorthose and Strange (2004: 52) is examined, the 'expanded realm of artistic labour' turns out to be confined to small informal networks of independent producers. Whilst that realm may be increasing, it remains marginal in terms of employment and output. Overall, the problem remains that by shifting the focus from production to consumption, Lawrence and Philips (and others) are excluding employees and the employment relationship from the framework of enquiry. Such analyses are thus unable to answer the question – what is industrial about the creative or cultural industries?

As Lampel, Lant and Shamsie (2000) note in their useful overview, there are few empirical studies of cultural industries and even fewer of their management and organisation. That is one of the reasons why more long-standing analyses of cultural industries retain some of their influence. In his path-breaking essay, Hirsch (1972, 2000) argues that the expertise of record companies lies in their understanding of how to seek out and distribute musical items that fulfill a demonstrable public need. Within each firm, that expertise is dispersed between various clear functions – most notably at the 'input' and 'output' boundaries where individuals are employed to select from the enormous numbers of suppliers of 'art objects' and later to convince media 'gatekeepers' that such objects will connect with readers, listeners or viewers. What no one can predict, given variations in public taste, is which of these 'objects' the public will find novel and attractive. The 'solution' is to offer as many as is economically and logistically feasible with the certain knowledge that if at least some of the many different objects are purchased the profit realised will compensate for the costs of production of the rejected items. This is a strategy of 'over-production' and Hirsch regards it as characteristic of creative industries in general.

A similar conclusion is reached by Miège (1979, 1987), though from a Marxian or political economy tradition. The categories 'capital' and 'labour' are blurred in popular music, as they are in other creative sectors, yet Miège identifies the problematic nature of the use values attached to cultural goods. These industries became significant when cultural production became a site for the extension of the commodity form. However, in the transformation of cultural use values into exchange values, the imprint of the artist and his/her claim to authenticity (Peterson, 2005) must remain visible to the user, and the producer cannot predict how it will be received or whether it will sell in sufficient quantities. Creativity is, in various ways, part of the currency of exchange. Yet for Miège the end point is similar to Hirsch – the predominant explanation focuses on the spreading of risks through catalogues of products.

The best-known and more recent attempt to address the explanation of cultural industries comes from Richard Caves (2000). He also starts from the huge failure rate – described as the 'nobody knows' dilemma. Despite the title of *Creative Industries*, Caves uses creativity in a traditional cultural sense and is concerned with the emergence and economic characteristics of art as big business. For Caves, the high rate of uncertainty in such industries is resolved primarily through the contracts that have evolved between artists, intermediaries and owners. Each industry has developed standard contracts that are open-ended enough to reward success but also punish failure by non-renewal and other measures. Again, the creative work itself receives less attention but Caves does emphasise factors such as the diversity and hierarchy of skills in sectors such as film and television, and the temporality of work, typically through a series of projects.

A common feature of these analyses is a focus on the indeterminacy of *outcomes* in the cultural industries. Creativity is managed but the medium is more likely to be the contract, the product portfolio, or the distribution sphere rather than the labour process. Unlike classic industrial or service work, or even for traditional creative workers such as scientists and other expert labour, the tensions in the management of creativity are located largely outside the employment relationship.

We accept that indeterminacy of outcome is a key distinctive feature of cultural industries but would make two important qualifications. First, companies may seek to deal with indeterminacy of outcome at various points in the chain (Hesmondhalgh, 1996). This involves what we call *multiple points of management*: intervening in the supply of talent, the division of labour in the production process, the control of distribution, or the shaping of consumption. Second, much of this strategic choice can be explained by the nature of the activity. As Miège (1987) makes clear, we must talk of cultural industries; each of which may develop partly according to its own logic. What is efficient, profitable, or achievable in the film industry might not be in its musical equivalent. If this variance is the case, it makes sense to examine one of those logics and for these purposes we turn to the popular music industry.

Popular music, the record industry and cultures of production

Despite continuing colloquial references to the 'Entertainment Industry' and 'Tin Pan Alley' as metaphors for the industrialisation of music, there are considerable constraints to addressing popular music as a managed business. Music is a source of pleasure and artistic expression and, as such, is a key resource in the development of subjectivity and a sense of individualism (Frith, 1983). Furthermore, musical work tends to be judged on aesthetic criteria alone. Its makers are conceived of as individuals who are to be admired for their exemplary qualities and agency (Toynbee, 2000) and are, therefore, *anything but* workers whose creativity is subject to disciplinary regimes.

Even the most remarkable feature of this particular cultural industry – that the products of the record industry overwhelmingly fail to sell and sometimes they fail even to be *made* – reinforces the above view. Negus (1999) highlights the industry's 'rule of thumb' that only one in eight records released into the marketplace recoups its costs of production and makes a profit for the company that pays for its manufacture. What is notable about this rule of thumb is how comfortably the industry lives with these statistics – with the effect that, because it is inevitable, market failure is considered somehow 'natural' (Dannen, 1991).

The problem with the 'naturalisation' of market failure and the focus on it, is that it obscures the management of creativity within the record industry. While Hirsch (1972) can show goods falling at the 'output boundary' (because media 'gatekeepers' disallow them the opportunity of coming to public attention) and Caves (2000) can show us record (and film and book) company managers second-guessing the marketplace and utilising contractual clauses to cancel projects deemed as likely market failures. Neither can isolate many of the practices of management between 'looking for talent and marketing it' (Barfe, 2004: 337) that are *common* to success and to failure.

In recent decades, a different literature – Popular Music Studies – has undergone significant growth. For example, in the UK alone, we have seen work from Frith (1983, 1996), Negus (1999), Toynbee (2000), and Hesmondhalgh (2002). There is much that is instructive in these studies and other allied observations, and much that is understandable in the choice to be 'upbeat' and celebrate musical creativity. This is linked to the literature's own 'cultural turn' in the last decade, reflecting a desire to further bend the stick back from the pessimistic legacy of the Frankfurt School while, at the same time, retaining some approach based on political economy. But as Popular Music Studies became more interested in how culture acts on expression and understanding, and is organised to achieve these outcomes, the general explanation tends to over-sell the autonomy of music-makers and shifts the focus to the multi-layered relations between audiences and the industry, and to the packing and distribution of music to market segments. In this approach, the thorny issues connected with rights ownership, and with it the management of creativity in the music industry, are largely neglected. By proceeding from the worlds of music-making and music-use, the gap between creativity and consumption remains largely unfilled.

Making management visible

> I don't know why they won't let me go ... I just ask them to let me do my job and for them to do theirs ... it's all about the money. It's about the corporation (Singer-songwriter Nellie McKay on trying to get out of her contract with Columbia, quoted in Petrusich, 2005: 61).

One of the problems of analysis arises from the fact that direct managerial activity in music production is difficult to pin down – what exactly is the 'job' that Nellie McKay refers to? Corporate managers are not on stage with rock groups, in the booth with DJs or in the studio with record producers. Their power tends to be re-located to other areas of the commercial process and as dispersed and indirect, it is easy to diminish or to ignore entirely that popular music *performances* become popular music *products* substantially as an outcome of a managed business process.

To make managers and management visible, we can re-cast the making of popular musical products as an outcome of a combination of competences and, therefore, of specific types of creativity associated with them. This approach in turn opens up the 'value chain' of popular music to closer examination – from the origination of music texts, to the value-adding of signing, producing, marketing, promoting, and distribution of these (by now *transformed*) texts by staff either employed directly or sub-contracted by record companies. We argue that there is a double articulation in the management of creativity associated with the record industry, which is necessitated by the fact that musicians create music, but companies produce records. In this sense it is misleading to refer to 'individual inspiration versus creative systems' in cultural industries (Lampel *et al*, 2000), as the former can only enter the market through the latter.

In all production processes, the firm is meant to be 'expert', to know its own business as the sequence described by the conversion of raw materials into saleable products through labour input organised in and through technologies; and to understand its market and to produce goods that will succeed there. At the apex of the corporate hierarchy of the conglomerates that dominate the industry, the strategic role of senior management is to debate and decide the direction of revenue streams across their portfolio of artistic activities (Negus, 1999). However, given the 'nobody knows' principle, much necessarily rests on the delegated authority assigned to second tier production managers.

If we take the recently conglomerated Sony–BMG as an example, this was less a merger of two *corporations* than an amalgamation of their separate music divisions. As the *Financial Times* noted, the company was seeking $350m of annual savings from the deal and planned to re-invest some of this saving in artist development (Burt, Malkani and Pesola, 2004). The first priority of the merged company was to recompose the existing staff base so that the employees regarded as the key creative personnel were retained (and new ones hired) *before* considering which of their acts to retain, which to dismiss and which new ones to contract.

In other words, the first order 'creativity' is to establish that a production process is in place that can be effected and actualised through the practices and imaginative insights of appropriate personnel (creative individuals) who will be kept 'on track' by senior managers. These personnel will then engage 'artists' with a view to locating then 'developing' them, leading to releasing recordings of their work.

Given the nature and number of production decisions taken about a record *as a product*, there is no universal sequence or managerial recipe at play. At which point managerial intervention is made and its precise character will depend, to a large degree, on the nature of the act, its genre and the scale of the investment. Indeed, the value chain in popular music diverges from an anticipated norm in that, while 'value adding' through distinctive, sectional expertise is demonstrable, it is not as sequential and as demarcated as may be the case in other industries such as film. This is contrary to the view articulated in Hirsch's influential study.

... no product can enter the societal subsystem (e.g. retail outlets) until it has been processed favorably through each of the preceding levels of organization, respectively.... This model assumes a surplus of available 'raw material' at the outset ... and pinpoints a number of strategic checkpoints at which the oversupply is filtered out (1990: 133).

Hirsch represents cultural production as a 'Markov Process'. Such a process is a stochastic one: the next step in the process depends only on the current condition of the process, not on any cumulative momentum. In the film industry, the nature of production lends itself to repeated bouts of second-guessing the market in a way that is characteristically Markov: buy the film rights, hire the screenplay writers, revise the script, hire a producer, identify locations, hire crew, assemble the cast, and so on – with capital released only if those who hold the purse-strings are convinced that further investment is justified. Here, the 'value chain' is more obviously a series of 'linked' decisions and events, but pop music is not like this. In the record industry, it is popular perception that when acts are found they usually come with their own material that simply requires to be recorded and released (hence 'recording' industry); but, in practice, 'simply' misrepresents what is always an extremely costly commitment. It is costly because, in order for a released record to stand any real chance of market success, it needs to be produced, marketed, promoted and distributed effectively.

Considered in this way, while there are indeed stages at which record companies might 'pull the plug' on a project, these are far fewer than those available to film companies. The cost structure of large record companies requires that its employees are constantly engaged in producing records, while the operating condition that 'nobody knows' demands a constant stream of new signings and new releases (the UK trade publication *Music Week* regularly reports in excess of 200 albums released in any week). Under these circumstances, senior management's agreement to release can often come after many of the key value-adding activities have been accomplished but before the 'marketing spend' is sanctioned.

This is a key juncture and many acts 'fall' at this point, but it would be a mistake to believe that recording companies necessarily stay out of the production process and business of influencing creative content, focusing their attention solely on marketing and related activities. While the promotion and persistence of music genres is an attempt to provide templates that narrow the risk, the prior managerial environment of the act conditions whether marketing spend is sanctioned. Our argument is that there are multiple points of management and that interventions vary from act to act and so cannot be conceived of in terms of sequence or a universal template.

That is not to say that common features in the value chain of popular music cannot be identified, and the following section seeks to explore these commonalities in more concrete terms.

Re-examining the value-adding chain

The value chain in popular music begins with the creative efforts of song-writers and music performers. Very few of these attract the attention of record companies and fewer still go on to make profit for those companies (and earn a living for themselves). Major record companies are identified as those that enjoy their own sales and distribution apparatus, along with 'in house' Artists and Repertoire (A&R), marketing and promotions depart-ments. 'Independent' companies lack the ability to distribute physical product, and may also choose to 'buy out' marketing and promotion. A further distinction will be that some independents will be genre-specific, unlike 'majors' who still tend to seek and retain broad rosters of signed acts.

Because the industry requires a constant stream of new acts with mass sales potential, senior business managers expect to concede direct oper-ational control over record-making to this second tier of management. These individuals will be allowed 'space' to be creative – in the sense that they exercise their own distinct sensibility in selecting the 'right' acts from all of those on offer to them and will then go on to make the 'right' records with them in the face of the almost endless aesthetic choices that make up the recording process.

As Negus (1999) shows, the signing process is less the result of scouring for talent than an outcome of networks that reach from the offices of pro-duction managers out into localities. What aspirant acts need is an invest-ment of capital by local entrepreneurs and/or the expertise of a manager who will help them gain the attention of record companies. Record company managers do not directly access the creativity of signed acts. Not only will the act have been self-managing its creativity from the outset, they will be likely to be guided in some or all aspects of their working lives by an 'artist manager' of their choice.

Therefore, when A&R departments of major record companies choose new signings from the multitude on offer to them, the 'value' of (new) music lies in their *selecting* it for production, rather than their discovering it as a finished object of already great worth. This latter is the entire premise of the now hugely influential reality television shows *Pop Idol/American Idol/X Factor* – that 'talent' is 'out there' and requires only to be 'spotted' by those who possess this ability. But, of course, the exposure and public sympathy talent show contestants win by participating in such shows acts as a self-fulfilling prophesy where their subsequent sales success is concerned. In the UK, winners *and* losers of reality television shows have gone on to sub-stantial success; notably, and respectively, Will Young and Girls Aloud; Gareth Gates and Liberty X.

The creativity of artists and managers is circumscribed by the need to feed the market, or more precisely record company perceptions of what the market wants. As an American A&R executive notes:

> I have to go chase after these bands I don't give a shit about. Like, their music, I think, is just garbage. And I find myself asking questions that I never would have asked. 'What do they look like?' Or, 'can she dance?' ... really stupid stuff like that. It's about what's going to get it on television, what's going to get it on MTV... What's going to turn into mall fare' (quoted in Bowe, Bowe and Streeter, 2000: 352).

Ultimately, value in this particular cultural industry is *extrinsic*. Musical creativity, at least from a commercial perspective, is an outcome of the power of record companies to make judgments of commercial potential and to support those judgments with an apparatus geared to achieving success in the marketplace. Their management of each 'project' will be governed by judgments about the extent and nature of corporate effort – more or less directive with regard to repertoire, image, style, 'story' and so on. While managerial objectives remain consistent, managerial *execution* takes place on a case-by-case basis. In this situation, it is the nature and effect of recording contracts (and other) contracts that allows this flexible exercise of power.

From contract to completion

As Caves argues, the key and crux of management in 'creative industries' revolves around the nature of the contract that seals the agreement to initiate production. Where the record industry is concerned, the contract, for the purposes of law, equalises, quite artificially, two signatories who are vastly differently resourced. In return for the assignment of a pop act's recording rights (the intellectual property it alone enjoys in its original, creative work), that act is meant to receive the distinctive services of the record company. Amongst those services is that of record *producer* – the selection of which is potentially the most direct intervention into the actual exercise of creative labour. Even well-established artists can find that if the company does not like the finished product, they will assign another producer to change the sound – as happened to Fiona Apple when the production of her album *Extraordinary Machine* by Jon Brion in early 2003 was not signed off by Sony–BMG, then re-produced by Mike Elizondo, to be released in late 2005 (http://www.freefiona.com).

A contract is what it says, namely a *recording* contract, not one that pledges to release, market and promote any ensuing recording. The contracted pop act, whilst a business in its own right, has no mechanisms (save the abilities and acumen of its own manager) to monitor, audit, specify, direct, control, predict, or to meaningfully evaluate the actions taken (or not taken) by its contracting partner. This was the substance of George Michael's dispute with Sony (see Jones, 2002) and his failure to have his recording contract (and by implication *all* such contracts) declared void as a 'restraint of trade' had confined signed pop acts to this disadvantageous position.

The overwhelming likelihood of the market failure of released records is what helps Caves pose his questions but to consider the only strategy as the zero-sum game of a contract with options that favour one party over the other does not clarify how this strategy is *enacted*. This failure rate is not simply a product of over-production at the level of the industry – too many records chasing too few customers – it is a function of the coping strategy adopted by record companies. The coping strategy is that music originators are *over-signed* – too many acts within the company compete for the attention of managers.

It is in the everyday experience of fulfilling a record contract that Cave's 'humdrum inputs' demonstrate their value, albeit in an incremental and diffused manner. Not only must a pop act work with others in the recording of its music but the act must also concede access to them as an entire entity – what is marketed is *more than* music, it is the 'uniqueness' of the act, its look, its 'story', as well as its sound. In granting that their contracted partners are 'expert' in production, in most circumstances it is only those acts that co-operate most closely with their assigned managers that stand a chance of making it all the way through the process from signing to supported release. In this sense, branding and image management does not start after, but takes place *during* the production process. Six months before they had even released a record, British indie band Keane employed Moving Brands, a company specialising in 'truly holistic identities' to create an image for the band. This is so contrary to conventional ideas of rock authenticity that it remains something of an industry secret, 'It's like a theatre;' suggests one of my contacts. 'They don't want to show you behind the scenes, in case people stop believing what's on stage' (Petridis, 2004: 4).

What this means for *all* signed acts (and not simply newly-signed ones without a 'track' record) is that they can never be sure whether their album will be released or, if it is released, whether it will be marketed – a decision normally made by a combination of production and corporate management. In recent years, the most high-profile victim of a decision not to pursue a contract was EMI's decision to 'drop' Mariah Carey in 2003 after the release of only one album of a five album contract. Move down the hierarchy and such decisions multiply, with often devastating consequences for the career of the artist, as happened to country singer Robbie Fulks whose critically-lauded album – *Let's Kill Saturday Night* – was promoted, then he was dropped from the Geffen label following a merger between PolyGram and Universal Records (http://robbiefulks.com/articles/?id_00046).

Net value?

It is increasingly apparent that aspects of the music business – whether peer-to-peer file-sharing or self-production and distribution – are being conducted in cyber-space. Commentators are increasingly hailing the extent that the internet enables buyers, fans and artists themselves to by-pass record companies as a major disruption to the conventional business model in the cultural industries. As the editor of the web version of the music magazine *New Musical Express* notes, 'As a musician, it is already possible to write, record, and distribute music without signing a record deal at all' (Perreau, 2005).

Whilst the relations between the music industry and the internet remain fluid, the response to the initial wave of file-sharing demonstrates that the resilience, power and capacity for adaptation of the record companies should not be under-estimated. Within a few years, these companies have largely recovered the ground lost and, through huge investment in legal downloading services, have re-located the existing business model (with its attendant exclusive ownership of intellectual property rights) seamlessly, if not entirely painlessly, to the web. After several false (and expensive) starts, the Applemac 'ITunes' initiative has contributed to the swelling success of 'legitimate' downloads – for example, by the end of 2004, paid-for downloads of single tracks had outstripped physical sales by one third (http://news.bbc.co.uk/1/hi/entertainment/4242571.stm). This strategy of incorporating potential threats into an adapted business model has been employed before when, in the late 1970s, the major record companies used the new independent and seemingly 'alternative' companies as 'unofficial A&R men' to filter out non-commercially viable punk bands before signing those bands deemed commercial (Savage, 1991: 515).

The pattern of over-exuberant hype, then re-appearance of business as usual, follows that for the web and publishing more generally. In the early days, many believed that 'the Internet had also altered, perhaps irrevocably, how the individual can influence the corporations from which they purchase goods and services. Suddenly anyone with access to a computer and a modem can be a publisher' (Bailey, 1999: 3). Within a short time, prominent evangelists had already ceded defeat in the net wars as small companies, independent start-ups and niche markets were increasingly swallowed up by the big IT and media conglomerates such as AOL, Microsoft, and Viacom (Grossman, 2001; Rosenberg, 2001).

However, whilst the new forms of direct access to production and distribution for pop bands may not herald 'a joyous new musical socialism' (Barton, 2005: 5), it would be misleading to claim that the situation in the music business remains unchanged. One of the success stories of 2005 in British pop was the Arctic Monkeys whose local management team used a combinatory strategy of music industry networking (with the successful management company Wildlife) and fan-driven 'blogging' (through www.livejournal.com) to create media interest in the availability of their entire repertoire. Exploitation of online viral marketing strategies saw them reach number one in the UK sales chart in the first week of the release of their (by then) much-anticipated first single – to be followed by the largest first day sale of any album in UK history. More and more up-and-coming bands collect their own marketing data from live audiences and host web-sites and run blogs in the hope of consolidating a fan-base as a strategy for attracting record company attention.

Nevertheless, in the wake of the Arctic Monkeys' hit single came the £1m record deal with Domino Records, an independent company that relies on EMI for international marketing and distribution. What the web is enabling is not a new business model, let alone a triumph of autonomous creativity, but an alternative route into the traditional model that may by-pass some of the initial forms of corporate management. Even that remains unclear. As Barton (2005) admits, the A&R and marketing departments of record companies are adapting to the new media by offering free downloads for new acts and strong online marketing campaigns. Rupert Murdoch's media empire has already bought up myspace.com, the main web forum to listen to and discuss new bands. These initiatives are part of a wider re-configuration whereby record companies are looking more seriously at the licensing opportunities arising from other new media platforms – an extension of the synchronisation rights that come with the acquisition of recording rights (Barfe, 2004).

The story, however, does not end there. A more interesting sub-plot is that the web is enabling a much greater number of genre artists – from old-fashioned soul to alt-country – to survive without a record deal with the major labels. The editor of the soul music magazine, *Echoes*, observes that an artist is able to create a body of work without any pressure to conform to label expectations or A&R tampering: 'so they make their own album, they put it out on their own label, they sell thousands copies ... They have a career, a good living' (quoted in Egere-Cooper, 2005: 13). Whilst the survival of craft production in the niche markets of modern capitalism is notable and welcome, it is worth remembering that the sales of all alt-country acts combined is unlikely to match a single album from the manufactured country-pop of Shania Twain or Garth Brooks.

Conclusions

Our review of the general literature on creative and cultural industries has argued that little explanatory power resides in what might be called expanded conceptions of each set of 'industries'. Nor is creativity as such robust enough to carry the conceptual or empirical weight laid upon it in many recent writings. The distinctive characteristics of creative labour are best understood within particular sector and market contexts. With respect to the record industry, we have shown that there is something between creativity and consumption. Musicians may *self-manage* their own creativity but within a framework whereby production and business managers set the terms of access to resources and influence and ultimately to the market-place. This double articulation of creativity across the value chain shows considerable continuity with past practices. Though more dispersed, with the multiple points of management referred to earlier, is arguably cumulatively more managed than many conventional work settings.

There are limits to how far this preliminary analysis of how creativity is managed within the record industry can be generalised to all creative or even cultural industries. Some work is clearly more creative than others and there are typical and often long-standing patterns of tensions or polarities in its management. For example, the tension between autonomy and control has long been central to the management of expert labour, and many firms adopted mixed forms of control and dual professional and managerial career structures.

Whilst it is reasonable to point to commonalities across all types of management of creative work, including paradoxes such as reconciling creativity and routine, flexible and integrated activities, a general template for managing creative intensity has limited application. A more grounded approach would distinguish, for example, between the different categories and characteristics of creative work in the cultural industries (film, popular music, theatre), scientific-technical industries (bio-technology, pharmaceutical), traditional professions (law, medicine, academia), and new media (software, graphic design, web-based work). The last three of these categories have traditionally relied on some version of responsible autonomy to manage highly skilled work that utilises specialist knowledge (Friedman and Cornford, 1989). Such issues and approaches have re-emerged in a number of sectors under the guise of 'knowledge management'. For example McKinlay's (2002) case studies of pharmaceutical firms illustrate the complexities of managing the tensions between creativity and control and the boundaries between tacit and explicit knowledge in an industry under greater pressure to speed up the time from 'molecule to market'.

Knowledge workers in an industry such as pharmaceuticals share some similarities with the indeterminacy of outcome found in cultural industries in that project teams can spend years developing drugs that never reach the market. But such knowledge-intensive commodities are not symbolic goods dominated by aesthetic attributes. As McKinlay (2002) shows, the focus of new knowledge management initiatives – whether through enhanced means for monitoring projects and their outcomes or electronic cafes to share experiences – is firmly on the labour process. Furthermore, in such companies the 'creatives' produce outcomes under the loose supervision of the hiring company – they are valued and valuable because they create intellectual property that is automatically owned by that company. In the record industry, there is a need for intellectual property to be assigned to the company through the medium of the recording contract. Once intellectual property rights have been assigned, the musician loses power: the company owns the copyright and will work on and with it as the company sees fit – creativity, here, is appropriated rather than directly managed.

This example illustrates why we have also argued that a narrower conception of cultural industries has some analytical purchase. Whilst we reject a particular version of creative distinctiveness based on the subordination of economic relations to matters of culture and exchange value to sign value, we do recognise that the indeterminacy of outcome characteristic of the cultural industries can only be partly resolved in and through management of work relations. There is now the technological means to manufacture an 'appropriate' sound through the production process. As music publisher Eddie Levy comments, 'with the technical input of the studios now, you're going to make my dog be able to sing, but you're not having any impact on the US market. And it's not really doing anybody any good' (quoted in Barfe, 2004: 340). The danger is that such a 'manufactured' sound may detract from the symbolic value of the goods. Moreover, that value is inscribed through 'a cycle of authentication involving everyone active in the field' (Peterson, 2005: 1091). Each pop record is a performance that derives in part from the personalities of the performers. Miège's point is crucial here, as the imprint of the artist must remain visible to the user, then the company has, by definition, access not just to a quantity of the act (a number of recordings) but to its central quality – the uniqueness that the 'personalities' concerned bring to the 'project' as a whole. The act itself becomes a commodity and is treated as such, but the focal point for the management of creativity is more likely to be employment relations, specifically contracts, image and intellectual property rights. To return to a point we made earlier, this requires a managerial environment between (initial) creativity and (eventual) consumption.

However, sector specificity remains a constant factor. As Miège (1987) made clear, there are cultural industries: each of which may develop partially according to its own logic. The skill sets, organisational hierarchies, reward systems and employment structures pertinent to the film industry, fashion or repertory theatre are often as different as all cultural industries are to the manufacturing sector. For example, in the film industry 'projects' can grow into 'blockbusters' under the control of a contracting company whose primary contributions to creativity are finance for development and the apparatus for marketing and distribution. While, superficially, this is what record companies offer musicians, the latter begin their creativity *away from* the direct supervision of record companies but substantially on their conditions.

If comparative analysis across cultural industries relies ultimately on bottom-up, detailed pictures of what is going on in different industries or groups of industries, we have only been able to indicate the desired direction rather than the finished product. Furthermore, a wider analysis of how the record or any other cultural industry works requires links to be made between the management of tensions inside and outside the employment relationship, situating developments in the labour process within the structural changes taking place in the relevant industry and institutional contexts, as well as the impact of new technologies such as peer-to-peer distribution and supply-side factors. Finally, tensions and conflicts require agency as well as structure, and are manifest between the producers of creativity and the company or its agents, and between temporary alliances of particular agents and acts against others. This can be conceptualised as a struggle over the terms of creativity but that struggle always has to be located in specific organisational and social contexts.

REFERENCES

Adorno, T. and Horkheimer, M. (1979) *Dialectic of Enlightenment*. London: Verso (first published 1947).

Bailey, L. (1999) The triumph of the individual. *New Statesmen*, 1 November, 7–9.

Barfe, L. (2004) *Where Have All the Good Times Gone? The Rise and Fall of the Record Industry*. London: Atlantic Books.

Barton, L. (2005) Our tunes. *The Guardian*, 23 December, 5–6.

Bowe, J., Bowe, M. and Streeter, S. (eds) (2000) *Gig: Americans Talk About their Jobs*. New York: Three Rivers Press.

Burt, T., Malkani, G. and Pesola, M. (2004) The state of the music industry (3 parts). *The Financial Times*, 17–19 November, 12–13.

Caves, R.E. (2000) *Creative Industries*. Boston, Mass.: Harvard University Press.

Coy, P. (2000) The creative economy. *Business Week*, 21–28 August, 38–43.

Dannen, F. (1991) *Hit Men: Power Brokers and Fast Money Inside the Music Business*. London: Vintage.

Davis, H. and Scase, R. (2000) *Managing Creativity*. Milton Keynes: Open University Press.

Department for Culture, Media and Sport (DCMS) (2001) *Creative Industries Mapping Document*. London: DCMS (first printed in 1998).

Department for Culture, Media and Sport (DCMS) (2002) *Regional Cultural Data Framework: A User's Guide for Researchers and Policy-Makers*. London: DCMS.

du Gay, P. and Pryke, M. (2002) *Cultural Economy: Cultural Analysis and Commercial Life*. London: Sage.

▶

►

Egere-Cooper, M. (2005) New soul legends. *The Independent*, 25 November, 12–13.

Florida, R. (2002) *The Rise of the Creative Class*. New York: Basic Books.

Frith, S. (1983) *Sound Effects: Youth, Leisure and the Politics of Rock and Roll*. London: Constable.

Friedman, A. and Cornford, D. (1989) *Computer Systems Development: History, Organisation and Implementation*. New York: John Wiley & Sons.

Frith, S. (1996) *Performing Rites: On the Value of Popular Music*. Oxford: OUP.

Grossman, W. (2001) *From Anarchy to Power: The Net Comes of Age*. New York: NYU Press.

Healy, K. (2002) What's new for culture in the new economy? *The Journal of Arts Management, Law and Society*, 32(2), 86–103.

Hesmondhalgh, D. (1996) Flexibility, post-fordism and the music industries. *Media, Culture & Society*, 15.3(3), 469–88.

Hesmondhalgh, D. (2002) *The Cultural Industries*. London: Sage.

Hirsch, P.M. (1972) Processing fads and fashions: An organization-set analysis of the cultural industry systems. *American Journal of Sociology*, 77, 639–59, and in Frith, S. and Goodwin, A. (eds) (1990). *On Record: Rock, Pop and the Written Word*. London: Routledge.

Hirsch, P.M. (2000). Cultural industries revisited. *Organization Science*, 11(3), 356–61.

Howkins, J. (2001) *The Creative Economy*. London: Penguin.

Jessop, B. and Sum, N.-L. (2006) *The Cultural Turn in Economics: Towards a Cultural Political Economy*. Aldershot: Edward Elgar.

Jones, M. (2002) Learning to crawl: The rapid rise of music industry education. In M. Talbot (ed.), *The Business of Music*. Liverpool: Liverpool University Press.

Jones, M. and Thompson, P. (2001) Between rock and a hard place: Creativity and commodification in the music industry. Paper to the *19th Annual International Labor Process Conference*, University of London.

Lampel, J., Lant, T. and Shamsie, J. (2000) Balancing act: Learning from organizing practices in cultural industries. *Organization Science*, 11(3), 263–9.

Lash, S. and Urry, J. (1994) *Economies of Signs and Space*. London: Sage.

Lawrence, T.B. and Philips, N. (2002) Understanding cultural industries. *Journal of Management Inquiry*, 11(4), 430–41.

Leadbeater, C. (1999) *Living on Thin Air*. London: Viking.

McKinlay, A. (2002). The limits of knowledge management. *New Technology, Work and Employment*, 17(2), 76–88.

Miège, B. (1979) The cultural commodity. *Media, Culture and Society*, 1, 297–311.

Miège, B. (1987) The logics at work in the new cultural industries. *Media, Culture and Society*, 9, 273–89.

Negus, K. (1999). *Music Genres and Corporate Cultures*. London: Routledge.

Perreau, B. (2005) Internet idols. *The Independent*, 25 November, 15.

Peterson, R.A. (2005) In search of authenticity. *Journal of Management Studies*, 425, 1083–98.

Petridis, A. (2004) We're gonna make you a star. *The Guardian*, 8 July, 4–6.

►

▶

Petrusich, A. (2005) Nellie McKay: Princess of the protest ditty. *Paste*, 19 December, 60–3.

Pink, D. (2001) *Free Agent Nation*. New York: Warner Business.

Pratt, A. (2002) New economy: a cool look and the hot economy. Unpublished mimeo, London School of Economics, but see similar article in *Information. Communication and Society*, 5(1), 27–51.

Rosenberg, S. (2001. Assimilating the Web. Salon, 26 June. http://archive. salon.com/tech/feature/2001/06/26/looking-up-the-web/index.html

Savage, M. (1991) *England's Dreaming: Anarchy, Sex Pistols, Punk Rock and Beyond*. London: Faber and Faber.

Scase, R. (2002) Create harmony, not harnesses. *The Observer*, 4 August, 10.

Shorthose, J. and Strange, G. (2004) The new cultural economy, the artist and the social configuration of autonomy. *Capital & Class*, 84, 43–59.

Smith, C. (2002) Creative labor: Content, contract, control and customer. Unpublished paper, Royal Holloway, University of London.

Toynbee, J. (2000) *Making Popular Music: Musicians, Creativity and Institutions*. London: Edward Arnold.

Working in the Creative Economy: Risk, Adaptation, and the Persistence of Exclusionary Networks

4

Susan Christopherson

Introduction

Our world is one in which gender, race, and age have played profound roles in the choices people make. These categories tend to define the risks we are willing to take to pursue our dreams; they also motivate our tendency to feel more comfortable working with those who seem similar to ourselves. These realities are particularly salient in the Hollywood industry. It is a highly competitive industry dependent upon creative talent, freedom of expression, and more than a fair amount of good luck. It is also an insular industry that white males have traditionally dominated, where employment opportunities rest squarely on personal networks steeped in gender, race and age.

Hunt (2007: 14) for the Writers Guild of America

The concept of a 'creative economy' encompasses the idea that a new international division of labour is emerging in which advanced economies retain a comparative advantage in a set of economic functions, including those that emphasise creativity, innovation, and culturally specific production. These functions are characterised by a labour process and work organisation that differs significantly from that of routine production The literature on creative work has explored some of these differences, including: 1) entrepreneurship and self-employment; 2) labour flexibility; 3) network-based work organisation, and 4) project-based production.

In one of the most comprehensive analyses of creative industries, Caves (2000) presents a model of creative work in which:

1) Training and education inculcates values of self-expression over a realistic assessment of the ability to earn a living from the creative pursuit.

Teachers whose own livelihoods depend on valuing self-expression over an economic rationale reinforce the primacy of self-expression.

2) Competitions organised by gatekeepers and intermediaries are developed to evaluate contestants on proficiency, audience appeal, and the ability to perform under pressure. These competitions also serve as 'trade shows' to showcase talent and enhance the power of intermediaries in the production process.

3) Gatekeepers and intermediaries identify aspiring 'stars' on the basis of their personal trajectory and attempt to shape their 'brand' and market prospects via promotion. In this identification and promotion process, the creative worker's network (connections, school, movement) is very important to successful marketing. It is also critical to obtaining work experience, which, in these industries, is more important than educational credentials. It is within sequential projects that creative workers build their skills, experience, and careers.

4) The production process and its outcomes are fraught with risk and uncertainty. These uncertainties extend to the workforce, encouraging multiple strategies to reduce risks.

At the heart of Caves' model is a set of contracts, between the creative worker and the intermediary; and between the creative worker and the gatekeepers based on the high- risk nature of these industries. These contracts attempt to distribute risks and potential rewards among the creative workers, the intermediaries, gatekeepers, and (where appropriate) product distributors.

The analysis of creative work by Caves and other researchers has tended to emphasise differences among industries and occupations, comparing work in the advertising or fashion design industry with that in the theatre, for example. So academic debates have been about whether project work in an industry is accurately described and interpreted or about individual strategies in a high risk creative work environment. Much less attention has been paid to questions of change and adaptation in production organisation and the work process over time. In part, the static and horizontal character of the analysis of creative industries and creative work is attributable to their fairly recent claim to attention. Possibly more significant, however, is the tendency to consider creative industries as *sui generis* and set apart from the context of the economic institutions that construct incentives in market economies.

A reflexive approach

Creative work is, however, not a static phenomenon. Worker identity and the work process itself changes in conjunction with the strategies of firms and organisations in creative industries, and as the workforce adapts to new forms and levels of risk. While the idea that work is constructed in conjunction with changes in technology and industrial structure is well-established, for example, in studies of the advent of 'Taylorism', the analysis of temporal change has been neglected in creative work. This neglect can be explained, in part, by the disconnect between creative work and the broader economic institutions that govern labour, capital and product markets. Because creative workers are perceived as exceptional, their work process has been set apart. Creative workers' goals and strategies are depicted as driven by personal, internal motives (as Caves suggests) rather than influenced by the political and economic context within which they work. To fully understand creative work, however, we have to integrate the analysis of enduring features, particularly high levels of risk and uncertainty, with the political and economic context that constructs the level and distribution of risk. That context differs in time and space, affecting chances for (and definitions of) success, workforce strategies, and the work process.

One perspective useful to a more contextualised understanding of creative work is that of 'reflexive capitalism', which recognises changes in risk as characteristic of contemporary economies (Beck, Giddens and Lasch, 1994). To make the case for a contextualised, reflexive approach I focus on the media entertainment industries, particularly film and television. These industries are important both because of their international markets and production centres but also because work in these industries incorporates all the key dimensions of a creative economy: high risks, innovation, creativity, entrepreneurship, project-orientation, and high degrees of complex coordination. These industries are also valuable as cases for reflexive approaches to creative work because the economic and institutional context in which work is carried out in these industries has changed dramatically over time. While I focus on the most recent period of change in this analysis, my goal is to illuminate the relationships among market governance incentives, firm strategies and the situation of the creative workforce. Since, as Caves points out, creative industries begin from a standpoint of high-risk ('nobody knows') changes in the distribution of risk and adaptive strategies are key elements of an analysis of change over time.

My central hypothesis is that as U.S-based media conglomerates have positioned themselves *vis-à-vis* changing global markets and production centres, they have altered what they produce and how they produce. They have moved from producing a diverse portfolio of films for national and global markets to a more exclusive focus on global 'blockbusters' aimed at a young male market. Despite the level of capital investment necessary to these mega-projects, they are less risky (because of global mass market appeal, repurposing for a sequence of ancillary markets, and merchandising potential) than producing mid-size films aimed at less predictable niche markets. So, the conglomerate portfolio is filled out by independently produced and financed films aimed at more limited markets (adults, women, national cultural markets etc.).

Conglomerate strategies in broadcast and cable television have also changed, emphasising cost reduction in the large corporate broadcast organisations and dramatic expansion of low-end production, particularly in 'non-fiction' programming for cable television. Given the overall profile of industry production, it is at this low-end that labour demand has substantially increased since the late 1990s.

These changes in what is produced and how it is produced have had important implications for the expanding industry workforce. Labour demand for example, has become bi-furcated between a core of A-list talent and crew, and a large peripheral workforce that must necessarily rely on work outside the entertainment industries to obtain their livelihoods. The B-list or 'middle class' of the industry workforce has shrunk as a proportion of the overall workforce. This has important implications for the ability of workforce entrants to obtain the experience necessary to build a career.

The production process in both film and television continues to be organised around high-risk project-based work. As mid-range opportunities have declined, pre-existing networks show a tendency to pull in and go with the reliable and familiar despite the expansion of a large and diverse labour supply and creative resources. So, one manifestation of workforce adaptation is the rise of defensive exclusionary networks including the dominance of all facets of the most risky (but also most lucrative and prestigious) end of the industry production spectrum, that in film, by white men.

To draw the causal links between competitive conditions, producer strategies and labour force adaptation I examine how labour demand has been influenced by changing competitive conditions in the media entertainment industries, and how these changes have affected the strategies of a key intermediary – the project producer. I then look at workforce trends including the emergence of a smaller core and larger peripheral workforce and changing conceptions of work and professional identity. Finally, I look at one key form of workforce adaptation – exclusionary networks.

The evidence to examine the relationship between industry structure, risk, and workforce adaptation comes from a study of industry patterns that included forty interviews with directors, producers, leaders in both unions and guilds, and studio owners as well as analysis of proprietary data and publicly available data on industry production trends and employment (Christopherson *et al*, 2006).

As a first step to understanding workforce adaptation to increasing risk, I review what is known about the contemporary entertainment media labour supply.

Labour supply: workforce expansion in a 'post-professional' setting

Questions concerning employment in the entertainment industries have always been difficult to answer because of the project-oriented character of production. Even the most successful entertainment industry worker has multiple employers during the course of the year, spells of intense work, and spells of unemployment. Using ES202 or social security payment reporting data, the Entertainment Economy Institute (EEI) (EEI and the PMR Group, 2004) found that a very broadly defined entertainment industry workforce grew at rate of 35 per cent in California between 1991 and 2002, more than twice as fast as the overall California workforce. And, the core workforce, those whose incomes were continuously made from entertainment industry employment at least 75 per cent of the time, grew 17 per cent between 1991 and 2002. What is more significant than this growth rate, however, is that core workers declined as a *share* of the total workforce, from 38 per cent in 1991 to 33 per cent in 2002. So, while the workforce was expanding, a smaller portion of the total workforce was able to derive a full-time income from work in the entertainment industries.

With concentration in the film and television industries, employment in firms in film and television production has also concentrated in Los Angeles with 63 per cent of total employment in 2004 (Christopherson *et al*, 2006: 14). Employment in firms in the second largest centre of production, New York, has stagnated and there are indications that the proportion of the New York workforce that is made up of independent contractors has increased (Center for an Urban Future, 2005).

This shift in employment patterns is especially significant in broadcast television, which historically has employed more people in medium and large size firms (Christopherson *et al*, 2006; Hunt, 2007).

As in many other industries, in the US, large media firms are paring down their production workforces to an essential core and using temporary workers and self-employed workers on an as-needed basis. However, increased use of a flexible labour supply is only part of the story; a change in the absolute size of the labour supply is another important dimension. The expansion of the labour supply has been stimulated, in part, by the success of higher education media training programmes. In these programmes, which have proliferated in Los Angeles and New York as well as in other cities, students learn a wide variety of production skills and are introduced to new technologies that cross conventional union professional and craft jurisdictions. They learn how to produce on 'shoe string' budgets and to work very rapidly and under severe time constraints. They learn to work in efficient multi-functional production teams. When they graduate, they are 'hybrids', writer-directors, director-camera-operator-editors, who make up a flexible, independent contractor workforce perfectly suited to the high growth segment of the media industry – production for cable television. In some respects, this workforce has more in common with their young colleagues in New Media than they do with their elders who work in broadcast television and medium to high budget film (Batt *et al*, 2001).

Working style, expectations, and a cultivated amateurism separate this 'free agent', entrepreneurial workforce from the establishment professionals that populate the traditional entertainment media guilds and unions. Although there is still considerable intersection (and even some merging) between the professional worker with a defined role and the multi-functional media production team member, the contemporary workforce appears more segmented and differentiated than it did in the 1980s when the major divide in the US workforce was defined by union or non-union status. (Christopherson and Storper, 1988).

Labour demand: the impact of changing competitive conditions on the extent and allocation of risk

The context for producing and distributing media entertainment products has been affected by the integration of global markets and decreasing transport and communications costs which have allowed producers to access less expensive skilled labour pools (Christopherson *et al*, 2006). The conditions affecting the workforce are inexplicable, however, without reference to changes in the structure of the industry and the reemergence of a highly concentrated and consolidated media entertainment industry in the U.S.

Specifically, labour demand is being shaped by industry restructuring and by the differential opportunities for profit from various types of products. While options (such as UTube) have increased for amateur distribution of entertainment products, the options available for earning a living as a 'creative worker' in entertainment media are limited and have become more constrained with greater industrial concentration.

In television, for example, concentration has led to a decline in the number of competing product distributors and has increased cost pressures and risks for programme producers. They have, in turn, re-allocated risk to the workforce.

A Directors Guild representative, testifying before a US Federal Communications Commission hearing in Los Angeles in October 2006, described the impact of concentration on television production. In his testimony he noted that in 1993, about 66 per cent of network television programmes came from independent producers while the networks produced 44 per cent. In 2006, independent producers produced only 22 per cent of network television while 76 per cent was produced by the networks themselves.

In the film industry, ownership concentration has been associated with changes in types of films produced and distributed. Production has become bi-furcated into big-budget blockbusters, distributed by 'The Majors', costing an average of $100 million to produce and market, and a lively and growing independent film sector with films typically costing less than $10 million. Independent films comprise over half of the total film output (though only 5 per cent of total revenue), and account much of the total growth in production numbers. What has been declining is the middle budget film.

The reasons for shifts in film production are complex. As the entertainment media industries have concentrated, the cost of producing and distributing a feature film has increased dramatically (Jones, 2002). Among the reasons for this increase are accounting rules for the industry which were changed in 1981 as new distribution venues for entertainment products emerged (Fabrikant, 1992). These rules permit the (now) conglomerate owners of multiple distribution venues to distribute the costs of marketing among theatrical release, network television and cable, and to rapidly write-off the cost of a product while at the same time increasing their bottom line (in current profits) by longer-term estimates of future revenues from these multiple outlets. This accounting strategy encourages the conglomerates to extract high advertising and marketing costs from their distribution outlets and raises the overall cost of marketing and advertising the product. This strategy, not coincidentally, raises barriers to entry from non-conglomerate controlled producers.

The control of multiple distribution markets by a handful of firms has spawned strategies to squeeze more profits out of products, both old and new, by multiplying the venues in which they can be distributed and increasing their value through cross-market advertising. Films produced by Universal are advertised on NBC, the conglomerate's broadcast television network, and hyped through its news and information programming. Theatres owned by the conglomerates advertise its other media products. Libraries of old television programmes and films are mined to find anything that could attract an audience, fill cable hours, and attract even small advertising dollars. The goal is to control audience share and to fill distribution outlets as cheaply as possible.

The fastest growing media entertainment sector in the early 2000s is the television sector and particularly cable television. The character of production for cable is significant because television production has outpaced film production in Los Angeles and New York since the mid-1980s and much of the recent growth has been concentrated in low cost production for cable television networks (Scott, 2004). So, while the number of productions has increased in Los Angeles and New York, much of this increase appears to be in low budget productions for cable distribution.

This is a mixed blessing – cable television provides work and sustains the media production complex but the work is poorly paid and rarely provides the benefits that have come to be associated with the unionised media entertainment industry. Thus, there are plentiful projects but meagre rewards, either for producers or for the workforce.

Concentration and consolidation, combined with changes in the labour supply have affected the production context for a key intermediary in the production process – the product producer. While a few producers can make a living in blockbuster films, most producers organise projects in independent film and broadcast and cable television. They face a very different set of conditions than existed twenty years ago and have responded by developing new financing, production, and labour strategies.

Changes in the production process: producer strategies in television and independent film

At the centre of the changing production process is the producer, who frequently initiates the production process and is primarily responsible for financing the project as well as for coordination and completion. Broadly speaking, the producer faces a set of pressures that emanate from the character of demand in the media entertainment industry and as a result of the economic power exercised by distributors and their associated gatekeepers.

Demand at the low end and the emergence of Wal-Mart model – supplier competition, lean production and loss of creative control

Growth in demand is at the low end of the production spectrum. The entertainment media industry is bi-furcated as described above and fewer mid-range films or quality television programmes are being financed and distributed. Producers and producer/directors, especially those not already established, enter an industry that is closer to a Wal-Mart model of continuous cost pressure on suppliers to reduce production costs and retailer (distributor) driven definition of the product and production process.

This model is defined by increased competition for financing and loss of creative control over the product. The control that the producer has over the product is reduced and cost pressures increase. This model has encouraged strategies to: 1) tap unconventional sources of financing, particularly place-based incentives; 2) use lean production methods made possible by new technologies and multi-skill training and 3) increase the reputation value of the product with product financiers and potential distributors by going with the 'tried and true' among the industry workforce.

Increased competition for financing and the search for public subsidies

As one producer/director who has worked for public broadcasting in Canada and the U.S. described: 'The networks are more unstable. The economics are just not there. The distributors are empty. They are shells. They used to be full of people on contract. (Now) they want to work with people who are reliable and produce at the lowest price' (personal interview, September 9, 2007).

And from another producer/director who has worked in supplying programming in both commercial and public television, 'I don't see the (economic) model. Budgets are lower and production values are lower. Schedules are crazy and you are expected to just churn out the stuff' (personal interview, September 5, 2007).

Media conglomerates have increasing power over producers. Just as Wal-Mart squeezes its suppliers, the media conglomerates squeeze the producers. Overall, the costs of getting a programme distributed have increased because of expanded marketing on the various platforms (including network and cable television) in which the product will be distributed. Because of this cost structure, production and distribution of a film requires multiple financial partners. The media conglomerates (who control the distribution gateways) frequently assume only a minor position in the investment. Producers must engage in complex co-financing deals, looking for finance capital wherever they can find it.

The bargaining position runs only one way, however. US television networks, for example, have adopted the strategy of demanding a financial stake in any pilots that are picked up for the primetime schedule. Even advertisers have noted the implications of this shift, warning that 'broadcast networks are more interested in financial deals than putting the best shows they can find on the air'. (Advertising Age, 1999 cited in Bielby and Bielby, 2003). This strategy reflects both the increased power over distribution access held by the conglomerates and their ability to shift risk for project development. According to Bielby and Bielby (2003:590) 'to reach the prime-time schedule, the supplier has to agree to forgo a share of the future revenues'.

In the world of documentary production, (as has historically been the case in the music industry) producers may pay to have their product distributed on major television networks. 'They paid us $3500 for the programme and the E and O (Errors and Omissions) Insurance was $3400. We ended up paying to have the product shown on a major public television channel.' (Personal interview, September 9, 2007).

Because of the increased individualisation of the production process and the difficulty of breaking through into the key distribution venues, would-be talent may have to pay to compete for the attention of gatekeepers. One variant of the 'pay to play' scenario is 'The ... Idol model' in which all the risks and costs of developing an entertainment product are assumed by the talent (or as they are now known, 'participants'), who are used as a revenue source for popular reality programmes.

This model is also increasingly prevalent behind the scenes in the media-financing world.

Film festivals, for example, are an entry point for film makers but also have become a money maker for entrepreneurs who set up festivals, inviting all comers to submit entries (for a fee, that is). There are now 122 festivals in North America. A website that coordinates all entries (www, Without a Box) enables the festival promoters to make money from the submissions and to reduce their processing costs.

And, in another example, in the highly competitive documentary world, competitions such as the Toronto 'Hot Docs' documentary forum, charge entrants who compete in a competitive arena to make a pitch for their project in front of a board of potential financiers. They have twelve minutes. 'If you can't get their attention in the first two minutes, you're dead.' (Personal interview, September 9, 2007).

The substantial number of documentaries entered in the competition is winnowed to a selection of entrants with reasonable chances of success. Observers of the competition (in the arena) are also charged high fees to watch the presentations.

The competition for financing has driven producers and their corporate sponsors to look for national, regional, or state subsidies to provide them with production cost advantages (primarily in labour costs) or direct financing for the film or television product. In many cases these production location choices are forced on the director by the conglomerate for which he is supplying the programme or film. Locations are now determined on the basis of economic criteria rather than on aesthetic grounds or in relation to the story.

According to one film office director:

The power has shifted from the 'Creatives' to the 'Suits'. In other words, if you don't have a large incentive, you are not considered. Many projects are now budgeted with specific incentives in mind before a director is hired.

A recent example captures the workings of the new financing-oriented public subsidies programmes:

Earlier this year, ABC was set to film a pilot episode of a show. The production was all ready to shoot, But then something happened?

'The company calculated [that] their gain from state of Georgia's tax incentive would be about $300,000 on a $4.5 million project,' says City of Savannah Tourism and Film Services Director, Jay Self. 'But the state of South Carolina could offer them a cheque for $680,000.'

So the entire shoot decamped the Coastal Empire and headed for the Holy City, $380,000 richer than when they started. The catch: The script had to be changed to reflect the location.

And they mean that literally. Whereas the state of Georgia offers production companies a base tax incentive of 9 per cent (twelve if you shoot in an economically depressed area like Fulton County), that's in the form of a credit that can be taken off the company's bottom line later.

But South Carolina's much more generous new 20–30 per cent incentives are made all the more valuable because they're *rebates*, not credits. In other words, the production company gets a big fat cheque soon after it wraps.

Savannah Times

Although simplifying what is a complex set of decisions, contemporary production decisions suggest a model in which:

1) Low budget productions have expanded and concentrated in the major production centres (Los Angeles and New York) because of the inexpensive non-union labour supply and because they are too small to take advantage of financing incentives offered in alternative locations.
2) Mid-budget productions in film and television have decreased as a proportion of total productions. They are more likely to take place outside major production centres in order to tap public subsidies and to use (at least partially) non-unionised crews. Talent retains employment in these projects but has decreased creative control.
3) High-budget blockbuster productions are likely to be co-produced by major companies so as to reduce competition and depend on major financing and subsidy packages. They are more likely to be filmed in international locations. They utilise unionised A-list craft and talent in order to reduce their substantial financial risk profile.

The creative workforce in a changing industry production process

For much of the creative workforce in the entertainment media industries, tie recent period of industry restructuring, which has combined expansion at the low end of the product market, high end retrenchment, and re-location of production for middle budget projects, has produced heightened anxiety over income expectations, and anger over a loss of creativity and pressure to produce too much too fast. Even in this historically high-risk industry, the recent period has been one in which the rewards of working in media entertainment are more elusive than ever.

Together, the bifurcation of the film market and cost cutting by network television have limited the number of mid-range productions that have traditionally composed the 'bread and butter' jobs in film and television. The combination of these trends in historically unionised major employment venues along with the expansion of the labour supply and the emergence of cable television have created a new bargaining climate for the media industry workforce.

Information on workforce trends is limited because of the project nature of work in these industries. By combining publicly available data with proprietary information from guilds and unions, special studies and a series of interviews, however, we can piece together a picture of how changes in the risk profile of the industry are expressed in workforce patterns.

Labour segmentation and deepening of the core-periphery divide

Changes in entertainment media production have been interpreted differently by the so-called talent or above the line workforce and the skilled craft workers who compose the below-the-line workforce. At the top end of the creative entertainment media workforce, producers, writers and directors complain about the loss of creative control, and tighter production deadlines and budgets, as well as loss of residual payments that sustain them financially during the dry periods when they are not employed on a project. They attribute these changes directly to industry conglomeration and the decrease in competition. Older established 'talent' particularly men, are, however, more likely than new entrants to be able to maintain their connection with higher budget film and broadcast television productions (Hunt, 2007). Thus, the new environment is associated with patterns and processes of labour segmentation that separate craft and talent workers and also separate the traditional white male workforce that has dominated industry employment from a growing, younger, and more ethnically diverse and female workforce that is more entrepreneurial and antagonistic to union representation.

As has already been described, the most important change from the mid-1990s onward is increasing demand for low budget productions to fill endless cable networks. Many programmes for cable networks are produced within small 'turn key' budgets by producers, whose profit margin depends on saving on labour costs by, for example using crews not on standard union contracts.

At the same time there is a larger supply of labour vying for a pool of less remunerative or reliable jobs. And, the opportunities for employment in higher budget, unionised productions have been eroded by slow growth in feature film production, the tendency of film-makers to shoot outside the US in order to obtain financing through co-productions, and a decrease in the proportion of the more expensive and labour intensive scripted productions (such as dramatic series) for television (Epstein, 2005). So, while the number of marginal productions for television is increasing, producers of medium to high budget feature films have also been under pressure to cut costs. The pressure to reduce total expenses (emanating from rising star salaries and product marketing costs) has focused particularly on 'below-the-line' or skilled craft labour costs because this work is perceived as less important in adding value to the product and acquiring necessary financing.

When we look at information from New York on changes in employment by occupation, those occupations connected with television production have seen increased work hours. Within the talent workforce, the earnings of New York-based Screen Actors Guild members have stagnated. By contrast, members of the American Federation of Radio and Television artists, who work primarily in television, have experienced a 33 per cent increase in workdays over the period 2000–2003. Work has also been higher in television for background actors (formerly called 'Extras') with 80 per cent growth in workdays between 1995 and 2003 in television productions shot in New York. Work for members of The Directors Guild has also increased in television with increased workdays in television production in the 2000–2005 period. Since cable production work is more frequently done in studios than on location, there has, not surprisingly, been a significant increase in working hours by studio mechanics. Their work hours in television production increased 40 per cent between 2000 and 2003.

Another 'craft' group benefiting from increased television production are editors, whose work hours in New York doubled between 2002 and 2003, and increased 25 per cent between 2003 and 2004. Editors are extremely important in growing production types such as reality television, which use editing to produce a story from hours of shooting with only a minimal script. The number of editors employed actually declined during this period indicating that those editors employed are working more but that the risk of unemployment may have increased. Because of the increased demand for editors across production types, it is not surprising that the only occupation in which the percentage of women increased on major film productions was editing by 1 per cent (Hunt, 2007).

Although below-the line or entertainment industry craft workers are most affected by the restructuring of the industry and the ability of entertainment conglomerates to squeeze producers in order to extract higher profits, the changes wrought by industry concentration affect even the most creative segments of the industry. According to one veteran film-maker, 'in cable, residuals (payments for each showing of the product) for writers, actors, and directors are a percent of the producer's gross. But if that producer is a network who self-deals the rights to their cable company... there is no compensation for that. Suddenly you discover that the 11 or 12 per cent gross residual among the three guilds that has been fought over for so many decades is virtually meaningless, as rights are simply self-dealt among related entities' (Hill, 2004: 20).

Anne-Marie Johnson of the Screen Actors Guild described the impact of these changes in her testimony at the Federal Communications Commission Hearings:

As actors, we find the continued consolidation of media companies has drastically limited our ability to individually bargain our personal services agreements.... the networks decide what the top-of-the show rates are, in a parallel practice. Some networks will even tell you they only pay 50 per cent of the going rate. Take it or leave it. This salary compression cripples the middle class actor's ability to make a living.

(http: //www.sag.org, 2006).

Increasing employment in television has combined with two other patterns: 1) increasing bifurcation in the incomes of above-the-line or talent, indicated by data on SAG members in both LA and New York; and 2) a narrowing of the income gap between people employed in the entertainment media and the median income of all people employed in California (EEI, 2004). Although these trends are only suggestive and require more definitive research, they point to changes in the relative position of media entertainment workers and to a relative diminution of their income advantage relative to other occupations.

Hourly wages in the media industries remain high, but reports from the unions indicate the work has become harder and less predictable than it was in the early 1990s. One common complaint is that producers attempting to cut costs will reduce shooting days by requiring overtime work from the production crew. While long working hours are legendary in the media entertainment industry, the boundaries that circumscribed abuse appear to have broken down as unions have lost power over industry practices and as there has been an increase in the proportion of productions made on 'shoe string' budgets.

The expansion of low budget production for cable, the growing labour pool, and slow growth in the more lucrative (for labour) production segments, such as feature film and broadcast network television series, partially explains why increased employment and production numbers in Los Angeles, and more recently in New York City, are combined with high levels of worker dissatisfaction and a sense of increased risk.

The decline of professional and craft identities and the rise of the hybrid, crossover workforce

The sight of the TV journalist who comes alone to a reporting scene, conducts interviews, and then sets up a camera and records herself is now a common one. It reflects a broader trend made possible both by technological change and multi-skill training that allows media companies to reduce the number of people engaged in producing a media product. In some cases, such as news journalism or documentary production, the entire project is carried out by a single individual who frequently does the writing, directing, camera work, editing and promotion for distribution.

The demand for low cost (meaning low labour cost) productions to fill time on conglomerate-owned cable networks has fostered the use of non-unionised labour. In addition, production types (most notably reality television) have emerged in which skilled labour inputs are minimised or provided free-of charge (for advertising purposes). In general, distributor control over production has increased and cost pressure on production intensified for a variety of reasons, (including increased marketing costs). The use of terminology such as programme planner to replace writer obscures roles in the production process and avoids union jurisdiction. The shift to participants (to replace actor or performer) avoids employment contracts and shifts accountability from the programme distributor and producer to the individual who willingly participates in a programme 'event'.

The labour politics emerging in the wake of the restructuring of the media entertainment industry have been influenced by three major tendencies: 1) an increasing labour supply across occupations and an increase in the proportion of industry workers employed as independent contractors (Center for an Urban Future, 2005: 2) changing labour demand, especially increasing demand for a flexible, inexpensive production workforce for cable television; and 3) pressure on producers from media distributors to identify production strategies that will substantially reduce costs and directly finance productions.

With these changes the still powerful media unions have faced powerful challenges. An already complex union and guild terrain has become more difficult to interpret because of shifts of power among collective bargaining units. Unions representing the workforce for television have experienced growth and increasing work hours for their membership. In unions whose members work in both television and film, such as the Directors Guild, it is television employment that is contributing more to total income. This shift has caused old rivalries between film and television-based unions such as The Screen Actors Guild (SAG) and American Film, Television and Radio Actors (AFTRA) to re-emerge, as well as talk of mergers.

Basically, however, talent and some prestigious craft guilds (such as the Cinematographers Guild) have focused their attention on retaining the shrinking number of good jobs for their members and want to ignore the entrepreneurial, multi-skilled, hybrid workforce that is growing at the periphery of the industry. According to one officer for the Directors Guild, 'These are bad jobs. We don't want to have anything to do with them' (Personal interview, April 2005).

Reflecting the exclusionary character of responses to increasing risk, attempts to unionise the fast developing low-end workforce are absent or failing. The Writers Guild reports, for example, that the proportion of its younger membership (under 30) dropped 42 per cent between 2000 and 2005 (Hunt, 2007).

The continued significance of exclusionary (old boy) networks

Competition over a declining proportion of 'good jobs' in the major production centres has put pressure on established worker networks. Evidence from recent studies of the workforce indicates that despite educational programmes in media that are training women as well as men and women from a variety of ethnic and racial backgrounds, the most stable and career-oriented jobs in media entertainment continue to be held disproportionately by white males. While the overall labour supply has become more diversified, that diversification has had little effect on employment in the most lucrative parts of the industry or in jobs that build careers over the long term.

To the contrary, there is evidence that in the media industries, defined by their avowed creativity, openness to innovation and emphasis on self-expression, high risk favours members of the 'old boy's network'. This pattern is not one that will disappear with the dying of the dinosaurs, however. A survey of new media professionals indicates that similar patterns have emerged in this newer and younger industry (Batt *et al*, 2002).

The film industry is notorious for its high risk-high return profile, requiring years of networking, investment in skills, and, most important, access to work opportunities in order to build a career. While educational training may provide an initial entreé, for example as a lowly production assistant, it is the ability to self-finance one's career for a number of years, along with luck and the right connections that construct the road to success. Studies of students in media programmes and their career paths note that even the ability to get a foot on the career ladder depends on continued parental financial support for a series of 'internships' beyond graduation (Holgate, 2006). Students without affluent parents and carrying significant educational debt cannot afford this route.

Even for those with established credentials, breaking through the barrier of established male networks is difficult. The situation of women in film demonstrates that creativity and willingness to take risks is not enough. In 2006, women comprised only 15 per cent of all directors, executive producers, producers, writers, cinematographers and editors working on the 250 films with the domestic gross in the U.S. This figure is the same as it was in 1999 and is down 2 per cent from the high of 17 per cent in 2005.

Possibly even more noteworthy, the incomes of women employed in creative positions in the media entertainment industries are not keeping pace with those of their male colleagues. The income gap between male and female writers belonging to the Writers Guild of America increased from $24,000 in 1999 to $40,000 in 2005 (Hunt, 2007).

The exclusionary pattern extends to minority writers for whom the earnings gap with white male writers reached a 15-year high in 2005 (*Ibid.*).

How do we explain the fact that white male-dominated networks appear to be able to maintain their hold over livelihood sustaining jobs in these high-risk creative industries? Of course there is not a single explanation, and many of the causes resemble those associated with labour segmentation and exclusion across industries. For example, women and minorities have been more likely to enter the television industry and that industry has undergone considerable restructuring, including downsizing, and moving toward subcontracted rather than in-house production. Women and minorities have also been ghettoised – women in places such as 'the family network' and minorities in production companies oriented toward production for minority communities. What one takes away from the available evidence, however, is that creative industries are not so different from other industries and are shaped by many of the same institutions that determine access to career-building opportunities.

What can an approach that is sensitive to time and institutional context add to our understanding of creative work?

The study of creative work is in its infancy and great strides have been made in understanding how individuals makes choice in high risk creative industries and how work is organised around projects and networks. Much of this work, however, takes the creative industries and creative work as exceptional and set apart from the incentives and institutions that influence work organisation and individual choices across the economy. This preliminary analysis of employment patterns in the film and television industries suggests that it would be useful to take another look at how common economic features, such as those constructing discrimination on the basis of race and gender influence both the capacity to take on risk and the resources one brings to high risk enterprises. Second, the story of the media industries demonstrates that while all creative industries may be high risk, they are not risky in the same way. The degree and nature of risk changes over time and can be affected by the incentives that emerge from different market governance regimes. The media industries, always high risk, have become more risky since the mid-1990s and the opportunities to earn a livelihood or build a career have deteriorated. A better analysis of risk as it is constructed across time and space would add much to the understanding of creative work and creative workers.

REFERENCES

Batt, R.S., Christopherson, S., Rightor, N. and Van Jaarsveld, D. (2001) *Net Working, Work Patterns and Workforce Policies for the New Media Industry.* Washington D.C.: Economic Policy Institute.

Beck, U.A. Giddens and Lash, S. (eds) (1994) *Reflexive Modernization: Politics and Tradition in the Modern Social Order.* Stanford, CA: Stanford University Press.

Biebly, W. and Biebly, D. (2003) 'Controlling prime-time: Organizational concentration and network television programming strategies', *Journal of Broadcasting and Electronic Media,* 47(4), 573–96.

Caves, R.E. (2000) *Creative Industries: Contracts Between Art and Commerce,* Cambridge, Mass: Harvard University Press.

Center for an Urban Future (2005) Creative New York. from www.nyc-future.org

Christopherson, S. (2002) Project work in context: Regulatory change and the new geography of the media. *Environment and Planning A,* 34, 2003–2015.

Christopherson, S., Figueroa, M., Gray, L.S., Parrott, J., Richardson, D. and Rightor, N. (2006) 'New York's Big Picture: Assessing New York's Position in Film, Television and Commercial Production. A Report to The New York Film, Television and Commercial Initiative.' Available at ILR.Cornell.edu.

Christopherson, S. and Storper, M. (1988) 'The Effects of Flexible Special-isation on Industrial Politics and the Labour Market: The Motion Picture Industry', *Industrial & Labor Relations Review,* 42/3, 331–47.

Entertainment Economy Institute (EEI) and PMR Group (2004) *California's Entertainment Workforce: Employment and Earnings (1991–2002).* Los Angeles: The Entertainment Economy Institute.

Epstein, E.J. (2005) *The Big Picture, the New Logic of Money and Power in Hollywood.* New York: Random House.

▶

▶

Fabrikant, G. (1992, July 12) Blitz hits small studio pix. *New York Times*, 7.

Hill, L. (2004) Can media artists survive media consolidation? *The Journal of the Caucus of Television Producers, Writers and Directors, XXII*, 17–21.

Hunt, D. (2007) Whose Stories Are We Telling. The 2007 Hollywood Writers Report. Writers Guild of America West, Los Angeles, California.

Jones, M. (2002) *Motion Picture Production in California*: Report Requested by Assembly Member Dario Frommer, Chair of the Select Committee on the Future of California's Film Industry.

Koch, N. (1990) American packed expansion. *Channels*, 20–8.

Lauzen, M. (2007) 'The Celluloid Ceiling: Behind-the-Scenes Employment of Women on the Top 250 Films of 2006'. Unpublished report. San Diego State University, Department of Communications, San Diego, California.

Manly, L. (2005, June 20) Networks and the outside producer: Can they co-exist? *New York Times*, C1–C7.

Scott, A. (2004) The other Hollywood: The organizational and geographic bases of television-program production. *Media, Culture and Society, 26*(2), 183–205.

Scott, A. (2005) *On Hollywood: The Place, the Industry*. Princeton, NJ: Princeton University Press.

Walker, S. (2007) 'Women on Top', *Toronto Star*, September 15, Section E, 1, 3.

Part II

Creative Labour in Practice:
Film, Theatre and Television

Getting In and Getting On in Hollywood: Freelance Careers in an Uncertain Industry

5

Keith Randle and Nigel Culkin

Introduction

This chapter explores issues related to employment in the US film industry, reporting on a study carried out between June 1999 and March 2002 around the themes of 'getting in, staying in and getting on' in Hollywood (Los Angeles). The study set out to explore the experience of freelance workers within a sector changing rapidly at both a global and local level (Wasko, 1995) and is part of a wider comparative project concerned with similar issues in the UK.

The study reported here has grown out of earlier work concerned with the nature of employment and management in the UK film industry (Blair, 2001; Blair, Grey and Randle, 2001), with the relationship between the US and UK industries (Culkin and Kerrigan, 1999; Blair and Rainnie, 2000; Kerrigan, 2000) and with a comparison between the industries in the two countries (Blair, Culkin and Randle, 2003).

For those with an interest in film-related employment in the UK, the location decisions of US majors are of considerable importance. While some US film production does take place in the UK, Canada, Australia and Mexico have also been seen as benefiting from 'runaway' or 'offshore' production – the tendency for film-making traditionally carried out in Los Angeles (LA) to take place in other locations.[1] Runaway production was a major issue for our interviewees and was felt by them to be affecting the ability of LA-based film workers to find work; but it was also the case that other events outside of their control such as technological change, strikes (or threatened strikes) in sub-sectors of the industry, or the cataclysmic events of 9/11 could have serious effects on the availability of work. Against this background of uncertainty, individual freelancers had adopted a range of strategies for finding work and making careers. Networking was a key strategy for all of our interviewees and the importance of good contacts is revealed as paramount. When work is scarce the quality of these networks may determine whether a freelance career continues or ends.

We begin with an account of the importance of the entertainment industries to southern California, and film and television more specifically to LA, and then consider some of the sources of uncertainty in those industries. Next we provide a brief note on the background to employment relations in film and television. This is followed by a description of the method the research team adopted in order to identify and contact freelance film industry workers in LA. A major section reports findings on how freelance workers experienced and were responding to change in the industry over the period of the study before we finally draw some conclusions.

The Hollywood film industry

The entertainment industry is crucial to the economy of southern California, growing by more than a third in the last decade of the 20th century (EEI, 2004) while film and television production in Los Angeles County alone accounts for more than a quarter of the total employed in entertainment (LMI, 2005). When the multiplier effects[2] of payrolls and employment are taken into account, the film industry probably contributes more than US$25 billion in payroll and nearly 295,000 jobs to the LA economy. With employment in aircraft, missiles and spacecraft falling (EDD, 2005) these industries are arguably now the dominant employers in LA.

Film production is labour intensive, with up to 85 per cent of the cost of production attributable to labour costs. This can be divided into above the line or 'talent' (40 per cent), below the line or 'crew' (33 per cent) and post-production (12 per cent) costs (KPMG Peat Marwick 1988).[3] Film production costs almost doubled in the decade to 2003. However, the total cost of delivering a film to the consumer, with marketing costs nearly tripling over the same period, has increased even more dramatically.

Entertainment industry statistics showing the number of days of location shooting in LA County reveal a shift away from film towards television production (EIDC, 2005a; EIDC, 2005b; EIDC, 2005c). With the total number of production days rising by 60 per cent, a 55 per cent decline in film production between 1997 and 2003 is disguised. Television production, at the same time, has almost tripled, absorbing unemployed feature film workers and largely propelling the industry.

The entertainment industries in the US are characterised by a set of unusual features (Gray and Seeber 1996). Of particular importance in the context of this chapter is the fact that they have an exceptionally high level of unemployment and are dominated by casual employment on a project-by-project basis. One Californian study (EEI, 2004) found that the 'jobs-to-workers' ratio, which indicates the number of jobs available for each worker, ranged from a low of 0.67 in 1993 to a high of 0.79 in 1997, where a ratio of less than 1 suggests that more than one worker is available for every job. This indicates that almost half of all entertainment workers relied on non-entertainment jobs for their primary income. The same study also found that in 2002 entertainment workers in production had an average of 2.3 employers, and workers in production services 2.6, compared with 1.7 for workers who earned their primary income elsewhere. This underlines the highly uncertain and competitive environment in which entertainment workers operate.

Sources of uncertainty in the audio visual media industries

There is general agreement that during the 20th century technological changes[4] have comprised the single most important influence on employment and industrial relations in the electronic entertainment and media industries (Brown, 1996). We have considered the impact of this 'disruptive technology' elsewhere; at a global level (Culkin and Randle, 2004; Culkin, Morawetz and Randle, 2006); at UK national level (Culkin and Randle, 2004); and at a UK regional level (Randle and Morawetz, 2005). Digitisation has no doubt aided, and will continue to aid the rise of regional film production centres in North America and around the world forming a (qualified) challenge to the LA film cluster (Lukinbeal, 2004; Scott, 2005).

If Hollywood has historically been the first choice for the majority of US producers to make their movies, many other countries now offer aggressive competition seeking to attract US investment through a combination of tax breaks, active promotion of the country as a production location by government agencies, lower labour costs, reduced union influence and the weakness of their local currencies against the US dollar.

By far the most successful country following this strategy has been Canada.[5] Several US industry reports have been published, claiming very significant job losses to Canada (CFTPA, 2004; FTAC, 2004; DGA/SAG, 1999; CEIDR, 2002) as a result of runaway production. However, these suggestions are not undisputed as a report (Neil Craig Associates, 2004) produced for the Canadian Film and Television Production Association demonstrates. Canada has been mimicked in its approach to targeting US production by a string of nations spanning Europe to Australasia and South Africa. As the Hollywood Majors are spending more money on fewer films (*Variety*, September 5, 2004) this translates to more competition by locations for projects, hence the targeting of capital by competing nations has become more aggressive. These nations may, however, find themselves engaged in a 'race to the bottom' as they are forced into continually increasing their financial incentives in order not to lose production to other locations.

Moving production out of the country, however, is not without its drawbacks, as one director notes:

> Depth is a big problem even in Toronto. Let's say you only bring the stars, so you need a supporting actress in her late 30s – but anyone who's got the goods has already gravitated to LA. It's even more of a problem in a place like Halifax because then it's as if you're casting community theater. (*Variety*, September 5 2004)

Locations outside of LA may thus lack the critical mass of talent which means that their financial attractiveness is moderated by the absence of appropriately qualified and skilled actors or crew members. A critical question for the LA industry is to what extent can other countries replicate the dense network of workers that a location such as LA offers? When production and post-production tasks are multiple but disintegrated, and assembled through dense networks of subcontractor relationships, then locations that possess such dense networks are necessarily limited, and cost alone for discreet functions, such as post-production work, may not offer the competitive features of the Hollywood cluster.

One argument sees the future of the Hollywood industry as comprising mainly non-production jobs, with LA remaining as a centre for the industry's deal making, financing and advertising (*Variety*, September 2 2003). The pronouncements of Askoy and Robins (1992) and Hozic (2001) to the effect that Hollywood is now effectively 'footloose', are however challenged by Scott (2005) who argues that these are 'both exaggerated and premature'. To put the impact into context, Scott maintains:

> So far, runaway production has not seriously undermined the vitality of the Hollywood film industry, and it may never become life-threatening, at least in the more creative segments of the industry. (2005: 55)

Scott's comments suggest that the degree of embeddedness of the LA industry is high and the long-term impact of producers location decisions will be mediated by the fact that there are few places in the world where a critical mass of talent is so tightly clustered. However, he is also suggesting that for below the line workers the future may not be quite so assured.

This brief review of the context in which freelance workers in the Hollywood industry operate suggests that there are a variety of factors impacting upon the ability to find work in Los Angeles. The number of movies being made, the impact of new digital technologies and the location decisions of the major studios are crucial in the medium to long term and as later sections will demonstrate, less predictable events can have sudden and dramatic effects on the opportunity to work. Against this background workers have varying degrees of attractiveness to employers; some are more highly skilled than others and/or have worked for them previously and are thus a known quantity. Finally, we will suggest, some workers have more developed networks of contacts than others and in an environment of declining work opportunities this may prove crucial to survival in the industry.

Employment relations in the US media industries

The US entertainment industry as a whole is highly unionised, although patterns of unionisation are changing as above the line unions have been growing while below the line membership has fallen. This latter tendency is accounted for by both technological change and moves towards non-union production in some sectors (Gray and Seeber, 1996). Christopherson (1996) has described the current organisation of production in the motion picture industry as more integrated in terms of distribution and production than at any time since the studio system dominated US film making in the 1930s. However, this growing integration has been achieved through a flexible subcontracted network system ('virtual integration') which developed during the 1970s, rather than by re-adopting an in-house form of production. In taking this approach major distributors use contract and investment to integrate the various functions involved in the production of entertainment products, rather than ownership and employment of personnel. The resulting structural workforce flexibility, it has been claimed, has significantly contributed to the success of the entertainment industry in California (EEI, 2004). In an industry that continues to experience cyclical trends, project-based (un)employment has become a fact of life for the entertainment workforce.

This system, while offering some economic advantages for employers, has not been without its drawbacks for them and as the new structures developed during the 1970s negative implications became apparent in the form of a loss of control over the maintenance of a skilled labour force. Furthermore, the unions were strengthened when they stepped in to fulfil roles previously played by the employer and to negotiate around issues far wider than simple rates for the job. They were involved in the development of a roster system which had the twin functions of maintaining lines of seniority and certifying skill and experience, the creation and operation of a health and pension scheme (The Motion Picture Health and Welfare Fund) into which employers paid on the basis of employee on a union contract, and a 'royalty' scheme connected to the outputs of production (Christopherson, 1996).

During the 1950s the roster system[6] was supported by the major studios, as it served as a certification and screening device for labour while allowing them to shed overhead. The system allowed craft unions to control labour supply and maintain seniority rights. However, the 'vertical disintegration' which characterised the period following the decline of the vertically integrated studio period of the 1930s and 1940s, meant that skills had to be acquired over an extended period of intermittent project work, rather than through continuous employment in a studio. While craft unions were able to control the supply of labour through this process, those undertaking apprenticeships were subject to greater hardship and eventually the frustration of those seeking to enter the industry, employer objections to union control over labour supply and new production technologies led to the development of initial training programmes which have become the preserve of the film and television schools (Christopherson, 1996).

As a result of these changes in the ways skills were acquired, over time the heterogeneity of the workforce increased and the culture of production within the industry began to change. During the 1990s and related to these changes the unions began to lose members as non-union films were made, production fled to other parts of the world and concessions were made to what were seen as wealthy and even greedy studios (Wasko, 1995).

While union membership is still seen as a goal for many entrants, bringing as it does health and social security benefits and signalling a degree of experience across the industry, the extent of change in the industry (see Christopherson, 1996 for a full account) has meant declining control and influence for the unions. With employers increasingly offering only 'flexible working' (fixed-term, freelance contracts) and unions unable to wield their former, quite significant power in placing film workers in employment, freelance workers are increasingly having to rely on developing their own strategies for acquiring skills, finding work and making careers in the industry.

Research method

The recruitment of participants for any longitudinal survey is problematic, with design issues such as the creation of a representative sample identified as a key problem (McDonald and King, 1996). Nevertheless, while more complex to design than their cross-sectional counterparts, they still need to strive to construct a sample that can reflect the population it seeks to represent. However, when we are faced with a population which is difficult to accurately define and access, our view on what value we should place on the pursuit of representativeness needs reassessing.

We decided to employ a panel study, a form of a longitudinal study involving a set of base measures followed by a succession of follow-up interviews (Oppenheim, 1992). For this study the base measures included: educational and family background, routes of entry, work patterns to date and union membership status. Freelance workers represent a particularly disparate group, giving rise to difficulties in identifying suitable subjects and gaining their cooperation. Participants were contacted via email based on a searchable database (http// www.crewnet.com). Since email penetration in the US was high in 1999, especially in California and in the media industries in general, we suggest that this represents both an innovative and effective method for collecting data relevant to our subject group. The degree of accessibility we encountered may well be linked to the position of freelance workers in the labour market. It was our experience that film workers invariably had several email accounts, a pager, mobile and landline telephones and a fax number. Contact information was made readily available on CrewNet, which appears to us related to the need for workers operating within the freelance industry to be easily contactable at all times.

The existence of the database is itself an indicator of the pressure on individuals to raise their personal profiles. The résumés held on the database gave names, postal and email addresses, fax and pager numbers as well as brief details of educational/training background and recent productions that the individual had worked on.

Several occupations key to the production phase were targeted and, randomly selected individuals in the LA area were contacted via email and invited to take part in the study. This approach secured a good response, with 25 per cent of the 180 contacted agreeing to take part in the interview programme. The next step involved plotting the addresses of those who had indicated willingness to take part in the study on a detailed street map of Los Angeles. By far the majority were based in the West Los Angeles area and most of these in the West Hollywood district. In the event it was possible on the first visit to arrange in depth, semi-structured interviews with twenty three individuals in both above and below the line occupations as well as a number of representatives of IATSE (International Association of Theatre and Screen Employees) affiliated unions.

Although the research team offered to travel to meet the film workers on their own ground, all but one was prepared to come to them. This prompts the question of why freelance workers were willing to travel at their expense and in their own time to take part in an academic study. The issue was raised with several of the interviewees and drew two broad responses. The first was related to a desire to 'pay one's dues' – recognition that a willingness to give something back to others involved in industry related activity was to the mutual benefit of all. The second response was concerned with the potential benefits that might accrue from the encounter in terms of contacts or information. Both responses can be seen as a comment on the nature of freelance work in the US film industry as a highly relational activity, which is further borne out by the empirical material examined in later sections of the chapter.

This methodology may also raise further questions concerning bias in the sample of interviewees. For example are individuals who choose to put their résumès on CrewNet likely to represent a less successful group who need to take every opportunity to raise their profile? Furthermore, are those with the time and inclination to travel to meet academic researchers likely to represent a group at a stage where every tenuous contact needs to be explored in case it constitutes an opportunity? If so, it could be argued that findings which appeared to demonstrate difficulties in obtaining work might be more closely related to the marginality of the subject, rather than, for example, the economic environment.

In the event the profile of respondents, while not including any Oscar nom-inees, did include people with over 30 years of experience and some who had earned six figure salaries over a relatively lengthy period. The inclusion of the resumes, on Crewnet, of established and successful freelancers, was an early indication of the need for film workers to make use of every available oppor-tunity for self-marketing. However few, if any, respondents were able to report any tangible benefit from the presence of their résumè on the database and none had directly gained paid employment from it. While we cannot claim this to be any more than speculation, we believe that given the networked nature of employment-seeking in the industry such open and non-relational forms of information are of limited value in finding employment.

A further arguable shortcoming of the study in its first phase was the relative shortage of respondents representing craft occupations especially those in the lighting and camera departments (grip, gaffer, best boy, clapper loader, focus puller). As these are members of the larger departments within a production crew their absence may have proven significant. Firstly, it may be that camera crew tend to gain jobs as a coherent team and form what Blair (2001) refers to as a 'semi-permanent group'. Secondly, a lack of response from these occu-pations might indicate that they are less affected by variable demand, are more consistently in work and consequently are less available for interview. We were subsequently able to remedy this by using a 'snowballing' technique – asking interviewees to arrange for us to meet their own contacts in these occupations.

While the argument put forward in this chapter is qualified by the for-going account, we nevertheless maintain that the study provides us with a valuable picture of the current issues associated with entering and finding continued employment in what has become a largely freelance industry.

Employee strategies in a climate of uncertainty

In this section we explore some of the circumstances surrounding entry into the industry, the conditions under which freelance employees are expected to work, and the strategies they use to find work and to develop careers in film and television. Getting into the industry can take place through one of several routes. Full-time positions are generally restricted to specialised suppliers and services directly related to production such as laboratories, locations services, prop and wardrobe and film stock. In the Hollywood industry, however, virtually all positions in film production itself are now freelance. One author advising newcomers on getting into the film industry, lists amongst the advantages of freelance work 'the opportunities to choose your own job' and 'to work when you want to'. In short he continues, 'being a freelancer gives you a level of freedom that you can't have when you're committed to a full-time job' (McHugh, 1999: 8). Evidence from the freelance workers interviewed as part of this study suggests that, in practice, such freedom is largely negated by the difficulties experienced in finding work.

A text aimed at those aspiring to enter the US entertainment business emphasises that while an element of luck and access to a mentor may be important, 'networking' is central to achieving a successful career (Tepper, 1999). This appears to be widely acknowledged both within the industry and amongst academic observers of the industry. Our interview subjects acknowledged the centrality of their networks to their ability to find work:

> ... if I'm looking for work there's five people I call and if those people don't know someone who knows something, then I'm in trouble ... (Matt, First AD)

A wide range of personal networking strategies were reported. Examples, however, include; always having résumés at hand and keeping them up-to-date or ringing up contacts from the set when in work, rather than waiting until you are out of work. This latter strategy can be seen as a way of, demonstrating one's desirability as an employee, indicating usefulness as a contact who may have 'inside' information and avoiding being seen as over instrumental ('[s]he only rings when [s]he wants something').

The importance of networking is such that it cannot be abstracted from the production task and maintaining one's network and seeking work becomes a central part of the job. The following respondent felt it *was* the job:

> ... finding and negotiating work is the hardest part. Doing the work is fun. Finding the work is the job. (Margery, script supervisor)

Despite intensifying competition for jobs as a result of the changing production environment, there was some evidence from the study of increased collaboration between individuals in seeking and securing work. For example, in the case of script supervisors, who tend to work individually, there being normally only one attached to each production, union meetings were seen as an important opportunity for networking and information exchange. One script supervisor described how she shared a subscription to one of the job information services available with two other young women in the same occupation, even though they could be in competition for the same vacancies.

Working for free

Those taking part in the study worked in a range of different media industries; independent and feature film, commercials, music video and television. The routes interviewees had taken into the business were equally diverse and are not explored in detail in this chapter however, no-one had simply fallen or drifted into the business. A strong motivation to make a career in the entertainment industry appears to be a pre-condition and is essential in order to overcome the high barriers to entry.

An unusual feature of the entertainment industry is that individuals are frequently expected to work without payment in the early stages of their careers (although this can also be a feature of 'getting on' and changing roles further into a career. We will return to this in a later section). Many of our panel reported having spent some time working for free or for 'deferred payment' (a share of the profits if the film makes money). Additionally whole crews are often 'hired' for free on, for example, low-budget independent productions. While such a crew is likely to consist largely of aspirant entrants, it is the case that more experienced crew members might from time to time agree to work in this way. This might happen if, for example, they are not currently in work and the production represents an opportunity to network with new talent or if they want to move on to a new role and a Director is willing to allow them to operate, for example, as a Director of Photography rather than Camera Operator. From time to time working for free might constitute a favour for a friend or contact working on a low or no budget production. A Director of Photography on music videos describes a dilemma:

> ... one director I've worked with, he financed his own little DV film ... I don't know how it turned out. I was supposed to shoot it for him, but at the last minute I got a couple of jobs in a row. So it was like 'sorry'. But it was going to be a kind of freebie for him. I can't do that if I get a job. You help out as much as you can, but if you get paying jobs that's kind of a little bit more important. So I had to pull away from him ... and I haven't talked to him since. What do you do? ... (William, DOP)

However, those in work were conscious of the growing pool of aspirant film workers seeking entry into the industry, many coming through the film school route, who were prepared to work long hours for free or for 'copy and credit'.[7] A young script supervisor felt that there were many unscrupulous producers who were prepared to take advantage of this situation:

> ... I've only been here for about six months and I've only worked on one feature ... The work is free and that's just the way it is, if you don't have a lot of experience, you have to work for free a lot. And I've attached myself to a bunch of different projects that never came to fruition and it's just a lot of talk, a lot of producers just lying, basically it's just flat out lying, saying 'oh, we're going to get this movie rolling in about a month here, we'll keep in touch with you, you know, ... It's all free work, and I can only work for free so much, yes, so it's hard in the very beginning ... (Andre, script supervisor)

Internships are quite a common entry route to the industry, generally through one of the film schools, and take the form of a short unpaid apprenticeship. The purpose is to gain practical film making skills. There seems to be a general recognition that skills are learned 'on the job' and that the formal training of a film school education does not equip graduates to work in the industry.

Others had begun by working, again often voluntarily for film-related businesses such as the camera rental houses as a way of learning about the equipment and making contacts in the production sector itself:

> ... what I did was I went to all the rental houses here in Hollywood and volunteered my time, which is the great secret by the way ... for people who want to get into the film business ... and I was lucky, I hooked up with some very nice people who I still know over at the rental house ... (Robin, Camera Operator)

It would be difficult to provide concrete evidence that working for free is on the increase specifically as a result of pressures on the industry through, for example, runaway production. It is probably true to say that the advent of working without pay is closely related to structural changes in the industry that came about as a result of the 'virtual integration' of the 1970s. As apprenticeship schemes sponsored by the studios declined and film schools became the key source of training, gaining practical experience became an individual responsibility. Combined with this the development of the low budget independent production may provide opportunities to work for free. Having said this, where work is scarce for whatever reason, freelancers may be prompted to work for free as a networking strategy:

> ... you do it for free just to meet people, which is what a lot of people do, and I've actually ... I've thought about it when it gets lean, you know, its

like, well maybe I should, just to get on the set and see people and make some new connections ... (Tudor)

Family support

In many cases, those we spoke to indicated that sporadic work in the industry would be supplemented, or even sponsored by other forms of part-time work either in parallel or between unpaid jobs. In practice it seems unlikely that any form of regular part-time work would be possible while working in the industry given the long and irregular hours worked by crews in production. For the majority of those taking on casual employment outside of the industry, this was likely to consist of bar or restaurant work which could be dropped quickly, and where another job was relatively easy to find later once the production was over.

Several of our panel, however, had access to family support, suggesting that individuals from wealthier backgrounds might be better able to sustain themselves through periods of unpaid or very low paid work:

> ... I have also been very lucky to have a mother and father that helped support a career in the film business. And I do have friends that are in the same boat. And its one of the things that unfortunately is really necessary ... some way to finance the time that you have here ... because you're either going to be working for free to get experience, or your going to be working for some pay, some free ... or you're going to ... the bottom line is ... going to drop out ...

The following interviewee was fortunate to be able to supplement his earned income from film work with unearned income from investments:

> ... I'm gonna give it five to ten years ... it's called paying my dues... and coming from a business family, I never like having all my eggs in one basket. I've invested a lot in the stock market. I've done things so I have a certain little income ... (Keith, Director of Photography)

In some cases support from the family might involve direct handouts, though in others access to other forms of paid work might be critical. In one case a young script supervisor, who claimed she had rejected financial support from her family, talked of having supported herself with a part-time job. When questioned about how she accommodated this work with the varying demands of film work she explained that her job was with a relative's company who accepted that if script supervision work had become available it would take priority.

An Independent Film Director at an early stage in his career, who was heavily involved in producing 'ethical' commercials, was able to gain financial backing for his current project partly as a result of having family contacts outside of the film industry:

> ... to be honest with you ... I'm starting this one up because I have some investors in Beverley Hills and in New York that are going to help me out ... my dad's, sort of, business associates ... (Chris, Independent Film Director)

There seems little doubt that parental influence has always been an important factor in entering film careers, perhaps most obviously in the number of actors and actresses who have mothers and/or fathers in the same occupation. The precise dynamics of this process are beyond the scope of this chapter but we can speculate that this is likely to consist of a combination of the availability of role models, of being brought up within a network of parental contacts and a movie making culture, and of location. That this extends beyond the above the line occupations is indicated by the comment of an expatriate British camera operator who referred to the 'three generation camera dynasties' that existed in LA. Perhaps what is changing is the importance of direct parental support to bolster aspiring entrants through the lean times early in a career. If a previous generation of entrants were disadvantaged by a lack of family background in the industry to help ease them into a job with a studio, the new generation have the double disadvantage that even if an opportunity to work on a movie presents itself they may not have the financial support to carry them through the early days of working for free.

'Getting on' in the industry

Even those who had got into the industry and begun to make a living, receiving paychecks on a fairly regular basis, may be forced back into working for free in order to 'get on', that is, to move up to a higher level occupation. An aspirant Director comments:

> ... I've been [working] 'union' as an actor for a long time, but I'm kinda starting all over again as a Director, where I'm working for credits, and I'm working for free practically. I've only been paid on a couple of jobs recently ... and in a production role ... (Tony, Actor/Second Assistant Director)

Once again the pattern seems to be that in order to acquire a reputation as a trustworthy crew member in a new role, skills have to be acquired on the job by working for a low rate or for free. This might require the individual to go back to working in low budget/independent movies where in addition to gaining experience he/she can also make a new range of contacts and join new networks. This suggests that on the more speculative projects, where the financial risk is greater we might expect to find more labour working for free. A camera assistant explained it:

> ... I moved up from Second Assistant to First Assistant, it's the same thing so what you end up doing is going back down to the bottom of the budget range and you work with people ... and you try to find people who you think are moving up themselves ... (Robin, Camera Operator)

The problem for those wishing to make a career move from say, clapper loader or focus puller to camera operator, is that within the networks an individual will be known by his/her current role and work will come forward on that basis. Avoiding being 'pigeon-holed' therefore means having to refuse work in that area and going through what the following respondent referred to as a 'starvation period':

> ... you're working as an electrician or best boy electric, in lighting, and people are starting to like you and you're making money, but you wanna be a DP, so still you're shooting this project on the side, and the problem is, the more you work as an electrician or best boy, electric, or Gaffer that's what anybody who meets you is gonna remember you as, that position, so after a while you have to say, 'you know what, I wanna be a DP', so then you make that leap, I'm only doing DP, so there's this starvation period, you know, where you're shooting things and not getting paid, but you wanna just be a DP, and if you can last that some people think of you as the DP ... so you get to the point where you're making money doing it, that's when you've made it. I happen to be in a starvation period ... (Keith, Director of Photography)

The implication of a 'starvation period' is that in the industry there is a degree of separation between jobs and that the idea of a career of continuous steps between inter-related activities, as might be characterised by the internal labour markets of corporate institutions, does not fit. There are clear breaks between jobs which require aspirants to go back to square one and acquire training, experience and contacts often by working once more for free. At the same time there is an understanding by respondents that learning for new jobs is nevertheless reasonably structured, and that this represents a temporary period of job transition.

Experiencing uncertainty

The impact of runaway production

In the past, as production moved to other states within the US, LA-based workers could travel from project to project. However, under Canadian Immigration and Union rules the only foreign occupations allowed to work in the country are above the line: directors, producers and stars. Consequently, above the line occupations have been employed to manage Canadian, below the line, crew during the principal photography (filming) stage. A young Independent Film Director referred to a meeting with representatives from a Canadian Film Commission:

> ... they were like, slick, they were like serving everyone coffee, and you know, I expected a foot rub or something, that's how much they were kissing your ass. It was great ... but what they're doing is they come down here and they tell, like, independent producers like myself, they say 'hey, if you bring your film up here we're going to give you tax breaks, you know, they offering me free location and a tax break ... and they were going to match funds for my film. (Sean, Independent Film Director)

Interviewees were asked what proportion of the previous year they had spent in work, was it for example 50 per cent in work 50 per cent looking for work? A line producer felt that this was an over estimate:

> ... it's more than that, it's probably 60:40 or maybe even 65:35 looking for work more than working, it really is ... (Todd, Line Producer)

While the above ratio seems fairly typical, a number of (below the line) interviewees stated that they and their peer group worked less during this year than in previous years. In the 2002 interview round, Adam, a sound recordist stated that in the 20 months since his last interview out of around 600 possible working days he had worked on '... probably 100 of them ...'.

This supports the contention (*LA Weekly*, 13.8.99). that it is 'working class Hollywood' (the film crews and support services such as equipment rental and catering) that is being hit disproportionately by reductions in employment opportunities. A camera operator commented:

> ... Definitely the big thing that you've seen ... I've seen it in the last couple of years ... is this huge and increasing divide between the fortunes of people who are in the executive part of this industry and people who

are in production. When I first got to this town this was basically where the executive and management side of the business was, and this was also the centre of production ... and that is shifting. I mean, there is pain at all levels, but the real pain is on the production end ... (Robin, Camera Operator)

And a young first Assistant Director was having second thoughts about staying in the business:

... I'm recently thinking about ... 'do I wanna live my life like this?' as I've watched the industry decline over the last three years ... everyone I know is making less money now than they were two years ago, everyone I know is having trouble finding good work, everyone I know is complaining that the jobs have gone to Canada ... (Matt, First AD)

A Director of Photography with nearly forty years experience in the industry, interviewed as the start of this study in 2000, commented that the shift to Canada was:

... terrible, it's absolutely devastating, it has completely removed the possibility for me to work in American pictures for the last year and a half or thereabouts ... it's so horribly impacted now that the really good guys and women that do what I do, they're out on the street looking, having a hard time getting jobs ... it's because of this migration to Canada and other foreign places so ... and it's built up a lot of resentment to widen the gap between producers and below the line ... (Peter, DOP)

The final sentence is a suggestion that the beneficiaries of runaway production are the production companies and a layer of the 'above the line' creatives. The evidence here is from a well-established head of camera department with many years experience and a successful career behind him, who seems to be suggesting that the migration of work is something that had begun to impact on him over the previous 18 months.

A Wardrobe Supervisor with 32 years in the industry had been very vocal in her opposition to runaway production during a first interview in 2000 and was actively involved in the IATSE campaign to promote 'countervailing tariffs' for US producers taking production out of the country. She felt the migration of work had a major impact on jobs in her trade:

... My union used to top out at 1,000 people, now its 1,800 people, probably of that 1,800, eight hundred do what I do, so there have to be 800 jobs for us, and there aren't ... and there probably never will be again, because of this runaway ...

Asked for her assessment of runaway production two years on she replied:

> ... I notice it more now, but it doesn't affect me as much. It happens ... so
> the anger that was coming out a couple of years ago has died down quite
> a bit ...

She continued, talking about runaway production to Australia and New
Zealand:

> ... they have enough crafts people in New Zealand and Australia to do 2
> or 3 huge pictures a year, but they can't support an entire industry, a
> national industry and that's what they're finding in Canada ...

and went on to say that that when production reports come out they often
showed TV pilot shows being produced in Canadian cities but that many
subsequently returned to LA:

> ... Talking to producers who go up there all the time, they are doing
> an extra day of production because unless you get one of the two or
> three crews in Vancouver or Toronto, maybe five in Toronto, they're still
> grabbing high school kids for the bottom of those crews. There's so much
> production they don't have the trained people ...

There were frequent comments on the availability of appropriately experienced and qualified crew in Canada and others which suggested that the
impact of an influx of production into the country had been to make crew
there unwilling to tolerate the terms and conditions accepted as normal by
the Hollywood crews.

Strikes and 9/11

Despite concerns about runaway production, it was clear that this was not
the only environmental factor affecting the ability of our panel to find work.
Robin, a camera operator who was trying to break into a Director of
Photography role, speaking in March 2002 talked about his previous year's
work:

> ... I started getting some really good jobs as an operator (camera opera-
> tor). Most of last year, 2001 was really taken up with that. I ended up, let's
> see, I did B camera on Planet of the Apes and then I did some stuff that
> was actually assisting, but I did another big chunk on Training Day ...
> Most of last year, in fact all of last year was operating ... that took me

through I guess about to the end of summer 2001 and then everything closed down and I've been out of work for about seven months now ... (Robin, Camera Operator)

What do you think caused the drop off?

Two things ... I worked virtually solidly, as did everybody else in this town for six months between the beginning of 2001 and June, because everybody was rushing everything they could find into production because ... they were worried about the SAG strike ... we all knew there was going to be a fall-off after that ... and there was, basically it stopped ... nothing new was being green lit ... they had actually co-ordinated everything, so that everything was wrapped before June.

He continued:

... then 9/11 happened, and everybody went into this collective frenzy about 'oh my God, is the public going to accept what we've put out, is everybody going to reject buying movies or are people going to require completely different kinds of movies, and there was this kind of... you had to be here ... total collective angst ...

These patterns were confirmed by other panel members. The Screen Actors Guild (SAG) commercial strike[8] had caused a drop off in work for many with no involvement in the making of commercials whatsoever. There was a belief that as commercial work dried up the most experienced and most well connected found work in other sectors and the shake down effect pushed the less experienced and less well connected to the margins of the industry. This worked in the opposite direction as the threat of an across the board SAG and WG (Writers Guild) strike loomed towards the summer of 2001. Studios strove to get as much production 'in the can' as possible before the onset of the strike. This opened up opportunities for crew to work more or less continuously and for some to break into the higher roles they aspired to. However, the events of September 11, 2001 were to have the effect of virtually closing down the industry. Several reasons have been put forward as to why this happened; studios became anxious about the sensitivity of audiences to the messages and images contained in their output; both restrictions on flying and a fear of flying constrained business activity and investors became more cautious about committing capital to high risk projects. Virtually all of our panel of interviewees commented on the impact of 9/11, from increased security on the lots where they worked which slowed down production activity, to the absence of opportunities for employment.

Conclusions

This chapter has demonstrated the importance for the freelance entertainment worker of creating, maintaining and extending a network of contacts in order to maximise the opportunities to work. This is to a greater extent (though notwithstanding the fact that some are born into networks) within her/his control. Furthermore, we have seen that a range of factors outside of the control of the individual freelance worker in the entertainment industries can have a very significant impact on his/her ability to find work at any given time.

In LA a number of factors are combining to impact upon the nature of, and prospects for, work in the US (West Coast) industry. While technological changes are having some impact on the way the industry is structured, and may prove significant in the longer term, of more immediate significance is the tendency for production to 'runaway' from the US to locations where state incentives, a lack of union organisation, lower wage rates and weaker local currencies are having the effect of cutting costs, sometimes considerably.

There is some debate about the precise extent to which runaway production is impacting on jobs in Hollywood and whether this represents a permanent and critical movement. Both the literature and interviewees refer to productions, for example TV series, which have runaway only to return for a variety of reasons, not least because of a shortage of sufficiently experienced and talented labour. Nevertheless runaway production has clearly been felt by our panel to be in large part responsible for what they currently see as a tightening of the jobs market. Consequently, while Scott's (2005) prediction that runaway production may never threaten the life of creative above-the-line Hollywood may hold out, its impact on increasing the work uncertainty of below-the-line 'working class Hollywood' seems less questionable.

Respondents in this study were, then, highly aware of the continuing local problem of runaway production and the impact of changing technologies but also raised the more immediate impact of strikes (or even anticipated strikes), or unanticipated events such as 9/11 on the jobs market within the sector. In the case of the newer entrants to the industry there is little direct previous experience with which to compare their current experiences. 'Getting in' remained a matter of perseverance, active networking, family background and support, and last but probably not least, luck.

Established freelance film employees, however, were experiencing difficulty in maintaining previous levels of employment and were able to broadly quantify the decline in paid work. In terms of 'getting on' in the industry, previously established freelancers reported that making career advances, in effect, meant going through a 'starvation period' during which they may be obliged to work for free, or for 'copy and credit' once more, often in the independent or low budget sector, before building up a resume and profile which would allow access to the better paid, generally unionised work with the majors on feature productions. This repeated process which may be experienced as stressful and uncomfortable by freelancers and which will have a formative influence on the quality and character of their non-work lives may nevertheless present itself as a rational strategy for employers in a project-based industry characterised by a large surplus army of willing labour.

The long run effect of vertical disintegration of the film business and its replacement by a virtually integrated industry has been to intensify insecurity for those employed on a freelance basis and this has a major impact on the way that employment is experienced and the ways that lives are lived. As Baines (paraphrasing Mariussen and Wheelock, 1997) points out:

> ... when large corporations have delegated risk further down the line, to subcontractors, to smaller firms, to a more flexible workforce, and to the self-employed, the overall result has been to transfer a business risk onto the household.

The reality of freelance work is demonstrated by our panel. Leisure becomes work as 'seeing friends' means looking for job opportunities; the family becomes a source of continuing financial support, well beyond the years of higher education, as periods outside of paid employment mean falling back on parents; children become an unsupportable burden as periods in work mean long hours, and periods outside of work mean living on reduced streams of income; training to acquire the skills to work and to move on in a rapidly changing industry becomes the responsibility of the individual, to be gained more formally during periods out of work or on the job by working for free on low or no-budget productions.

Freelance working in the US entertainment industries provides a graphic picture of the insecurity and uncertainty of project-based employment in the creative industries. Nevertheless, this is a 'structured uncertainty' where these features of the industries are well known, understood and to a great extent accepted as a fact of occupational life. If jobs in the creative industries are seen as replacing more traditional industries and freelance working replaces more permanent modes of employment, then increasing numbers of workers may well find themselves shouldering the burden of delegated risk against such a background of structured uncertainty.

The authors would like to acknowledge the help of Norbert Morawetz at the University of Hertfordshire in updating statistical and economic data contained in an earlier version of this chapter.

Notes

1 Essentially there are two forms of runaway production – 'creative', which departs because the story takes place in a setting that cannot be duplicated at home and 'economic' – in which the prime consideration is a lowering of production costs.

2 A number of economic multipliers (a measure of the total economic impact of a particular industry) have been used for the film industry. It has been assumed to be between 1.6 and 2.12 and to be 3.1 for wages and 3.6 for goods and services by the Monitor Company (DGA/SAG 1999).

3 These are average percentages. With some films featuring star actors or directors talent costs may well exceed 40 per cent, while on a high concept special effects film (e.g. Star Wars) the costs for post-production and 'crew' will make up the biggest part of the budget.

4 For example; cable TV, satellite technology, miniaturisation of equipment, home video and pay-per-view.

5 For a detailed analysis of the Vancouver film industry see Coe, 2000 and Coe, 2001.

6 Under the system the studios and independent producers sign contracts with the unions whose members are on rosters based on the amount of seniority they have acquired across the industry as a whole. This serves as a certification and screening device. Employers looking for labour would consequently approach the union who would seek to ensure that available work was spread evenly amongst its members. Thus the union was afforded a degree of control over who worked on what production.

7 This refers to the practice of providing individuals who have worked on a production with a video copy of the product, and of formally acknowledging their contribution. Credits are an important legal requirement in establishing entitlement to a share of any profits that might be made by the film where there is an agreement for deferred payment. They are similarly required in order to be entitled to 'residuals' (residual or supplemental payments) – income generated when a work is reissued in another medium (e.g. 35mm film to video or to television).

8 A strike by members of the Screen Actors Guild working in advertisements over residuals (royalties). This was seen as a key issue in determining compensation in the sector. A central part of the case for SAG members is that the more frequently an advertisement is shown or the more widely [for example when it moves to another technology platform] the greater the degree of 'typecasting' of the actor. This might mean that the association of the actor with a particular product cannot be overcome so easily and the degree of exposure makes it more difficult for him/her to find follow-on work.

REFERENCES

Askoy, A. and Robins, K. (1992) 'Hollywood for the 21st century: Global competition for critical mass in image markets', *Cambridge Journal of Economics*, 16, 1–22.

Blair, H. (2001) '"You're Only as Good as Your Last Job": The Labour Process and the Labour Market in the British Film Industry', *Work, Employment and Society*, Vol. 15, No. 1, 149–69.

Blair, H. and Rainnie, A. (2000) 'Flexible Films', *Media Culture and Society*, Vol. 22, 187–204.

Blair, H., Grey, S. and Randle, K. (2001) 'Working in Film: an analysis of the nature of employment in a project based industry', *Personnel Review*, Vol. 30, No. 2, 170–85.

Blair, H., Culkin, N. and Randle, K. (2003) 'From London to Los Angeles: a comparison of local labour market processes in the US and UK film industries', *International Journal of Human Resource Management*, 14:4, June, 619–33.

British Columbia, Ministry of Management Services (2002) February, BC Stats: *Exports December 2001*.

Brown, L. (1996) 'Technology Transforms', in L.S. Gray and R.L. Seeber, *Under the Stars: Essays on Labor Relations in Arts and Entertainment*. Ithaca and London: Cornell University Press.

(CFTPA) Canadian Film and Television Production Association/Nordicity Group Ltd (2004) *Canadian Film and Television Industry Profile 2004*.

(CEIDR) Center of Entertainment Industry Data and Research (2002) 'The Migration of Feature Film Production From the U.S. to Canada and Beyond', *Year 2001 Production Report*.

Christopherson, S. (1996) 'Flexibility and Adaptation in Industrial Relations: The Exceptional Case of the U.S. Media Entertainment Industries', in L.S. Gray and R.L. Seeber, *Under the Stars: Essays on Labor Relations in Arts and Entertainment*. Ithaca and London: Cornell University Press.

Coe, N.M. (2000) 'The view from out West: embeddedness, inter-personal relations and the development of an indigenous film industry in Vancouver', *Geoforum*, 31: 391–407.

Coe, N.M. (2001) 'A hybrid agglomeration? The development of a satellite-Marshallian industrial district in Vancouver's film industry', *Urban Studies*, 38, 1753–75.

Culkin, N. and Kerrigan, F. (1999) *A Reflection on the American Domination of the Film Industry: An Historical and Industrial Perspective*, University of Hertfordshire Film Industry Research Group, Working Paper No.4.

Culkin, C. and Randle, K. (2004) 'Digital Cinema: Opportunities and Challenges', *Convergence*, Vol. 9, No. 4 Winter 2004, 79–98 (Special Edition on Digital Cinema).

Culkin, N., Morawetz, N. and Randle, K. (2006) 'Digital Cinema as Disruptive Technology: Exploring New Business Models in the Age of Digital Distribution', Ch9 of S. Van Der Graaf & Yuichi Washida, *Information Communication Technologies and Emerging Business Strategies*. Hershey PA: Idea Group Publishing.

DGA/SAG/Monitor Company (1999) 'US Runaway Film and Television Production Study Report'.

▶

▶

EDD (Employment Development Department)/California Labor Market Information (2005) Data Library, [online] www.labormarketinfo.edd.ca.gov, January 25, 2005.

EEI (Entertainment Economy Institute) (2004) California's Entertainment Workforce – Employment and Earnings 1991–2002.

EIDC (Entertainment Industry Development Corporation) (2005a) Production Days: Television [online] www.eidc.com [January 25, 2005].

EIDC (Entertainment Industry Development Corporation) (2005b) Production Days: Features [online] www.eidc.com [January 25, 2005].

EIDC (Entertainment Industry Development Corporation) (2005c) Total production days, [online] www.eidc.com [January 25, 2005].

FTAC Film and Television Action Committee (2004, June 28) 'Comments on Unfair Trade Practices Task Force', [online] www.ftac.org [March 20, 2005].

Gray, L.S. and Seeber, R.L. (1996) *Under the Stars: Essays on Labor Relations in Arts and Entertainment*. Ithaca and London: Cornell University Press.

Hozic, A.A. (2001) *Hollyworld: Space, Power and Fantasy in the American Economy*. Ithaca: Cornell University Press.

Kerrigan, F. (2000) *Market Research in the European and US Film Industries*, University of Hertfordshire Film Industry Research Group Working Paper No.5.

LA Weekly 13–19 August 1999.

LMI (California Labor Market Information) (2005) *California Regional Bulletin*.

Lukinbeal, C. (2004) 'The rise of regional film production centers in North America, 1984–1997', *GeoJournal*, 59, 307–21.

McDonald, C. and King, S. (1996) *Sampling the Universe: The Growth, Development and Rise of Market Research in Britain since 1945*. Henley: NTC Publications.

McHugh, K. (1999) *Breaking into Film*. Princeton, New Jersey: Peterson's.

Neil Craig Associates/CFTPA (2004) 'International Film and Television Production in Canada – Setting the record straight about U.S. "runaway" production'.

Oppenheim, A.N. (1992) *Questionnaire Design, Interviewing and Attitude Measurement*. London: Pinter.

Randle, K. and Morawetz, N. (2005) '"Suddenly everyone's an expert": Digital Technology, Training and Deskilling in the UK Eastern Region Film Production Sector', *Society of Cinema and Media Studies Conference*, March.

Scott, A.J. (2005) *On Hollywood: The Place, The Industry*. New Jersey: Princeton University Press.

Tepper, R. (1999) *How to Get into the Entertainment Business*. New York: Wiley.

Variety (2003, September 2) 'Biz jobs leaving, study sez'.

Variety (2004, September 5) 'Fewer bucks for Canucks'.

Wasko, J. (1995) *Hollywood in the Information Age*. University of Texas Press.

Active Networking: Action, Social Structure and the Process of Networking

6

Helen Blair

Introduction

The concept and terminology of the network are being employed increasingly to describe and analyse the co-ordination of economic and social activity. The popularity of that framework is fuelled by a perception of the increased economic importance of information and knowledge-intensive products in the emergence of a new phase of capitalist development (Castells, 1996). The nature of such knowledge-based economic activity is contended by influential commentators to require new and fundamentally different forms of co-ordination (Castells, 1996; Hamel, 1996; Miles, 1986). This paper will explore the formation and nature of interpersonal networks using the labour market of the UK film industry as a case in point. The British film industry labour market is used as a relatively 'pure' context in which to illustrate this concept, as informal means of recruitment and selection are utilised almost exclusively. In distinction to previous network concepts, 'active networking' considers the influence of the social structure on network structure and individual action, conceiving that action as knowingly and purposefully performed.

It is the aim of the chapter, in advancing the concept of 'active networking', to develop existing understandings and theorisations of networking activity and the webs formed as a consequence. Active networking integrates objective position in social structure with the embeddedness of actors in networks of personal relations to provide a causal explanation for the resources and opportunities that accrue to individual network members. However, to avoid a static, structural conception, the activity of networking is also encompassed and conceived as a conscious, ongoing and active process in which actors knowingly and instrumentally engage. That active process is understood as a product of, as well as an influence on, the wider social structures of which networks form a component. The dynamic representation of the net-working process, and the sets of relations produced and reproduced as a product, addresses a number of deficiencies within existing network theory and its application to job searching and mobility (both generally and with respect to the film industry). In balancing the influences of structural position and conscious individual action, a framework is provided for understanding the respective roles of networks and social relations in the labour market.

In developing this framework, the following section outlines the limitations of existing network theory, especially in its application to employment mobility. A number of conceptual difficulties will be commented upon, such as the assumption of passive transmission of job information and the minimised role of social structure in shaping work opportunities and network composition. 'Active networking' is then outlined to provide an alternative understanding of the process and form of networks. Following a brief introduction to the context of the British film industry labour market, the concept of active networking is illustrated through the experiences of a film crew drawn from a longitudinal case study of a film production (TeenComedy). The theoretical implications of 'active networking' are then discussed in conclusion.

Network theory: a role for social structure and process?

The examination of the structure and function of networks has significantly enhanced our understanding of the internal features and functioning of the network as a form of co-ordination. However, it remains the case that network analysis tends not to embed interpersonal relations within social structure. Such an omission, it is argued here, limits the explanatory power of network theory to explicate the existence of networks (see also Nohria (1992) for recognition of this difficulty), restricting analysts to attempts to theorise networks as static, 'closed' systems. Pierre Bourdieu's (1993) theorisation of the relationship between agency and structure provides a useful resource through which to examine the respective roles of social structures and action within networks. However, Bourdieu's conception of agency tends towards oversocialisation of human action (following Wrong, 1961) and so the opposing limitations of structuralism are highlighted in arguing for a conceptual approach to networking and networks which encompasses both instrumental human action and the influence of social structure upon those actions.

Socially constructed networks and the role of social structure

Fundamentally, network theory has built from the assumption that actors are embedded in a set, or sets, of personal social relations and that those relations exert considerable influence on the actions of actors and their outcomes (Granovetter, 1992: 33). Institutions and networks are thus explained as being socially constructed and action, within that context, as predominantly an outcome of 'material' personal relations (Granovetter, 1992: 47). At an individual level, the relational (or dyadic) attributes of networks, then, affect behaviour through relationships built up over periods of time and an individual's experience and interpretation of those interactions. The capacity of individuals to affect circumstances to their advantage, in job mobility for example, relies predominantly upon their relative position within a network and the accumulated 'social capital' available to facilitate and realise actions (see for example (Burt 1992)). At a network level, the structure of the web created by an individual exerts influence on behaviour via the resources that flow, or are impeded, as a consequence of the pattern of relations constructed. An individual's relational position, and nature of the linkages are contended to influence, for example, the information accruing to a network member (Granovetter, 1992; Burt, 1980).

While concurring that the actions of individuals are, in part, the product of their relations, and subjective experience of those relationships (with, for example, social pressure being exerted to behave in a certain manner (Granovetter, 1992; Knoke, 1992), to view agency as solely or largely the product of individual personal relations and network position, precludes or minimises the role social structure plays in influencing individual and collective action (Bourdieu, 1993; Althusser, 1970). Considering the more abstract level of social relations provides a causal drive for the existence and form of networks and the access provided to certain desirable resources. Therefore, not only is position within the network significant in influencing action but the objective position within social structure is also an influencing variable (Bourdieu, 1993). While resources flow via relations between individuals and those links are fundamental to transmission, the respective positions of network members both within the network and in social structure are important influences upon the type of relations formed and the resources respective parties are able to access (directly and indirectly). The tendency within network literature, to stress the particular personal relationship between individuals as predominantly socially constructed leads to a neglect of the objective positions of each individual actor.

In looking predominantly within networks to explain their existence, form and operation, research has concentrated on understanding structural and relational features. A network, as the object of analysis, has therefore tended to be considered as a self-enclosed microcosm in which variables such as density and size (Mitchell, 1969; Burt, 1980), and relationship types (tie strength for example) (Feld, 1981; Granovetter, 1973; Marsden, 1984) are isolated as determinants of the outcomes of network relations (see for example (Hansen, 1999; Ibarra, 1992; Murray, 1981). The intent of this critique, however, is not to disregard such network features as influences on the operation of webs of personal relations, but rather to suggest that they form intervening influences mediating the relationship between an actor's more enduring and general position in social structure and the outcomes of actions.

If the concept of network density is taken as an illustration, some of these difficulties can be elucidated. As a determinant feature of network 'performance'. The size of a network is held to be of considerable importance to its information provision capabilities (Burt, 1992: 62). For example, De Graff and Flap (1991) argue that people with larger networks gain higher paid jobs that those with smaller networks. A greater number of contacts is assumed to lead to an increased likelihood, and volume, of information flowing to the network member. This is the principle which is applied to network analyses in the film sector with a positive relationship between number of contacts 'possessed' and the volume of referrals and information received being assumed (Christopherson, 1989; Jones, 1996; Jones and Walsh, 1997). Number of contacts is, therefore, unproblematically treated as a determinant of job mobility. However, as Burt (1992) himself points out, size can be a 'mixed blessing'. He argues that very large, dense networks contain a high proportion of redundant contacts that provide the same information benefits as a consequence of their interconnectedness within the network (Burt, 1992: 65). Therefore, the effort expended in maintaining such a network is not rewarded by similar information benefits. Consequently, a sparser network where actors are not connected may accrue more diverse information even though it may be smaller.

Nonetheless, the network analyses dominating understandings of the film industry labour market tend to rely heavily on network size as a determinant variable of a successful film career. Against the backdrop of increased free-lancing following the breakdown of the studio system in the 1960's, Christopherson and Storper (1989) argue the labour market became characterised by a dual labour market segmented according to access to work hours. That access is in turn determined by the density of contacts within individual's networks (Christopherson and Storper, 1989: 339). This is very much echoed by Jones (1996) who builds her network analysis upon the assumption of that binary division and accompanying network densities. For Christopherson (1989), those in the core possess denser networks of personal connections which facilitate less employment uncertainty than those with fewer contacts in the periphery who are subject to greater employment uncertainty.

However, size and denseness alone cannot be considered the defining characteristics of information or opportunity rich networks. The structural position of actors in the network (Burt, 1992) and in social structure are important factors in the type of information and opportunities contacts are able to offer. In delineating active networking in the next section, it will be argued that networks are not built exclusively on the premise of density. Contacts, *per se*, are a necessary, but not sufficient, precursor to job mobility. It is the position of those contacts within the organisational hierarchy that determines to a large extent the resources accessible through the network relation. If one considers that networks are not 'closed systems' whose outcomes are determined by the particular, immediate relationships forming the web, then internal structure is less of a determining factor than Burt (1980) and others maintain (Feld, 1981). Alternative network structures become possible and viable. A dense network, as such, is one of a number of possible structural forms, as when concrete social positions are accommodated, a small number of contacts with 'well-positioned' individuals is a viable alternative network structure (Blair, 2001).

Social institutions, it is argued here, precede the existence of any given individual or network of individuals and to a degree enable or constrain their actions. It is the neglect of the more abstract level of analysis, unsurprising within a constructionist framework, which gives rise to the causality problems identified by Nohria (1992) within network literature. While network theory can very usefully explain some of the factors influencing individual behaviour, it cannot explain within its own term of reference why network members have access to certain resources and therefore the causes of network composition. This difficulty can then be seen to similarly stunt the development of theory concerning network formation as the reason for the inclusion and exclusion of individuals remains problematic. Relatedly, therefore, the social relations of which networks are a part (in the productive process and other social spheres) influence the process of network formation The concept of active networking attempts to balance to a greater extent the structural and relational facets of networking activity and form and to develop a theory of the network that integrates those two related stages of development.

A conscious, dynamic process

A key premise of active networking, in reaching a dynamic conceptualisation of the networking process, is the assumption that individuals undertake conscious job search activity, purposefully using network connection to source and transmit job information. This introduces the role of human action to networking activity and the structure of networks themselves. In this respect, a promising theoretical framework is proposed by Bourdieu (1993) and which attempts to integrate the respective influences of structural position and individual action. The concept of *habitus* attempts to free the notion of agency from what Bourdieu viewed as the false dichotomy of subjectivism/objectivism and provide an alternative to the agent as either conscious subject or mere 'bearer'. Habitus is somewhat abstractly defined as the system of 'durable, transposable dispositions, structured structures predisposed to function as structuring structures' (Bourdieu, 1980: 53). Sometimes described as a 'feel for the game', a 'practical sense', habitus conceptualises agency as being the inclination of people to act in a particular manner in certain circumstances as the result of socialisation. In this sense, these predispositions are the product of the objective social conditions of their socialisation and can further shape social structure via their transposability and adaptation to specific contexts. So for example, Bourdieu argues that members of a social class have a similar *habitus*.

This framework provides sound theoretical and empirical attempts to overcome the structure/agency dualism, integrating as it does, concepts of both social position and individual action. Curiously much of the network literature assumes a role for agency without ever explicitly conceptualising its nature or process. It is merely assumed that individuals shape their networks according to the determining logics of size and density, for example, and the outcomes of their action are only inhibited by the internal network structure. By drawing in social structure as an influencing factor on agency, Bourdieu's framework provides greater causal explanatory power than network theory alone.

The notion of agency proposed by Bourdieu is not dissimilar to that invoked by Granovetter (1995) in his influential study of informality in job mobility. The relative unconsciousness of the networking act is assumed by both, as it is viewed as a socialised predisposition to which explicit and strategic action does not apply. For Granovetter, the benefits of interpersonal relations in the job market flow through contacts meeting socially for purposes other than to discuss work opportunities. Job information is passed largely as a by-product of social processes not specifically enacted for that purpose. This is similar to Bourdieu's predisposed agent who tends not to act with strategic calculation because of his/her position in an objective social situation governed by social relations. Bourdieu does propose a simplistic structuralism because that the position of actors in different 'fields' (social spaces or spheres) is argued to provide dynamic interaction. However, it remains the case that actors do not predominantly act in a strategic manner when engaged in social processes. In many instances and social situations that analysis can be upheld, as Bourdieu (1984) illustrates, the process of networking requires a more explicit consideration of 'rational' calculation on the part of the actor.

The networking process can be initiated deliberately with particular outcomes intended as a result of their use. For example, Pfeffer (1976) argues that networks are used in conditions where high levels of uncertainty prevail and so transactions tend to be repeated with organisations or people with whom an individual has prior experience. Rather than assuming that informal mechanisms are 'happy coincidences' or by-products of predispositions, a conceptual requirement exists to understand the networking process as an explicit, conscious activity. From the outset, therefore, the important role of human agency is established in facilitating labour market mobility. Individuals consciously act to make and maintain contacts with other individuals and groups, assuming that a variety of forms of information or opportunities for work will be more readily available as a consequence.

Commentators who tend towards understanding networks as consciously enacted tend to assume the only barriers to successfully transmitting network resources lie within the network itself. It is the structure of the network (Burt, 1992), or the types of relationships formed (Granovetter, 1973) that are the causal influence on the 'success' of the network. These explanations tend to assume a ready-formed, static network and fail to incorporate the process of network formation and its influence upon the network constructed and under constant reconstruction. Active networking proposes that there are wider social influences in operation during formative and maintenance stages. As such, the composition of a network is not a variable over which an actor has complete control and strategic intent does not necessarily result in the planned outcome.

Active networking

Active networking encapsulates and combines conscious search procedure and the informal nature of information flow evident in the film industry context. It emphasises, therefore, the consciousness with which a variety of relationships are formed and maintained to facilitate that exchange. Active networking can be defined as: 'the consciously enacted activity of initiating, building and maintaining a network of informal personal contacts with the purpose of influencing the outcome of actions, but which is conditioned by social structure (i.e. the outcome is the product of more than the personal relations of a network)'.

The characteristics of the process – conscious, informal, instrumental, ongoing

Active networking conceptualises as a conscious process, the formation and maintenance of informal personal networks and their associated information flows. This infers an awareness and degree of prior contemplation and intention on the part of actors in their valuation and utilisation of interpersonal connections in career development. Furthermore, actors undertake an assessment of the likely outcomes of their networking actions and consciously make decisions as to who and how to approach as potential network members. The process of contacting individuals, is then, considered to be deliberately and intentionally enacted rather than the coincidental or subconscious explanations of Granovetter (1995) and Bourdieu (1980) respectively. Rather than passive bearers of structural relations or habitual actors, the wilful formation and maintenance of interpersonal connections allows the shaping of job opportunities to be viewed as a process in which job seekers are actively involved.

A degree of instrumentality can then be argued to explicitly enter the process of networking, as job seekers form and maintain relations with those others they view as being able to provide resources that will enhance employment opportunities. So, relationships are purposefully sought and opportunities created to make contact with individuals. As network commentators have noted, these resources can flow either to or from the job seeker. Flows to individuals may take the form of information, access to further network connections, direct job offers or third party mediation on the seeker's behalf, while flows from may involve the transmission of information by the individual to other network members. Labour then is viewed as adopting particular strategies which are intended to result in desirable outcomes, such as targeting individuals in key hierarchical positions with information about themselves in order to enhance their likelihood of employment or recommendation. The timing of releasing information to contacts, or contacting network members for information can also be viewed as actively considered by individuals as prior to initiating a job search information may be disseminated as to the seekers skills, job requirements and personal qualities.

The composition of an individual's network is consequently in part the product of conscious calculation, as the building process involves the inclusion of others viewed as useful providers of various types of resources. Those contacts who provide such resources will be maintained as contacts, while those less 'productive' members may not be drawn upon as frequently and cease to be an active member of that particular network configuration. The network form is not a static one, with fixed membership and boundaries. As a consequence of the dynamic process of networking the composition and boundaries of networks are continuously shifting. Once a network is formed, individuals continue to form new contacts through a variety of social processes. The changing personal or work circumstances of individuals may lead to them becoming more or less desirable contacts and as both the seeker and their contacts circumstance alter (e.g. through promotion, or entering a new or different area of work) there is a continuous process of supplementing existing and previous interpersonal connections with new ones.

The active networking process, in part as a result of individual experience, is also a conscious one in terms of the methods of contact selected by seekers. Its explicit purpose is almost exclusively to initiate and develop informal, personal relations with other members of the labour market. In contrast, therefore, the more formal methods of presenting Curriculum Vitae or letters of introduction to potential employers, relationships are sought through more personalised media such as meetings or telephone calls. Impersonal third party mediators such as employment agencies serve a subservient role to that of informal connections through which individuals are recommended for, or offered, work. While Granovetter's analysis assumes that informality and consciousness of job seeking action are mutually exclusive, both form integral characteristics of active networking. However, that is not to success that those instrumental actions result in the desired outcomes, given the underlying structural influences outlined below.

The context of the process

As noted in the previous section and is outlined in the definition of active networking, this is not a process which takes place in a vacuum. The institutions of the labour market although actively reproduced and shaped by actors, pre-exist human action as a consequence both constrain and enable the deliberate action of networking. It is the case, then that both network and underlying social structure influence both the process and outcomes of active networking.

Individual job seekers are situated with a network context which consists of the membership, number of members, structuring of the relations, and relationship, or tie, types. The internal network structure and composition determines to some extent the benefits available to a given member. However, to understand the outcomes of individual action solely as products of the personal relations of the network is to assume networks are 'closed systems' which operated only at the level of individual personal relations. As Bourdieu (1980, 1984) contends objective structural position is an important determinant in the success or otherwise of action and access to various types of resources. The structural position of the job seeker in family, productive process or labour market structures presents an influential factor affecting the resources to which that individual has access. Those with family members present in particular industry labour market, for example, may be able in early career stages to draw on those familial relationships to build further network relations. Individual's structural position also influences the functions that different contacts are able to perform. A contact in a senior hierarchical position in an organisation is potentially more able to influence appointment decisions than a contact in a more junior position who may provide information but not be able to influence the selection decision directly. As such, the formation of a network, of whatever internal structural configuration and however many members, is not sufficient to effecting the desired outcome of job searches. Given the searcher's own structural position (access to industry contacts, skills, education etc.) they will be more or less capable of making these contacts and accessing the anticipated resource flows. The outcome of networking activity may then be more or less 'successful' depending on the resources a job seeker has prior access to as a result of their own structural position in addition to the structural position of their network of connections. Through family connections in an industrial sector, for example, a job seeker may have tacit industry knowledge that informs their actions and increases potential search success.

The structural position of actors is knowledge which job seekers assimilate, are actively aware of and endeavour to act in the knowledge of. This then influences the composition of a given network as individuals attempt to make contact with others who have, or can facilitate, access to desirable resources. To illustrate, in order to maintain regular employment in project-based sectors of the economy, seekers may require to have contacts at, or above, a certain organisational level (or more senior to their own position). These contacts are necessary as such individuals are in decision-making positions and can therefore appoint the seeker to a job without reference to more senior organisational members. Being 'known' to and by contacts of that type enhances job prospects, in addition to the information which may flow via other relationships. It is only through incorporating an understanding of the process of networking, and the structural influences acting on that process, that the causality of network composition can be explained. Although active networking is a consciously enacted process, it is also a reflection of social structures, and so individuals actions are the product of a complex interaction between their subjective understanding of the their position and the constraints and opportunities presented by their objective social position.

The outcomes of the process

To view a network as a dynamic form of social organisation, the boundaries of the web require to be understood as permeable and shifting. Once formed a network does not persist in that form, rather new connections are made on an ongoing basis and some connections may cease to be actively maintained. This has the effect of any given network being fluid and dynamic and requires networks to be studied and researched as such, rather than as entities of fixed structure and composition. Considering the process of networking as one which is continually reproduced, facilitates the analysis of network formation, and continual reformation, rather than pre-supposing an already-formed web. As a consequence, how individuals form networks is open to enquiry. For example, the degree of selection of individuals, the membership 'criteria' and how relationships are formed and linked within the web. The strategies employed in building networks provide important indicators as to the functions actors intend and understand their connections will serve and how they foresaw those intentions materialising.

As networks have conceptualised as having permeable boundaries, and their structure and operation influenced by underlying social structure, the opportunity is opened up for a greater range of network structures other than purely density or size (Blair, 2001). A small network with a number of individuals in influential structural positions may be as effective in the accrual of resources as a large network with fewer, or no, such individuals. OR, through having access to resources and the connections through which to disseminate them, network members in resource rich structural positions may offer to 'mentor' a less senior and experienced job seeker. This may involve, for example, the transmission of job and more general information to, and about, the seeker and job recommendations and offers. Therefore, there are more structural options of network structure possible when the underlying influence of social structure on individual and collective action are integrated into network analysis.

The film industry – a context of footloose labour?

As an illustration of the active networking concept, these sections describe and analyse the networking process in the UK film industry labour market. Whether it be project-based careers (Baker and Faulkner, 1991; DeFillippi, 1998; Jones, 1996), network organisations (Miles, 1986) or flexibly specialised production networks (Christopherson, 1989), film is an apparent signifier of broader changes underway in the structure and operation of economic activity. As in the USA film sector, the vast majority of the 10,700 people employed in film production in the UK (Creative Industries Task Force, 1998) work on short-term projects, in a freelance capacity, and re-enter the labour market with great frequency (Blair, 2001). The use of formal methods to attract job candidates, such as general advertising and application procedures, is not prevalent in the film industry in either the USA or Britain (Skillset, 1996; McHugh, 1999). The formation and maintenance of interpersonal network is critical to sourcing and gaining employment in that context (Blair, 2001; Jones, 1996). While recognising the importance of networks and networking to career development in many industries (see for example Coates and Pelligrin (1957) and Rees (1966)), the film sector provides a context in which there is almost exclusive reliance on such structures and relationships. It therefore provides rich empirical ground in which to conduct an analysis of the nature, structure and operation of networks.

Methodology

The empirical data used to illustrate the active networking concept, is drawn from a case study of a film production, TeenComedy (a pseudonym used to conceal the identity of the case study production). TeenComedy was tracked over a period of 18 months through the production process: pre-production, production, post-production, marketing and distribution to the release of the film. The case production was chosen as it conforms structurally to patterns of production and industrial organisation evident in the film sector (see Ellis, 1992 for descriptions of UK film production) and enabled a longitudinal study throughout the production process. Furthermore, due to the structuring of film production along project lines, TeenComedy employed a crew with wide industry experience through employment on a large number of film and television projects.

Multiple data collection methods were utilised in conducting the case study and facilitated an in-depth examination of the production process and the management of labour in an everyday context. Observation, interviewing and a questionnaire survey were the main data collection methods employed as through triangulating the data collected (Denzin, 1970) the validity and reliability of findings could be enhanced. Each of the methods also gave access to a range of different types of data which enabled multiple sources of evidence to be utilised, with for example quantitative information on employment patterns and qualitative information on attitudes and perceptions being gathered. Twenty in-depth, semi-structured interviews were conducted with a cross-section of crew members from different departments and at varying organisational levels following principal photography (see Appendix 6.1). This enabled the themes and issues arising from observation and survey data to be probed further. It is this data which is reported predominantly here. Fictional names have been used to protect interviewee's anonymity.

Active networking in the UK film industry

A conscious and informal process

Film freelancers almost completely rely upon their networks of personal connections to provide information about work and industry news and job opportunities. As such freelancers seek out opportunities to meet and build relationships with other industry employees. For example, this can involve purposefully initiating contact with people to become 'known' to others offering employment:

> ... in the early days its phonecalls, its all the hard ... you know, to get yourself established and hoping that someone will employ me. [1]

There is also a degree of instrumentality involved in the means used to make contact others when building connections. As can be seen in the following quote, freelancers consciously consider the means they use in making relationships:

> So you can get in through CV, just persevering and cold calling. But what its best to do is essentially to phone up and say 'look can we meet'. You know, I'll come and meet you. I'll come and see you. I'll come and spend a day for nothing on the set or something just to get that contact. So you become a face rather than just a piece of paper ... that gets ... lost. [2]

Interactions between individuals are initiated with the specific purpose of acquiring information about job opportunities, as opposed to Granovetter's assumption that the passing of job-related information is a by-product of other social processes:

> if your talking about 'kow-towing' to people because they give you jobs, its not something I've ever.. (pause) although lots of people do it. I mean you ingratiate yourself (that's a terrible word, ingratiate yourself) possibly to certain people who are going to have, who you know are going to get jobs. You have (slight emphasis) to be nice to people but that comes down to the fact that that's what's dif-ferent to, for instance, having a permanent job in a factory or whatever. [3]

There is also an awareness of the importance of maintaining 'good' relationships with those in the network likely to be influential in securing information and/ or opportunities and may also influence the information circulated by those contacts concerning the searcher:

> To get repeat jobs? Just being able to get on with people ... Em (pause) to be nice to people. I don't really like to suck up to the producers. I mean

I'll be nice to them and do my job but I won't (pause) grovel. And basically if people want you they'll call you. [2]

The development and maintenance of network relationships is therefore a conscious activity which freelancers consider and deliberately conduct.

The structural context of networking

In the search for work and in the building of networks, the structural position of the members of the networks is as important if not more so than the number or denseness of contacts. It is this structural influence which commentators such as Christopherson and Storper and Jones in the film industry and Granovetter (although to a lesser extent) minimise in their respective conceptualisations. Knowing people of sufficient seniority within the organisational hierarchy, as noted, is an important factor in securing information and job opportunities. The importance of position in social structure is significant in family, social and productive processes, with for example most freelancers getting into the film industry via family or friendship connections (Blair, 2001).

In the productive sphere, given the hierarchical nature of the recruitment and selection process, the structural position of a contact is a contributory factor in their ability to grant access to work. In most cases this meant more junior film freelancers required to be known by at least one head of their relevant department. As a middle ranking member of the sound department demonstrates:

So I have to know a [head of department] and recently .... luckily for me [Mr X] employs me but I have to know a [head of department]. [1]

This principle was reflected in numerous crew member's accounts of getting work:

our best friend was, corporate accountant to Eon Productions who produce the Bond movies. They had a cashier doing the payroll and the cashiering who wasn't really up to the job so I was offered three days a week on that doing the payroll. That very quickly snowballed to a full time job and I haven't looked back since basically. [4]

From more senior crew member's point of view, they are aware of being requested to grant access to resources on behalf of others because of their positional ability to realise such requests. As a senior manager comments: 'I'm constantly being asked whether I can get, you know, X's daughter or son an attachment'. [5]

During the process of building and maintaining a network freelancers include in their networks people in positions to influence job appointments. Active networking is resultantly an activity which is conditioned by the constraints and opportunities of the structures within which freelancers operate. The outcome of the relationships formed is therefore not exclusively the product of the interpersonal relationship but also the structures within which the relationships exist and are enacted.

Networking strategies and network composition

As Mitchell (1969) and Burt (1992) note, the structure of a network influences the behaviour of its members. A limiting aspect of current conceptualisations of networking and networks in the film industry is the adherence to one structural form: that of contact density. The experiences of the crew of Teen-Comedy suggest that active networking results in a number of different patterns of relationships, outlined briefly below, that each potentially lead to regular employment opportunities. Each of these network structures do precipitate a range of different behaviours among members in terms of searching for and securing work. The existence of such patterns refutes the atomised impression of the labour market inferred by Christopherson and Storper (1989). Freelancers can operate a number of network models and do not exclusively rely upon building a dense network of contacts. Critical to each of these strategies, however, is an ongoing contact with whom the individual retains a relationship and who, in job provision terms is more senior in the hierarchy. As noted above, this contact will often be a head of department or middle manager in a position to be able to offer a job directly.

The first network structure is dominated by membership of a 'semi-permanent work group'. This group comprises a number of individuals (usually those required to form a department) who work together on an almost permanent basis. The group will move from job to job as a unit with membership remaining the same. Therefore, ongoing contacts exist between each member of the group but also, significantly, between the head of department (who supplies employment opportunities) and group members.

> with [my present head of department] I mean basically I don't have to look for work because I knew that when he found work he'd ask me to do it. So he was looking and I could just sort of sit back which was really nice but that's a sort of very secure position that you kind of you pray to be in. [6]

Although these groups may remain stable for a number of years, their configuration is not career long as individuals may leave (for career progression purposes, for example) or may be expelled (if, for example, performance is not satisfactory). Questionnaire data from the case study revealed that over one third of the crew generally moved jobs with a group of people they had worked with before (see Blair, 2001 for a fuller discussion of the characteristics of each network structure).

The second dominance network structure was characterised by freelancers (either through choice or because they have yet to establish themselves in a work group) moving from job to job relying on the facilitation of a range of discrete contacts. This is the pattern that most closely resembles the network density espoused by Jones (1996) and Christopherson and Storper (1989). As opposed to relying upon a single head of department to secure work, the searcher may be contacted by, or contact, one of a number of people in their network concerning their availability for work. As a member of the TeenComedy crew contrasts the two patterns:

> With [my friend] its more like she's just waiting for a phonecall and I find her situation quite envious because she knows lots of people and lots of people use her. Whereas she finds my situation quite envious because I'm in with this team and we don't stop working and its very secure at the moment. So its sort of like, you know, two sides to it. [2]

Freelancers operating in this manner build up a large number of contacts on whom they draw for information and for job opportunities. The reduction of employment uncertainty, rather than taking place through a fixed set of working relationships, is more dependent upon a wide net of contacts in positions either to recommend, set up a job or offer a job directly.

The final network form evident comprised freelancers who were members of more loosely configured work groups and oscillated between individual and group movement. As a member of a group remarked about other heads of department regarding more loosely configured groups:

> ... a cameraman might have two or three operators that he uses who would have two or three focus pullers so I mean the combinations are there that you can have different faces. But as you do more I suppose you'd know people and you would have worked with them at some point – they wouldn't be complete strangers. [7]

Therefore, the people working in these groups are still known to the head of department and other group members but the configuration of individuals may alter and, in that sense, the group is less permanent than a semi-permanent work group. People who move between groups also use individual contacts. Such people have a range of fixed contacts from whom they either actively seek work or by whom they are offered work. As such, they can move from working in a group, to getting a job via a contact who has recommended them to an unfamiliar department head and staff.

Conclusions

The central concern of this paper has been to propose and outline the concept of active networking as a means of capturing the dynamic and conscious, yet structured process of networking and the interpersonal webs which are produced and reproduced by that process. The process of active networking has been characterised as conscious, instrumental and ongoing, as job seekers build and maintain personal, informal connections. As a departure from network theory, which almost presumes the pre-formation of a network, active networking considers the process of assembling a web and therefore enables the question of why they are composed of certain types of individuals.

Considering this question of how and why networks are formed cannot be answered from within existing network theory as the causality does not lie solely within a configuration of personal relations. In this chapter, underlying social structures and actors concrete positions in those structures have been integrated into the above understanding of the networking process as one in which individuals actively engage. As such the outcomes of network relations and the resources which may, for example, be accessed as a consequence, are not determined solely by the internal operation and structure of the web. The position of actors in wider social structures, such as family and in the productive process, are important determinants of their access to various types of resources. However, actors are not mere bearers of social relations, because, as was outlined above, they engage strategically in the networking process with the intention of effecting desired outcomes. It is the wider structures within which they and their network of relations are situated which exerts constraining and enabling influences on those action and which are not always transparent to actors.

REFERENCES

Althusser, L. (1970) 'Contradiction and Overdetermination', *For Marx*, pp. 89–128. New York: Vintage Books.

Baker, W.E. and Faulkner, R.R. (1991) 'Role as Resource in the Hollywood Film Industry', *American Journal of Sociology*, Vol. 97, No. 2, pp. 279–309.

Blair, H. (2001) 'You're Only as Good as Your Last Job: The Labour Process and Labour Process and Labour Market in the British File Industry', *Work, Employment and Society*, Vol. 15, pp. 149–69.

Bourdieu, P. (1980) *The Logic of Practice*. Cambridge: Cambridge University Press.

▶

▶

Bourdieu, P. (1984) *Distinction: A Social Critique of the Judgement of Taste.* Cambridge, MA: Harvard University Press.

Bourdieu, P. (1993) *Sociology in Question.* London: Sage Publication.

Burt, R.S. (1980) 'Models of Network Structure', *Annual Review of Sociology,* Vol. 6, No. 1, pp. 79–141.

Burt, R.S. (1992) *Structural Holes: The Social Structure of Competition.* Cambridge, MA: Harvard University Press.

Castells, M. (1996) *The Rise of the Network Society.* Maiden, MA: Blackwell.

Christopherson, S. (1989) 'Flexibility in the US Service Economy and the Emerging Spatial Division of Labour', *Transactions of the Institute of British Geographers,* Vol. 14, No. 2, pp. 131–43.

Christopherson, S. and Storper, M. (1989) 'The Effects of Flexible Specialization on Industrial Politics and the Labour Market: The Motion Picture Industry', *Industrial and Labour Relations Review,* Vol. 42, No. 3, pp. 331–47.

Coates, C. and Pelligrin, R. (1957) 'Executives and Supervisors: Informal Factors in Differential Bureaucratic Promotion', *Administrative Science Quarterly,* Vol. 2, pp. 200–15.

Creative Industries TaskForce (1998) *Creative Industries Mapping Document.* London: UK Department for Culture, Media and Sport.

De Graff, N.D. and Flap, H.D. (1991) 'With a Little Help from My Friend: Social Resource as an Explanation of Occupational Status and Income in West Germany, The Netherlands, and the United States', *Social Forces,* Vol. 67, pp. 452–72.

DeFillippi, R. (1998) 'Paradox in Project-Based Enterprise: The Case of File-Making', *California Management Review,* Vol. 40, pp. 125–9.

Denzin, N.K. (1970) *The Research Act in Sociology.* Chicago: Aldine.

Ellis, J. (1992) *Visible Fictions: Cinema, Television, Video.* New York: Routledge.

Feld, S.L. (1981) 'The Focused Organization of Social Ties', *American Journal of Sociology,* Vol. 86, pp. 1015–35.

Granovetter, M.S. (1995) *Getting a Job: A Study of Contacts and Careers.* Chicago: University of Chicago Press.

Granovetter, M.S. (1973) 'The Strength of Weak Ties', *American Journal of Sociology,* Vol. 78, No. 6, pp. 1360–80.

Granovetter, M.S. (1992) 'Problems of Explanation in Economic Sociology', in Nohria, N. and Robert, G.E. (ed.) *Networks and Organizations.* Boston, MA: Harvard Business School Press.

Hamel, G. (1996) 'Strategy as Revolution', *Harvard Business Review,* Vol. 74, No. 4, pp. 69–82.

Hansen, M.T. (1999) 'The Search-Transfer Problem: The Role of Weak Ties in Sharing Knowledge across Organization Subunits', *Administrative Science Quarterly,* Vol. 44, No. 1, pp. 82–111.

Ibarra, H. (1992) 'Paving an Alternative Route: Gender Differences in Managerial Networks', *Social Psychology Quarterly,* Vol. 60, No. 1, pp. 91–102.

Jones, C. (1996) 'Careers in Project Networks: The Case of the File Industry', in Arthur, M.B. and Rousseau, D.M. (ed.) *The Boundaryless Career: A New Employment Principle for a New Organizational Era.* Oxford: Oxford University Press.

▶

▶

Jones, C. and Walsh, K. (1997) 'Boundaryless Careers in the US File Industry: Understanding Labour Market Dynamics of Network Organizations', *Industrielle Beziehungen*, Vol. 4, No. 1, pp. 58–73.

Knoke, D. (1992) 'Political Organizations', in Borgatta, E.F. and Borgatta, M.L. (eds.) *Encyclopedia of Sociology*. New York: Macmillan, pp. 1480–4.

Marsden, P. (1984) 'Measuring Tie Strength', *Social Forces*, Vol. 63, pp. 482–501.

McHugh, K. (1999) *Breaking into Film: Making your Career Search a Blockbuster*. Princetown, New Jersey: Peterson's.

Miles, R. (1986) 'Organizations: New Concepts for New Forms', *California Management Review*, Vol. 28, No. 3, pp. 62–74.

Mitchell, J.C. (1969) *Social Networks in Urban Situations*. Manchester: Manchester University Press.

Murray, C. (1981) *Families Divided*. Cambridge: Cambridge University Press.

Nohria, N. (1992) 'Is a Network Perspective a Useful Way of Studying Organization?', in Nohria, N. and Eccles, R.G. (ed.) *Networks and Organizations*. Boston: Harvard Business School Press.

Pfeffer, J. (1976) 'Beyond Management and the Worker: the Institutional Function of Management', *Academy of Management Review*, Vol. 1, No. 2, pp. 36–46.

Rees, A. (1966) 'Information Networks and Labour Markets', *American Economic Review*, Vol. 56, No. 2, pp. 559–66.

Skillset (1996) *A Career in Broadcast, Film and Video*. London: Sector Skills Council for Creative Media.

Wrong, D. (1961) 'The Oversocialized Conception of Man in Modern Sociology', *American Sociological Review*, Vol. 26, pp. 183–93.

Appendix 6.1 – Interviewee Profile

Identity Number	Psuedynym	Skill Group/ Level*
[1]	Julie	Artistic/ middle grade
[2]	Susan	Co-ordination/ middle grade
[3]	Adrian	Technical/ head of department
[4]	Derek	Administration/ junior grade
[5]	Keith	Management/ senior grade
[6]	Liz	Co-ordination/ middle grade
[7]	Stephen	Technical/ middle grade

*The specific job descriptions of participants are not detailed as, given the size of the crew, there was usually one individual in each job grade. Identifying a person's job would therefore make their identification possible and violate the guarantee of anonymity given to respondents.

I Don't Know Where You Learn Them: Skills in Film and TV

Irena Grugulis and Dimitrinka Stoyanova

Introduction

One of the central areas of concern for any industry is the ease, capacity and competence with which the skills necessary for work are developed and reproduced in the next generation of workers. In the film and TV sector, such activities are of particular interest because of the structural changes which have occurred over the last two decades. The institutional bodies, organisational structures and other material conditions that contribute to (or detract from) skills development have undergone dramatic changes, shifting career paths, expectations and skill formation systems in their wake. For TV in particular, British industry has traditionally been dominated by the major broadcasters which catered for every aspect of production from the genesis of ideas to the broadcast of programmes (Saundry, 1998; McKinlay and Quinn, 1999; Saundry, 2001; Langham, 1996). Employees were provided with employment security (generally 'jobs for life') and strong internal labour markets facilitated skills development. Today, while the large broadcasters still employ significant numbers of workers, an increasing amount of production is outsourced to smaller, independent companies whose workforces are neither so secure, nor so stable, as those in the old vertically integrated broadcaster bureaucracies. In film this fragmentation happened earlier (Blair, 2001). Employment on British film production was never as constant as that in Hollywood under the old studio system, nonetheless studios did provide fixed points of stability and some long-term security. The industry is now fragmented and employment often project-based, but the demand for skilled workers and the need for skills development continues.

In this chapter we consider the form that skill formation now takes in film and TV and the implications of this shift. That form is unusual in two senses: firstly, because development occurs through the medium of a community of workers. Newcomers learn on the job through observation and discussion with their peers and their entry into a professional network (coupled with the effectiveness of that network) is key to skills development. To a certain extent this seems to follow optimistic predictions of the way expert labour will function in the future (Castells, 1996; Albert and Bradley, 1997). And research certainly reveals how effective professional communities can be at supporting skills development across formal organisational boundaries (see, for example Finegold, 1999; Blair, 2001; Piore and Sabel, 1984). Clearly this form of development encourages and supports rather different behaviours to those fostered by a skill formation system based on lifetime employment and strong internal labour markets and we might expect technical skills to be combined with strong social skills, impression management and self presentation as opposed to, perhaps, loyalty, independent judgement and rigorous professional standards. Such communities or 'learning networks' are still comparatively understudied so this group of workers are of interest not only because they are in transition (from one form of skills development to another) but also because the form that development now takes is that of a network.

This takes us to the second unusual feature of this research, that the network observed here is a regional one, rather than a cynosure of best practice. Existing research into professional communities tends to concentrate on exceptional areas: Silicon Valley for computers and software, London for film production, and the Emilia-Romagna district of Italy for fashion and design; all geographical concentrations of both organisations and individuals that act as magnets for further development. These studies are rigorous ones and succeed in engaging with both what networks are and the way they work but there are dangers as well as opportunities presented by the self-conscious study of excellence (particularly in the area of skills and training, where there is still a tendency to assume that any training is good training, see, for example Payne, 1991). Not all networks are so effective at skills development (Grugulis and Vincent, 2005) and not all skills development is confined to centres of excellence. In this chapter then, we present research into a mundane, rather than an exceptional network; an area where good practice could be observed, but which also had weaknesses and (perhaps most significantly) an area which was far more likely to lose skilled workers to the glamour and opportunities of London, than it was to attract such professionals from the capital.

Film and TV in Britain

Television in the UK has been a subject to significant changes over the last two decades. A series of legislative reforms in the late 1980s and 1990s led to a transformation of the way the sector was organised, as well as its industrial relations and employment practices (Ursell, 2000; Saundry, 1998, 2001; McKinlay and Quinn, 1999; Saundry, Stuart and Antcliff, 2005; Sparks, 1994). Sparks (1994) attributes the changes in the organisation of work in television not to the changing technology or institutional factors as others do (Barnatt and Starkey, 1994), but to economic and political pressures.

A detailed discussion of the industrial, technological, legislative and industrial relations changes can be found in Saundry (2001), Langham (1996) and Tunstall (1993). In brief, following the establishment of Channel 4 the configuration based on the exclusive presence of the BBC and ITV networks changed. Still, employment was based on permanent jobs and trade unions were very influential. The recommendations of the Peacock Committee in 1986 and their subsequent implementation in the early 1990s led to 25 per cent of programming being produced by, and purchased from, independent companies. Following this, a series of regulations covering advertising and franchising resulted in financial constraints for the main industry players, which, in their turn, led to profound changes in the structure of the employment (Saundry, 2001). The most significant of these was the rapid and dramatic increase in the number of freelance workers, both in the independent production sector and in contract work to major broadcasters. Typically, freelance labour consisted of staff who had been made redundant from the large broadcasters and individual workers who set up their own small independent companies. As Saundry notes, this blurring of the distinction between employers and employees further complicated the industry's industrial relations systems. But it did facilitate a relatively smooth shift to a freelance market, because the skills and expertise needed (including organisation-specific knowledge of the major broadcasters) could be supplied without interruption.

Another major change was the weakening of the trade unions, caused largely by redundancies and workforce reduction by the big broadcasters in the late 1980s, the internal reorganisation of work and outsourcing, and the attitudes of independent producers (Sparks, 1994). This had major implications for skills development since possession of a union card had acted as an effective barrier to entry. Extensive on-the-job training and slow progression to higher level work meant that trainees had numerous opportunities to consolidate their skills, were guarded against expensive mistakes on set and helped to act as a guarantor of competence. Taking away the requirement for union membership and the firms' obligation to abide by union terms and conditions effectively removed any threat of sanctions or reprisals for not conforming to this model of development.

At the same time, regionalisation, cost pressures, small scale operations and intensified competition all significantly constrained the scope for 'independence' on the part of the independent companies (Saundry, 1998: 156):

> Buyer-supplier relations within television were characterized.... by almost total dependence on broadcasting organizations. The main commissioning companies (BBC, ITV and Channel 4) enjoy a high degree of power as monopsonistic customers. In most independent productions, the commissioning company controls cashflow to the independent producer through the life of the project. Each item of the programme budget and schedule is subject to scrutiny. This extends as far as approving the personnel to be used on the production.

The result is that independent production companies which move from commission to commission have very limited resources to allocate to investment and development. Given this, and the fact that most employees are hired by the project and are therefore part of a transitory workforce not entirely under the control of the small firms, there are strong structural disincentives to invest in formal training.

In film, while individual projects are considerably longer than those in TV, there has been a similar movement towards the casualisation and marketisation of employment (Blair *et al*, 2003). This industry structure poses considerable challenges to skills development, especially for those in the initial stages of their career. The heavy reliance on on-the-job training in the absence of the supportive institutional structures that characterised the 1970s, generates a rather opportunistic form of skills development (Tempest, McKinlay and Starkey, 2004). According to Langham (1996: 85):

> The industry was (and still is) strongly biased towards 'on-the-job' training. This was all very well when the industry did take on some training responsibility ... Training will still be offered to core staff, but an increasingly large percentage of workers will be freelancers who generally will be expected to have received their training elsewhere.

There seems to be little question that skills development has changed as dramatically as the industry itself, but there is still an interest in and an engagement with skills development. Casualisation here has not eliminated training, rather it has changed it.

Community skills

Given the fragmentation of the industry, few small independent companies offer the type of formal training, structured progression and security of employment that characterised the big broadcasters. Instead, people are expected to learn through employment by taking part in various projects, watching others perform tasks, appreciating what production involves and working their way up through simple jobs to high skilled work. Crouch (2002) labels this type of skill formation the 'community' model. In it, specialised groups of workers such as university academics or computer software engineers, alliances of small firms involved in specialist areas such as design or innovation, and linked customer supplier networks collaborate (both formally and informally) to develop the knowledge and skills of those who work in the sector. Such knowledge is generally high level and tacit (Nonaka and Takeuchi, 1995) and so is very much a part of the individual who exercises it and is not easy to codify. More significantly, as it is passed on it is often developed, taken further and extended, which often makes it difficult to distinguish between 'learning' and 'doing'.

This has implications for the way skills are learned. Lave and Wenger's (1991) and Wenger's (2005) description of community-based learning (among midwives, butchers, tailors and recovering alcoholics) shows how integral doing work is to acquiring skills. Unskilled newcomers start by joining professional groups to assist, a process Lave and Wenger call legitimate peripheral participation. By mixing, socialising and occasionally living with the more established group members they learn occupational norms, valued attitudes and ways of working. And as they progress they are involved in more, and more complex, tasks. So learning to work well and becoming a full, legitimate member of the community are inextricably intertwined: '...it involves becoming a full participant, a member, a kind of person' (Lave and Wenger, 1991: 53). As Crouch (2002) notes, it is impossible to distinguish between further training and simply doing the job since the process of working itself effectively expands an individual's knowledge base. Indeed, he takes this further (p. 5884):

> The creative community therefore represents a skill formation system where most of the distinctions that are normally crucial to the discussion of this topic break down: if the community is strong enough, the distinction between collective and private goods breaks down; distinctions between levels of training disappear; even that between training and the job itself, and therefore that between the school and the market.

So training is indistinguishable from work and work involves social participation in a community of fellows. The scientist extends her knowledge by conducting an experiment, the designer is prompted to new and innovative activity by observing the designs of others and the doctor learns morally appropriate behaviour by listening to the discussion and reactions of his peers. Participation involves more than performing a specific task, it is the way that people learn the function of the whole enterprise, which:

> might include who is involved; what they do; what everyday life is like; how masters talk, walk, work, and generally conduct their lives; how people who are not part of the community of practice interact with it; what other learners are doing; and what learners need to learn to become full practitioners. It includes an increasing understanding of how, when, and about what old-timers collaborate, collude, and collide, and what they enjoy, dislike, respect, and admire. In particular, it offers exemplars (which are grounds and motivation for learning activity), including masters, finished products, and more advanced apprentices in the process of becoming full practitioners. (Lave and Wenger, 1991: 95)

In this model newcomers are not just taught how to do a job, they are socialised into a way of life with its own particular values, priorities and forms of behaviour.

Research methods

This chapter is taken from an ongoing study of work and skills the film and TV industry which concentrates primarily on freelance workers and those involved in small, independent companies. The focus of our analysis is sectoral. Clearly, we would not claim that the sector is the only influence on what skills development an individual receives nor that such an influence is deterministic. Nonetheless many material constraints and accepted norms will remain reasonably consistent, perhaps the more so here because the labour force is a mobile one and practices, ideas and assumptions are unlikely to be confined to organisational boundaries. According to Smith, Child and Rowlinson (1990), sectoral investigations can reveal insights at three levels: the 'objective conditions' of market structures and technology; the 'cognitive area' where ideas about 'accepted' and 'best' practices are generated; and the 'collaborative network' which offers formal and informal opportunities to acquire and diffuse knowledge (see also Arrowsmith and Sisson, 1999). In our study, our concern was not only with the practices adopted by organisations but also with the effect they had on individuals. Accordingly, detailed case study data was combined with semi-biographical interviews to provide both a means of triangulating information as well as additional perspectives on practice.

To date the project has involved some 46 interviews with industry professionals, trade unions and official and professional bodies as well as three months of participant observation by a researcher in a small production company. The majority of the industry professionals and the small production company were based in the north of England (with some additional interviewees from the south west). This was significant since both film and TV work in Britain is concentrated in and around London where the majority of companies, freelancers and commissioning organisations are located (a concentration that becomes even sharper around Soho). Regional film and TV production does exist and is officially encouraged with various locally-based government quangos providing limited match funding for projects in the hope of securing stable, creative jobs for their area; but while some individuals, specialisms or companies do remain regional (nature programmes, horse racing, certain popular soap operas), on most contracts and for many workers, companies are in competition with London.

The fact that this research focused on communities of practice outside London had implications for skills development. As noted above, much of the literature on communities of practice and learning networks concentrates on groups that have reasonably tight spatial boundaries or are centres of excellence. Many of Lave and Wenger's (1991) workers physically lived together; the collaborative networks of small firms in the Emilia-Romagna district in Italy relied heavily on trust, a sense of community and a shared Catholicism (Crouch, Finegold and Sako, 1999; Piore and Sabel, 1984); and the strong customer-supplier networks that characterise Japanese firms compensate for geographical dispersion by regular communications and strong social links (Fruin, 1997; Ray, 2002). Research among Chinese firms in Italy suggests that local networks can be subjected to increasing pressures and internal stratification (Ceccagno, 2004). However, it can be argued that the Chinese migrant's business networks are more stable as they are mobile and flexible being often parts of wider, global networks. Our networks were neither so strong nor so stable. The region was the focus of companies and workers but few there were confident of retaining skilled workers or of attracting others in. It was, without wishing to condemn our respondents, a local network rather than an exceptional one. Yet, in consequence, it may have far more interesting lessons to offer other locations and labour markets than the sites of best practice. This is a community of professionals who worked in an area which was not an automatic magnet for their peers. It is skills development among mobile and insecure workers who co-operated on individual projects but who might also choose to relocate (generally to London) for more, or more interesting, work opportunities. If, as some authors claim, professional community networks really are to become a key source of skills, then such groups are likely to be far more typical of the experience of the majority of workers than the glamour associated with either Silicon Valley or Hollywood. While recent research revealed the complex reality of the latter (Blair *et al*, 2003), the local character of the network and community we studied showed even more opportunistic skills development. This chapter focuses particularly on the first few years of individuals' professional careers. It considers the way they entered the industry, opportunities they had to learn and the way that work and employment were organised.

Getting a foot in the door

In order to learn from a community of workers it is first necessary to join that community and this proved a major stumbling block for many people. Film and TV have a reputation as glamorous and every small company we interviewed spoke of being inundated with calls, e-mails and CVs from potential newcomers requesting work. All those that participated in this study did take people on placements, observations or for (invariably short-term) entry level work but none could either cater for or even meaningfully sift through the applications they received. Realistically, there were three ways that an aspiring worker could secure experience. The first was simple serendipity, their request (or repeated requests) could arrive at the moment a project started or some aspect of their previous experience could match a project particularly well (as in the case of a science graduate, hired as a researcher for a science-based documentary). Or, they happened to be in the company at the time when someone was needed for particular work.

> So, I came for two weeks work experience ... then [the company director] kept me on. I, kind of, filled a niche at that time ... all the producers were freelance and they'd left all the paperwork to do. (Britney, Production Assistant)

Mary, an Arts graduate, currently a Researcher, left her job in a Real Estate company, and did a training scheme which involved community work filming. She was lucky to come across a production company which was just then screening CVs:

> Oh, it's such an annoying tale for other people, but I basically put my CV on the [agency] data base and I got a call from [company owner] directly saying 'Would you like to come in and have an interview for the position of a PA?'... And at that point I didn't know anything about independent companies... anything about television industry; nothing!

Daniel, a cameraman, remembered the old days when he started in a camera rental house, when his age and good luck granted him an entry:

> I just went along...at the age of 19–20 and said I wanted to work in the film industry, and that I was prepared to do anything to get a job in the

film industry. And I was a bit older than most of the people that they got on their waiting list, and I was just very lucky. It was as simple as that, it was luck.

The second way to get access was contacts. This was particularly important since at all levels the industry operated on personal contacts; information was regularly sought from co-workers and colleagues about an individual's competence, reliability and expertise and the impression someone created or the friendships they cultivated could make the difference between winning or losing a contract (Blair, 2001). For example Abigail, a director, got her first job at a production company while on a journalism training scheme with a big broadcaster:

> Actually, it was a mom of a friend of mine. I didn't know much about it, but she owned a small production company. So, she said, you know, 'We need someone to just do some research for a bit', and so I just went along to help out.

Adam, a sound recordist got his first job as a freelancer through a director whom he knew working in a college recording studio.

The third way was by effectively starting their own apprenticeships themselves. Much of the technology required to produce short films is within the reach (at least temporarily) of many young people and there were numerous examples of amateur activities which materially assisted initial job prospects. One aspirant director persuaded his (affluent) father to fund him and a team of friends with ambitions in lighting, camerawork, acting and design, to make a short film. Another produced his first film by borrowing money from his uncle and harnessing his mother's expertise in accounting. A third made music videos for a friend in a band then turned to designing websites and invited numerous media companies and the press to the launch of one.

For many these self- or un-funded projects were a consistent feature of working life and part of building experience. Amrita, a young director, recognised that one of the ways she was able to obtain work was by doing a great many projects for free and even established professionals might be persuaded into working unpaid on an interesting project run by someone who wanted to break into the industry. For others, these extra activities were ways of skill building in their existing job. Sam, a sound recordist specialising in wildlife, recalled his early days at work:

> Alongside that, in parallel, one of the methods of escape that I used from the studio was to take portable recording equipment out with me at week-ends and just go out into [the countryside] where I grew up and just use this equipment out of doors, and again just by practical experience, got to find

out what worked and what didn't. There was very little published in-
formation about it. In fact, there is a society that's still going called a
Wildlife sound recording society and I joined that in the end of the 1970s
.... And so there was a wealth of actual experience there from about
300 members worldwide who were very free with information exchange.
So I learnt a lot through that. Just ... although it's a very isolated activity
.... just through exchange of views, and magazines, and circulating tapes,
I, sort of, learned a lot of basics that way. But the best thing about it was
actually getting out there on my own and doing it, and finding what
works out and what didn't.

Once in, most people's first job was that of 'runner', the fixer, organiser,
ideas person and general factotum who deals with everything from arran-
ging interviews and filming schedules, to fetching tea, to ensuring that
somehow a herd of cows is available in the background on the dawn shoot
the next day. To a certain extent this mirrors the experience of our older
respondents who entered the industry in a range of capacities and worked
their way up to professional roles: from post-boy to cameraman, tea boy to
sound recordist and typist to producer-director. But there were also important differences between these occupational generations. Our older respondents may have undertaken lowly tasks, but their work was paid and the
community they joined was both stable and structured.

Work was very different for the younger interviewees. Many of these
entry level jobs were unpaid and all were short term, limited to the life of a
particular project. The companies we interviewed accepted people on these
free placements on a regular, if *ad hoc* basis and said that they only ever
accepted people who they might be interested in hiring, so that the placement effectively acted as an extended interview with the trainee learning
about the industry and hopefully gaining paid work on the next project.
However not all firms were so unwilling to sign up long-term free labour and
there were numerous tales of young workers employed for months without
pay. Moreover, even when the placement was intended to introduce a
potential employee to a potential employer, given the fragmented nature of
the sector and the erratic levels of work undertaken by small producers, good
workers were unlikely to move directly into a job. Instead many moved from
one unpaid placement to another.

Learning on the job: legitimate peripheral participation

Once hired (whether or not they were paid) the young workers became
peripheral members of the community, supporting preparation, filming and

production through a range of generally simple tasks. Entry was, after all, access to a low level job. It guaranteed neither a chance of being trained nor an opportunity to learn. Novices answered telephones, cleaned camera lenses, took continuity notes, held booms, fetched, carried and arranged aspects of the shoot. The people we spoke to all thought that such involvement with work was the best way to learn the trade:

> I think you'll find that most professional film makers will always say to you the best kind of training is to start as a trainee attached to a crew. You won't ever find better training than that. There is no training like it. (Christopher, cameraman)

> In a nutshell, most people learn on the job. It's not something you can really... study for. You have to be involved in the process, pick up your skills while you're working, really. (Matthew, cameraman)

> It's just experience, really, of how people work and how a film is shot and put together... It's just experience that you can only get on the shop floor, I think... you know... They can't teach you that in a classroom, I don't think. (Edward, sound recordist)

Most members of the film and TV community are happy to accept the trainees and greet new faces on set or in the office by finding out who they are, what sort of experience they have had, what their function is and offering to help by answering questions. Indeed, it is this social acceptance of developmental conversation that is the cornerstone of skill formation since traineeships and placements are irregular, of varying lengths and unstructured. Trainees are given tasks to do and may get involved with any aspect of production on top of their set roles. They can ask questions and most of the people they deal with are happy to answer. This process can work well. A combination of observation; accepting job roles, making mistakes and learning what should be done; and getting on with co-workers can guide the trainee in what is expected and how they should do it:

> The whole shoot lasted for 6 weeks ... Just from the day I started to the day I finished, all the mistakes in the world, I made them ... Within, like, 30 minutes the director knew that I didn't know anything ... He trained me ... He sat me down, and we had a coffee ... And, of course, I didn't write down whether it was overcast, or whether it was sunny, or whether it was windy ... The director had made a note of it, he knew, but asked me deliberately ... that was so useful. (Amrita, director)

> And there I was on my very first day and not knowing a thing about how to work as a clapper loader. .... So it was a very, very steep learning curve. The first time I ever put a clapper board on was with ...[name of a focus puller] and the first thing he said to me after the take was 'Daniel, don't do that again' 'cause obviously it was much too loud and much too close to his face. So, I never did that again. So you learn very quickly. (Daniel, cameraman)

But it did rely very heavily on individual trainees being prepared to take the initiative, ask questions, participate in tasks beyond their immediate jobs, stay late and get involved in every aspect of work. Initiative was vital and, as one employer pointed out, if you were shy, this sector was not the place to be. Those bold or inquisitive enough to engage learned a great deal:

> When I knew something was going on I'd say 'Can I stay in?' ... can I sit in and just listen? And when they were there with client just to learn how to talk to them, or when they're cutting I'd say can I just come and watch it? And I'd learn, and they'd be very open, and help you out like that. So, that's how I learned, really. (Oliver, executive producer)

Occasionally more formal training was provided in the form of bringing in a specialist for the trainee to talk to or sending them on a brief course, but this was rare and on-the-job training formed the core of skills development. Observation in particular could be valuable. Filming involves a whole series of inter-related tasks and everyone on set needs to be aware of what others are doing and adjust their activities accordingly. Takes can be ruined by poor continuity between scenes, unexpected noises or movements or lack of co-ordination between various activities. Peripheral participation not only allows newcomers to undertake a range of roles on set, learning from experience what each one does and how it fits into the whole, it also enables them to learn appropriate behaviours and note the frenetic and confusing activities before they have to do work that might suffer from that confusion. According to Oliver:

> It was like watching ... surgery, in a way .... You've got different people shouting and everybody knows what the other person's doing at one point, and they're talking about things that you have no idea what they are. And that's how it was like ... I didn't know what was going on, who was doing what, who was in charge of who and ... so you just, kind of .... stand and observe, make sure you're not in the way, and try to get a feel for ... for who's doing what, really ..., and what you should be doing, what you shouldn't be doing, when you should be quiet, when you

should step back and when you can, kind of, ask questions. And from there I just, kind of, really stick to the grips ... All I did on my first day was hold an umbrella above the camera, that's all I did, but, you're, kind of, watching stuff there.

Knowing another person's job could also help the inexperienced worker perform their own tasks better. Abigail was training to be a director and found editing work both helpful and illuminating:

And then in the edit room they gave me an editor who works with first time directors, who was very patient and basically did it all for me ... I didn't really know what I was doing, but I did learn, you take a lot in. And I also learned a lot of things I shot were wrong, or I needed extra things, because I didn't know, I couldn't ... like when I was actually directing it I didn't know how to shoot for the edit, so I'd learn, kind of, what I'd need next time I shot stuff ... It was quite revealing.

Most pointed out that the tasks they learned and the experience they acquired were 'not rocket science' and often this was true, with common sense and thought many people would be able to perform the technical aspects of the work our trainees learned. However, mistakes were almost universal and were certainly expected. It might be more accurate to note that while these tasks mainly required common sense that common sense was context dependent and our trainees learned it just as they learned about the way people worked on set and one task related to another. This knowledge was not complicated, but neither was it 'natural'.

Clearly individual projects were not intended primarily as vehicles for learning and often conditions were not ideal. Limited budgets and small production teams meant not only that there were fewer experienced workers around to ask questions of, but also that those who were there were likely to be hard-pressed and not necessarily willing to take time out to explain things to a new worker. It had not always been so. According to Emma, a researcher and writer:

the cameraman had .... a camera assistant, the sound man had a sound assistant, and the editor had an editing assistant. And it was a fantastic way for people to learn the trade, as there was ... the skill.

Smaller teams also meant that experienced operatives had fewer opportunities to discuss work with other professionals during production. One older cameraman noted with regret that he no longer had an apprentice to discuss individual takes with and felt that the quality and creativity of the end product suffered as a result.

Some established professionals took on trainees themselves. Most of these master-apprentice relations were informal. Some lasted only the length of one individual project. Others were of longer duration. One sound recordist we interviewed had a 'trainee' with him who followed him from project to project to learn the trade (terms and conditions were negotiated by the experienced sound recordist). Such relationships could also materially benefit the trainer. Sophie, a location manager spoke of being trained for her first few years in work by a more experienced professional. He taught her how to do the work, recommended her to friends for projects he could not do, assisted her with queries and took a proportion of her fee.

Occasionally limited budgets created opportunities for less experienced workers or those with ambitions to move from one role to another. Such progression was often difficult since, in the absence of any form of structured career path the way any individual got a better job was quite simply by being hired to do it, a risky choice for any small company when a badly made product could mean contacts would be reluctant to commission future work. As George, a director and employer commented:

> People come to us and say 'I want to be an editor', and you say 'well, I can't throw you at the deep end – you've got no experience. And they say, 'Well, where do I get it from?' You say, 'I don't know, really.' But I can't take a risk with a network programme ... So you tend to rely on the people that you do know, who are trusted.

However when budgets were tight, as they almost invariably were, and in the regions where the pool of skilled labour was small, compromises could be made. Sometimes these took the form of structured work experience, such as allowing someone to have a day's experience of directing under supervision during a reasonably long project. On other occasions people who had never directed or edited or produced before were hired for those roles for the whole project. When this happened the independent production companies took steps to ensure their risks were limited, staffing every other position with experienced workers who, although notionally doing other jobs, were knowledgeable and skilled enough to provide direction and support for their less experienced colleague. Indeed Amrita, a director, described how, in the first film that she notionally directed, most of the time she simply watched while the experienced cameraman put her ideas into practice.

Of course, not all sets and not all workers welcomed trainees. Since these new entrants represented either current or future competition for work in a sector where employment was insecure there were tensions between the older and younger employees (Lave and Wenger, 1991). Daniel's first job on set had been as a clapper loader, holding up clapper boards with scene and take numbers before each shoot to help the editorial process. However, his 'old school' camera operator neither told him that the boards were out of frame nor made any attempt to move the camera so the relevant information could be recorded so Daniel did not learn about his errors until the end of filming, eight to ten weeks later, while travelling home with the more sympathetic producer.

Moreover the brevity of most projects also limited learning. Each production could be very different, staffed by different people and requiring different types of subject knowledge in terms of content so that skills were not so much built up from a structured foundation as assembled, pick and mix style from a wide range of different options. Indeed one owner-producer described success in entry level positions as largely 'serendipity', pointing out that a researcher or trainee who had failed abysmally on one project might shine on the next. His willingness to forgive failures by entry level workers may have a structural foundation since his firm tended to take on trainee researchers for a period of several months rather than an individual project and during such placements he became accustomed to observing both triumphs and disasters. Blair's (2001) research suggests that tolerance is far more limited further up the hierarchy where a disaster on one project can materially affect an individual's chances of finding work elsewhere.

The lack of any form of structured progression also presented problems. For earlier generations a combination of formal apprenticeships, barriers to entry and official union structures meant that most spent a great deal of time learning the ropes and acquired a great deal of knowledge in the process. One worked as a warehouseman at a site supplying cameras to the film industry to gain his union card, by which time he knew a great deal about the equipment needed on set. Another spent his first two years cleaning equipment before being allowed to touch a camera. Under this system, long periods of learning and time served in jobs were a publicly accepted part of progression. New entrants knew what to expect and were provided with secure employment while working their way up the ladder and acquiring skills. According to Alexander, a producer-director:

There used to be ... it wasn't exactly a formal structure but we used to say that, you know, most people who start as a researcher, say as a junior researcher, we'd expect them to do probably three years as a researcher, you know, working a way to become a senior researcher. You need three years to, kind of, understand what you're doing .... And you know, we would give people opportunities [to develop] on simple things .... And then, once they could do that and they've been an assistant producer for a few more years, probably you get another three years, then we would think about making them into producers.

The skills needed for the more senior roles were still the same but workers' expectations had dramatically changed, partly because the fragmented nature of the industry now made progression opaque and partly in line with other social trends. Small production companies spoke of new graduates arriving and expecting to direct or researchers with only six months experience asking to be moved up the hierarchy. This had positive aspects: Christopher, a cameraman noted with approbation that it was no longer possible for the union to prevent someone working because they had no union card and the 'system' itself was certainly flexible enough to accommodate any amount of creativity and innovation but it did heighten the risk for small employers and goes some way to explaining their reliance on word of mouth and reputation in preference to previous job title in recruitment decisions. Their caution might also be explained by the fact that the ambitions of entrants were also built in to the system. The two aspects of work that each individual negotiated for at the start of a project were pay and 'credits', the way their name appeared at the end of the feature and the job title they were credited with. This was far from being a simple matter of individual ego and prestige since future job offers and standing in the community depended on such credits. When budgets were limited, small companies often kept their hired help happy by offering 'grandiose' job titles (Tempest *et al*, 2004: 1536). In the production observed as part of this research almost all the office staff were credited with something. It was a welcome and much appreciated gesture but it further distorted the already blurred line between job titles and skills.

Discussion and conclusions

In some respects this system of training has advantages. Film and TV is an area where technology has changed quite dramatically and a flexible approach to skills development has the capacity to capture these changes and leave individuals room to innovate. Moreover this is an industry in which on-the-job training has always been favoured and where qualifications are (at best) only an indirect means of entry to the profession. In Langham's (1996: 75) words, this industry '... certainly includes an obsessive fascination with film and a willingness to work long hours. In a world of fanatics, academic degrees and even vocational qualifications were (and still are to a large extent) beside the point.' This is not to say that qualifications were not used and useful. Our interviewees included engineers who praised their degrees and the skills they had gained, claiming to use them every day in work, as well as company owners who owed their break into the industry or had founded their company on the basis of friendship groups formed at university. But all agreed that the most valuable skills were those they had acquired on the job.

The flexibility of this form of development was further extended to the type of people who had access to it. In the absence of the closed shop and the need for a union card the various occupations were (at least theoretically) open to all. However, in practice, we found no evidence that this freedom effectively increased diversity. On the contrary, although our research was conducted in a region with a large ethnic minority population, few were represented here. Skills agencies expressed concern at this and special events were held to encourage black and minority ethnic workers into the industry. Other barriers were also apparent. Lengthy unpaid placements, a history of amateur activities prior to entry and access to work through friends and contacts may well have ensured that this sector stayed a middle class preserve. One union respondent noted with alarm the increasing homogeneity and gender stereotyping of job roles that had run parallel with the fragmentation of the industry. He argued that the large broadcasters had employed 'atypical' apprentices – men in makeup and women in cameras or engineering – but that subverting such gender roles was almost unheard of in smaller companies. In this instance it seems that flexibility did not bring diversity.

But flexibility is not necessarily the optimal criterion to seek in skills development and the community model of gaining expertise has some fairly obvious limitations. In particular, structuring a learning experience around the novice questioning the master places considerable responsibility on both parties to ask the right questions, observe the right activities and respond with the right answers. Learning through freelance work was, as Robert remarked, a 'hit and miss' process. Even when the questioning went well there were no formal structures to ensure that the learning was understood or could be successfully applied next time. In addition to this, those answering the questions or supporting learning might be in competition for jobs, now or in the future, with the trainees. The incentives to provide disinformation or simply not answer were quite significant and under the circumstances it is surprising, not that we found some resistance to trainees, but that we did not find more. It may have been that their status as real workers helped, that the culture militated against such practices, or simply that most workers in the industry were too generous to stoop to petty misinformation. Nonetheless, insecurity and community make uneasy bedfellows and the behaviours encouraged by one are more than likely to disrupt the smooth functioning of the other. More fundamentally for this industry,

while researchers had traditionally been involved in every aspect of production from preliminary ideas to final edit, and while this was seen as
the key element of learning the trade, budget pressures in small firms meant
that they might only be hired for the minimum length of time and many
finished their work before filming even started. Even when junior employees
did have access to the set their access to learning could be limited. As
Tempest *et al* (2004: 1535) note:

> The quality of experiential on-the-job learning depends on the challenge
> and diversity of the production role offered. The most challenging jobs
> tend to be concentrated in the hands of those with established reput-
> ations, creating important issues of exclusion from access to learning
> opportunities for many workers.

The fact that much of this research was undertaken in a region may have
increased the fragility of the network. As noted above, most of the research
into communities of practice has been conducted in stable work groups,
some very stable as participants were born, grew up and died in the communities in which they worked (Lave and Wenger, 1991; Orr, 1996). By contrast here, 'community' groups were very temporary, short-lived, often under
extreme pressures of work and existed only as long as the projects lasted, a
process exacerbated by the tendency of ambitious freelancers to relocate
to London in search of more or better work. Certainly, groups of friends
often re-formed on other projects and regional or specialist gossip tightened
links between members but no matter how welcoming these groups were,
opportunities to watch, participate and learn were restricted. Such mobility
seems to contrast with Blair's (2001) conclusions on the existence of semi-
permanent work groups where professionals at all levels would be consistently re-hired by a head of department and moving from one work group
to another might endanger an individual's chances of regular work. But
Blair's research was specifically focused on the film industry and (from the
references in it to exceptionally well-known box office hits), to the upper
end of that industry, where budgets are rather more generous. Many of our
participants would have welcomed the opportunity to either hire or work in
such semi-permanent groups since these not only made workers easier to
organise, they also offered a sort of collective guarantee of the quality of the
finished product. But in our study, when monies were spent hiring experienced workers for one stage of filming it was generally at the expense of
another. Senior workers tried to bring in trusted colleagues and often suc-
ceeded, as when Robert, a producer-director, hired a cameraman he had
worked with before, whose skills he trusted, but here such recruitment was
something to be negotiated.

The impact of restricted development opportunities was, perhaps, most clearly marked on the technical side of the work. Changes in technology meant that operating most of the systems was far simpler than it had been. Camera and sound were often combined, cameras were far more mobile than they had been (many were hand held) and editing software could be mastered in a few days. As a result the numbers of video journalists and multi-skilled operators increased and it became common, particularly on low budget productions for crew members (including directors) to take on additional functions. But this did not mean that the skills needed to use these technologies had disappeared entirely and most people also pointed out that one of the major contributory factors making these skills easier to learn was everyone's willingness to accept much lower standards. Robert, a producer-director commented wryly on the sound after finishing filming, 'Technically it was crap, but it's telly – no one will notice'. Quality standards for feature films were still high but for the regular short documentaries, comedies, news features, human interest, current affairs and cookery programmes which formed the staple diet of the independent companies a more pragmatic approach was taken.

What this effectively meant was that the returns available for technical skills were often limited. Technology had made tasks much simpler, most people saw much of the skilled work as 'common sense' and small companies were prepared to compromise on product quality so for some jobs, particularly camera work, standards and salaries fell. Several people noted this with regret. Technological innovation could have provided a basis for raising standards. Moreover, the story-telling on which film and television relies, often rests on a great deal of technical expertise, the knowledge of how an effect will appear on screen or the impact a sequence of shots will have on viewers. Without this sort of experience, without the practiced eye and the ability to create a certain image on screen it was felt that creativity would suffer. Other technical skills were both valued and much needed but the fragmented nature of the industry mitigated against any developmental activities. Studio directing in particular was an area of expertise regularly sought by the broadcasters but since few directors now worked in-house the old internal and expensive training programmes were no longer run: individual directors felt that the expense and time would be too great to commit to, the broadcasters that the risks of putting on a course for independent workers would be too high.

Our final comment on the efficacy of learning through communities of practice in this industry is the one that is most speculative and that is on the wastage of human talent involved. The people we interviewed were, by definition, the ones who had just entered or who had remained in the industry. We have no means of knowing, and it is no-one's business to collate figures on, those who do not stay. The system of placements, short-term and temporary work assignments, and paid and unpaid work means that turnover is rapid and firms often have little idea what happens to an individual worker once a project has finished. Some succeed, at least in the sense that they gain work regularly enough to support themselves; others accept very sporadic contracts or unpaid assignments to maintain their images of themselves as film and TV professionals, supporting themselves with other (less glamorous) forms of paid employment or through state schemes; many drop out entirely.

These shifting communities of practice do provide opportunities for skill formation but for both employees and employers such experiences are varied and variable. Challenging jobs, as noted elsewhere, are one of the most effective means of learning (Finegold, 1999). But challenging, changeable, insecure jobs in fluid groups where little consensus exists on activities, quality levels or standards may be taking flexibility one step too far.

REFERENCES

Albert, S. and Bradley, K. (1997) *Managing Knowledge: Experts, Agencies and Organisations*. Cambridge: Cambridge University Press.

Arrowsmith, J. and Sisson, K. (1999) 'Pay and working time: towards organisation-based systems?', *British Journal of Industrial Relations*, 37: 51–75.

Barnatt, C. and Starkey, K. (1994) 'The Emergence of Flexible Networks in the UK Television Industry', *British Journal of Management*, 5: 251–60.

Blair, H. (2001) 'You're only as good as your last job: the labour process and labour market in the British film industry', *Work, Employment and Society*, 15: 149–69.

Blair, H., Culkin, N. and Randle, K. (2003) 'From London to Los Angeles: a comparison of local labour market processes in the US and UK film industries', *International Journal of Human Resource Management*, 14: 619–33.

Castells, M. (1996) *The Rise of the Network Society*. Oxford: Blackwell.

Ceccagno, A. (2004) 'The Economic Crisis and the Ban on Imports: The Chinese in Italy at a Crossroads'. Paper for the 5th Conference of the International Society for the Study of Chinese Overseas (ISSCO), Copenhagen, May 2004.

Crouch, C. (2002) 'Skill formation systems', *International Enclyclopaedia of Business and Management*. London: Thomson Learning.

Crouch, C., Finegold, D. and Sako, M. (1999) *Are Skills the Answer? The Political Economy of Skill Creation in Advanced Industrialised Countries*. Oxford: Oxford University Press.

Finegold, D. (1999) 'Creating self-sustaining, high-skill ecosystems', *Oxford Review of Economic Policy*, 15: 60–81.

Fruin, W.M. (1997) *Knowledge Works: Managing Intellectual Capital at Toshiba*. New York and Oxford: Oxford University Press.

Grugulis, I. and Vincent, S. (2005) 'Changing boundaries, shaping skills: the fragmented organisational form and employee skills', in Marchington, Grimshaw, Rubery and Willmott (eds) *Fragmenting Work: Blurring Organisational Boundaries and Disordering Hierarchies*. Oxford: Oxford University Press.

▶

▶

Langham, J. (1996) *Lights, Camera, Action: Working in Film, Television and Video*. London: British Film Institute.

Lave, J. and Wenger, E. (1991) *Situated Learning: Legitimate Peripheral Participation*. Cambridge: Cambridge University Press.

McKinlay, A. and Quinn, B. (1999) 'Management, Technology and Work in Commercial Broadcasting, c. 1979–98', *New Technology, Work and Employment*, 14: 2–17.

Nonaka, I. and Takeuchi, H. (1995) *The Knowledge Creating Company: How Japanese Companies Create the Dynamics of Innovation*. New York and Oxford: Oxford University Press.

Orr, J. (1996) *Talking about Machines*. Ithaca and London: ILR Press/Cornell University Press.

Payne, J. (1991) *Women, Training and the Skills Shortage*. London: Policy Studies Institute.

Piore, M. and Sabel, C. (1984) *The Second Industrial Divide: Possibilities for Prosperity*. New York: Basic Books.

Ray, T. (2002) 'Managing Japanese Organizational Knowledge Creation: the Difference', in Little, Quintas and Ray (eds) *Managing Knowledge*. London: Sage Publications.

Saundry, R. (1998) 'The Limits of Flexibility: the Case of UK Television', *British Journal of Management*, 9: 151–62.

Saundry, R. (2001) 'Employee Relations in British Television-Regulation, Fragmentation and Flexibility', *Industrial Relations Journal*, 32: 22–36.

Saundry, R., Stuart, M. and Antcliff, V. (2005) 'Networks, Trade Unions and Television', *British Universities Industrial Relations Association Annual Conference*. Northumbria.

Smith, C., Child, J. and Rowlinson, M. (1990) *Reshaping Work: The Cadbury Experience*. Cambridge: Cambridge University Press.

Sparks, C. (1994) 'Independent Production: Unions and Casualization', in Hood (ed.) *Behind the Screens: The Structure of British Broadcasting in the 1990s*. London: Lawrence & Wishart.

Tempest, S., McKinlay, A. and Starkey, K. (2004) 'Careering Alone: Careers and Social Capital in the Financial Services and Television Industries', *Human Relations*, 57: 1523–45.

Tunstall, J. (1993) *Television Producers*. London: Routledge.

Ursell, G. (2000) 'Television Production: Issues of Exploitation, Commodification and Subjectivity in UK Television Labour Markets', *Media Culture Society*, 22: 805–25.

Wenger, E. (2005) *Communities of Practice: Learning, Meaning and Identity*. New York and Cambridge: Cambridge University Press.

Bringing Creativity to Market: Actors as Self-Employed Employees

8

Axel Haunschild and Doris Ruth Eikhof

Introduction

In team-based creative industries such as media, film, theatre and dance, the production of creative goods takes place in trans-organisational projects (Eikhof, 2006). Heterogeneous and constantly changing groups of artists and non-artists work on projects with tight time schedules and unpredictable outcomes (Caves, 2000). Individual success and careers depend on the success of projects and on (the reputation of) the partners worked with. This project-focused system of production and the strong motivation to produce 'art for art's sake' lead to both desire and necessity to organise individual lives according to the requirements of creative work and employment.

The aim of this chapter is to explore the effects project-based working has on individuals in a specific creative industry: German theatre. Whereas a number of studies on creative industries address the labour market level (Haak and Schmid, 1999; Menger, 1999; Benhamou, 2000; Caves, 2000; Baumann, 2002) or the economics of creative production (Heilbrun and Gray, 1993; Throsby, 2001), neither the way artists or creative workers develop strategies to cope with the uncertainties and labour market requirements they have to face nor the characteristics of the labour process in creative industries have attracted much attention (for exceptions see Dex *et al.*, 2000; Blair, 2001; Blair *et al.*, 2001; Fraser and Gold, 2001). This chapter seeks to fill this gap by analysing the project-focused work of theatre artists at an individual level by using the concept of 'Arbeitskraftunternehmer' or 'self-employed employee'. The analysis is based on 45 in-depth interviews in three major German theatres and in selected inter-firm institutions.

The *Arbeitskraftunternehmer* is a theoretical concept developed by German sociologists (Voß and Pongratz, 1998; Pongratz and Voß, 2000; Pongratz and Voß, 2003) to illustrate a highly market-oriented and individualised form of labour supply.[1] The term 'self-employed employment' was not coined to describe existing forms of work or employment and their specific underlying contractual arrangements. It rather provides an analytical framework for analysing a mode of labour use which, at the individual level, is characterised by the following three features: (1) a high degree of self-control, (2) self-marketing, and (3) economisation of life together with blurring boundaries between work and private life. According to Voß and Pongratz such usage of human labour is currently spreading and supersedes traditional forms of transforming labour potential into real labour. By introducing such an ideal type of labour use, Voß and Pongratz provide a clearly defined reference point for examining the labour process in different industries as well as current changes in the world of work. We will use the three characteristics of self-employed employees outlined by Voß and Pongratz to analyse our empirical evidence of how theatre actors experience and respond to working in a project-focused system of production.

This chapter shows how self-control, self-marketing and economisation of life shape work practices in theatres. For intrinsically motivated self-employed employees, working in trans-organisational projects leads to a seemingly paradoxical situation: individuals understand themselves as creative, self-controlled and intrinsically motivated bohemians (for whom 'art for art's sake' is a central professional value), but at the same time they have to be very clever as well as calculating managers of themselves as human resources. This situation not only requires continuously marketing oneself through social networks and maintaining one's employability, but also living a life fully committed to work. The chapter draws conclusions for a wider industry context from theatre actors' particular experience. We argue that interpreting actors as self-employed employees in the project-focused theatrical industry points at crucial features of such forms of work and labour usage in general. Since organisations increasingly propagate workers' self-control and demand self-economised workers who subject more and more aspects of their life under the requirements of work, we argue that our analysis of theatre actors can also help to understand wide-ranging changes of the labour process beyond the creative industries.

Research setting

Data used in our analysis of theatre artists as self-employed employees comprise qualitative empirical data and secondary data both collected by the authors. Primary data include 45 semi-structured in-depth interviews conducted between 2000 and 2003. The first set of interviews (ten interviews) was carried out in a German theatre (Staatstheater) financed by public subsidies and situated in a city with approximately 500,000 inhabitants.

Interview partners here included the theatre manager (artistic director), a senior administration manager, a director, a project coordinator, and several actors linked to the theatre by different contractual arrangements. The second set of interviews (five interviews) was conducted with representatives of inter-firm institutions: the national employers' (Deutscher Bühnenverein) and employees' (Genossenschaft Deutscher Bühnen-Angehöriger (GDBA)) associations, the state-run work agency for actors (ZBF), and a state-run theatre school (see also Haunschild, 2003). A third set of interviews (30 interviews) was conducted with theatre actors, *dramaturges*,[2] directors and a theatre manager in two repertoire theatres situated in a city with approximately two million inhabitants. The interviewees comprise ensemble members (actors on 1–2 year contracts, see below) as well as self-employed theatre artists. Additionally, informal discussions mainly with so-called free artists (see below) provided further information on theatre employment. Secondary data used include interviews with theatre artists in newspapers and practitioner journals, statistical reports, and information given on theatres' and inter-firm institutions' websites.

Work arrangements and institutional context

Unlike in most other countries, nearly all German theatres of artistic relevance are public theatres owned by cities or local states. These public theatres are repertoire theatres that stage a different drama every night, drawing on a standing repertoire of 15–30 plays for a season. Medium to large-sized theatres employ an ensemble of about 25 to 40 theatre actors. The contracts of ensemble members in Germany are temporary employment contracts with a duration of one, two or, rarely, three years. Therefore, they provide an example of work arrangements between freelancing and self-employment on the one hand, and permanent employment on the other. The 'Normal-vertrag Bühne' (NV Bühne), which is the result of collective bargaining between employer association and union, provides a mutually accepted framework for these contracts and it also holds for employed directors, stage designers and *dramaturges*. However, the NV Bühne covers less than one third of the actual work arrangements of the 10,000 professional actors estimated to be working in Germany. Actors that are not engaged on the basis of the NV Bühne in one of the 151 public repertoire theatres work either (a) as 'guests' engaged for a certain play, (b) as contractors employed in an engagement for (part of) the season, (c) in private, commercial or 'free' theatres, (d) as actors who are not exclusively theatre actors but work across the acting profession, e.g. film, TV and radio productions, or they are unemployed actors (Haunschild, 2004b).

Our research, however, focuses on members of theatre ensembles working for repertoire theatres. As our analysis will show, flexibility and mobility requirements as well as uncertainties concerning the future demand for one's labour power are crucial not only for freelance actors but for ensemble members as well. Before analysing how theatre artists perceive and cope with these requirements and uncertainties, the remainder of this section briefly describes some characteristics of the German theatrical industry.

The creative industries generally offer instructive examples of how institutional frameworks can provide some stability within a flexible labour market. Several studies of artistic labour markets marked by project work and high labour mobility emphasise the importance of trans-organisational networks and occupational or industrial communities as a basis for individual careers as well as for organisational recruiting activities (Faulkner and Anderson, 1987; Jones, 1996; Raider and Burt, 1996; Tolbert, 1996; Jones and Walsh, 1997; DeFillippi and Arthur, 1998; Blair *et al,* 2001; Sydow and Staber, 2002; Haunschild, 2003; Marsden, 2004).

In theatre, the process of rehearsing (typically four to eight weeks) and performing a play for a certain number of times constitutes a project-focused form of production. For the production of a play, theatre artists (actors, director, stage designer, costume designer, light designer) work together with technical staff providing the required technical infrastructure (light, costumes, stage). It is common practice in German theatres that the team members change from project to project, i.e. a selection of members of the ensemble works together with selected guest actors, guest directors and permanently employed technical staff.

During a theatre manager's period in office, the ensemble is more or less a stable group. Thus, the German theatre industry is project-focused but it is not totally organised as a dynamic network of trans-organisational projects (Haunschild, 2003). Nevertheless, theatre artists in the German theatre industry have to renew their employability on a project basis and their careers reflect a sequence of more or less successful and renowned projects.

The German theatrical employment system is stabilised by intra- and inter-organisational networks, an occupational community including 'professional' theatre artists and excluding non-artists, inter-firm institutions (GDBA, Bühnenverein) negotiating industry-wide formal rules of the game, labour market intermediaries (ZBF, agents) helping to match job requirements with artists' characteristics and skills, and, finally, an artistic or bohemian lifestyle functioning as a 'social glue' holding the community together and creating a fit between individual preferences and work requirements (Haunschild, 2003, 2004b; Eikhof, 2006; Eikhof and Haunschild, 2006). This institutional framework enables and restricts employers' and individual workers' strategies and helps participants to cope with labour mobility and career uncertainties.

Self-employed employees

Reviewing empirical studies into new forms of employment, Voß and Pongratz (1998, see also Pongratz and Voß, 2000, 2003) saw a new form of labour supply emerge. They described the main characteristics of this new form of labour supply in an ideal type, the *Arbeitskraftunternehmer* (self-employed employee). According to Voß and Pongratz, self-employed employment is characterised by three aspects:

(1) Self-control: self-employed employees exercise a considerable amount of control over the content and quality as well as the organisation of their work.
(2) Self-marketing: self-employed employees have to explicitly market their labour power on both internal and external markets. They are under a permanent pressure to demonstrate employability for future projects.
(3) Economisation of life: Self-employed employees subordinate their life to work not only by devoting more time and energy to work, but also by applying the (economic) logic of work to their private life.

As the *Arbeitskraftunternehmer* or self-employed employee is an ideal type, empirical forms of labour supply will comprise these characteristics to varying degrees. For instance, Arbeitskraftunternehmer *may* legally be self-employed (which implies a maximum level of self-control), but they can also be employees of a company, working in flexible networks (which may imply less self-control but more economisation of life compared to some self-employed). Voß and Pongratz's key argument is that with current trends in work (e.g. project work and temporary work) characteristics that have previously been restricted to self-employed workers become widespread in other forms of employment, including permanent employment contracts. They argue that the extent to which workers have to exhibit self-management and self-marketing skills to succeed depends not on their legal employment status, but rather on the actual enactment of employment relationships. For instance, competitive internal labour markets, as prevalent in consultancy, force permanent employees into behaviour previously only associated with self-employed professionals. Voß and Pongratz point out that current changes in work and employment alter the way individuals understand themselves as providers of labour services and that both understanding and the resulting behaviour are driven by the logics of marketing and economising ones work life and private life.

In the following we will use the three characteristics of Voß and Pongratz's ideal type to analyse work practices in theatre. We point out how each of these characteristics is represented in actors' work lives. In so doing we use an empirical example of workers who are by law employees, but who work in employment relationships that require them to act as self-employed or entrepreneurs of their labour power, in order to explore what an increase in self-employed employment as a form of labour supply could mean for the world of work.

Theatre actors as self-employed employees

Self-control

Voß and Pongratz point out how self-employed employees have to plan, organise and control their work themselves. But in so doing they work within constraints that are set by their contract partners. Project agendas, for instance, specify time, place, quantity and quality of work output and self-employed employees have to ensure that they meet these targets. Nevertheless, they exercise considerable discretion as to *how* they meet these targets. Voß and Pongratz summarise all activities of planning, organising and controlling work-related activities which are geared towards meeting work targets under the notion of *self-control*.

Compared to the ideal type description, theatre actors do not, at first glance, appear to have much scope for self-control. Theatre work is dominated by tightly knit time schedules of the daily rehearsals and evening shows. Both rehearsals and performances are scheduled on a short-term basis: the programme is set approximately a month in advance, rehearsals (which may take place in the morning or, depending on the cast of the evening show, at night) are set a week in advance and are often changed on a daily basis. Rehearsals are open ended and many nights are spent discussing work and life in theatre. Collective bargaining prescribes a three hour break in the afternoon, but since each rehearsal process has its own dynamics, those breaks are often not taken. As a result, actors have little say in the temporal aspects of work organisation. One actor illustrated this by saying: *'I was never able to promise my wife that we would go to the cinema the next day.'*

Yet, on top of rehearsal and show schedules, actors have to manage a substantial part of their work life themselves. They prepare for rehearsals by studying scripts and additional material, and sometimes engage in field studies of characters they have to play (e.g. meeting with disabled people) or in specific preparations such as learning an instrument or special body movements (e.g. karate, specific dance styles). In addition, theatre actors promote their public persona by giving interviews and liaising with the media, they participate in smaller events at the theatre (readings, PR activities etc.) or work on external projects such as film or TV productions. For successful actors, this may easily result in approximately 60 working hours per week, stretching Monday to Sunday.

In terms of work content, two main parameters of actors' work practices are scripts and directors. One would guess that since scripts prescribe words (and often movements) and directors have the ultimate authority as to how the play is going to be staged, actors might have little scope for influencing the content of their work. Our interviews both with theatre actors and with directors, dramaturges and drama teachers, however, contradicted this assumption. Most directors do not have a pre-set idea about the play, but ask the actors to offer their own interpretation of the role. In the words of a drama teacher, an actor's main qualification is to '*make an empty space come alive*'. This initial contribution is solely up to the actors, and their capability of transforming script material into a character that directors can work with crucially influences whether directors will want to work with the actors again. Directors will suggest rearrangements and modifications, but ultimately, initial interpretations as well as reactions to the directors' responses are left to the actors. This way of collaborating leads to a high awareness of one's own labour output. Our interviewees pointed out how, despite elements of spontaneity, they constantly assessed their own performance, both with respect to artistic criteria and in relationship to their colleagues: '*You are not only exposed to external judgement all the time, you also constantly monitor your own work. It is constant crisis and conflict, there is a low barrier to panic and you are always afraid that you will be cast for too little or too small roles – you are always afraid that theatre management and audiences will not love you enough*' (actor).

Taking into account the whole picture of actors' work practices, self-control plays a more dominant role for theatre actors than a superficial glance would suggest. Actors organise both work in the narrower sense of rehearsing and staging a play and in the wider sense of participating in external productions, collaborating with the media or preparing for roles themselves. Theatres only provide frameworks of tasks and schedules. Although actors may not exhibit the degrees of self-control common, for instance, for a self-employed physiotherapist, they exercise considerably more self-control over their work practices than employees in, for example, a bank or call centre, where work routines are more standardised. The notion of self-control seems to contradict the bohemian image of self-realisation commonly associated with artists. Nevertheless, our study shows that practices of self-control are essential qualities for a career in acting and that despite all bohemian camouflage (cf. Eikhof and Haunschild, 2006) they make up a substantial share of actors' daily work practices.

Self-marketing

Voß and Pongratz define a high degree of self-marketing as the second characteristic of self-employed employees. Self-marketing subsumes all activities directed towards advertising and selling one's own labour power on internal as well as external markets. Such activities include scanning the markets for future employment opportunities, making and maintaining contacts to potential buyers of labour power, actively selling oneself for future projects as well as generally enhancing one's employability by updating and developing skills. Voß and Pongratz point out that regardless of the formal duration of their employment contract, self-employed employees have to ensure their future participation in projects. Even workers on permanent contracts, such as, for example, key account managers in advertising, have to actively seek participation in future projects that ensure or advance their position within their company's internal market. As a consequence, self-employed employees are characterised by a high degree of market-orientation.

For theatre actors, the main focus is to be cast for roles, as only by being on stage can they demonstrate their acting capabilities, advance their careers and recommend themselves for future projects with their current employer and/or with new and external employers. Role assignments lie with theatre managers and directors. They assemble the project teams and decide on a play-to-play basis who gets to stage what throughout the season. If no appropriate role can be found for an ensemble member, the theatre manager will let this actor 'go for a walk' (while continuing to pay their salary) and staff the current productions with ensemble colleagues and/or guest actors. For financial reasons, theatre managers will try to avoid these situations, but the artistic quality of the play always dominates an actor's need to work.

The common employment contract for actors, NV Bühne, is a temporary contract (usually for one year) that can be terminated every autumn. Theatre managers will cancel contracts for instance if the actor has not performed well or has not been cast often enough in the previous season. This puts pressure on ensemble members to be included in a sufficient number of plays and in leading roles, and it creates a tense atmosphere during autumn:

> 'Of course, everybody plays it cool and acts like they do not expect an end of their time at the theatre. But hey, we're actors! If you look closer, you will notice tension and insecurity among all. Autumn is the time when you ask yourself: Have I played enough during the past season? Did I have enough leading roles? Did the directors show enough interest in me? Are there any signs that the theatre manager wants to keep me? Or worse: that he wants to get rid of me?' (actor).

Thus, the actors' key concern in marketing their own labour power is getting the right, i.e. prestigious or leading, roles. All interviewees agreed that role assignments depend on personal contacts. Friendships and acquaintances with directors, theatre managers, *dramaturges*, critics and other actors increase the likelihood of being considered for prominent roles. As a consequence, theatre actors market themselves by building up and maintaining a personal network throughout the whole occupational community. Key figures in these networks are theatre managers and directors, since both have the power to cast actors for plays at the theatre they are currently employed with, for guest roles at another theatre, for productions outside the theatre (e.g. film and TV productions) or even for a new ensemble contract at another theatre. Because of this dependence on powerful individuals, many actors equated professional success with *'being loved by the theatre manager'* (actor), as such 'love' ensures role assignments and career success.

In theoretical terms, an actors' personal network can be understood as his stock of social capital (Bourdieu, 1983, 1984). The higher in quantity and quality the social capital an actor can rely on, the more likely he is to be cast for interesting projects throughout the industry. Social capital reduces the uncertainties induced by the project-organisation of theatre production. Asked about how he could advance his career, a young actor's first answer was not *'perform better'*, but *'maybe I should increase my presence at premiere celebrations'*. This is a common reflection, which shows that theatre actors are very aware of the fact that social capital requires strategic investment. Social capital has a self-reinforcing effect: the more social capital an actor has already accumulated the easier it is to accumulate more. Frequently, the opportunity to build up or increase social capital will make participation in a project more attractive than the immediate monetary rewards offered. Even renowned actors will, from time to time, partake in low-pay projects that offer collaboration with interesting partners or an increase in social capital and reputation.

Our interviewees were very open about the impact of personal networks on careers. They explained that art is the ultimate criterion anything in the industry is judged against and that individual and subjective artistic tastes dominate staffing as well as programme decisions. Yet, most of the actors refrain from reflecting upon their activities in economical terms. *'Some colleagues are very active in networking at premiere celebrations. I don't do it'* stated one actor, and others described their network as a 'collection of friendships and acquaintances founded by chance'. Most respondents tried to give the impression that strategic investment in social capital was something only others were engaged in. These claims contradicted the authors' observations that virtually all ensemble members took care to attend premiere celebrations, even those who had been on stage at the theatre's second venue at the other end of the city that same evening or who had had an evening off.

On the one hand, work relationships in theatre have a much more friendship-like character than in other companies and thus it is relatively easy for the actors to masque self-marketing activities as 'interacting with friends'. For instance, they would ask a colleague they are friendly with to introduce them to a director he knows. On the other hand, the problematic extent to which friendships are used for self-marketing became obvious in some interviewees' reflections about theatre friendships: they complained that since every personal relationship had a potential economic value it was often hard to distinguish true friends from those who just try to advance their career.

Networking and the strategic accumulation and use of social capital are the main practices of self-marketing in theatre. However, the high degree of market-orientation Voß and Pongratz describe in their ideal type can be found in a number of smaller aspects as well. Actors are very aware of general theatre-related media coverage, reviews for individual plays and award nominations, all of which indicate their own market value in relation to that of their colleagues. Our interviewees also stressed the vital importance of all sorts of information about other members of the occupational community, such as changes of theatre managers, staff for new projects and the emergence and break-ups of personal alliances. Furthermore, the actors' market-orientation showed in their perception of theatre management. When asked to explain the main tasks of a theatre manager, most only named 'staffing plays' and 'approving ensemble members' participation in external projects'. Both are activities which indicate an actor's value on the internal labour market. Only few interviewees named general management activities such as representing the theatre in public or taking responsibility for the theatre's artistic and economic success.

Finally, our study showed that actors are very aware of their return on investments. They compare time and energy invested in a project to returns in terms of praises by the theatre manager and critics, money and future role assignments. When deciding about how to invest time and effort, they put their own career first and are not necessarily loyal to their employer. Considering their strong market-orientation, their constant awareness of their own market value on internal and external labour markets, their networking activities and their conscious calculation of the effective allocation of time and energy, actors can be described as highly involved with marketing their labour power and maintaining employability.

Economisation of life

As the third characteristic of self-employed employees, Voß and Pongratz define a phenomenon that is best translated as economisation of life. This concept tries to capture the observation that self-employed employees extend their work-logic into their private lives. Private aspects of life, such as family or leisure, tend to be dominated by different logics, for example the logic of parental affection, relaxation or entertainment. Voß and Pongratz point out that instead of acting according to these logics when off work, self-employed employees apply the economic logic of work to private life and calculate private activities in terms of a more calculative balance between investment and return. In most cases this means organising private life in a way that enables flexibility in terms of time and mobility in terms of space. For instance, renting a flat rather than buying a house or employing babysitters and housekeepers to increase temporal flexibility are typical practices of self-employed employees.[3]

In theatre, spatial mobility and temporal flexibility are indeed crucial. Ensemble members at larger theatres will stay five years on average; young actors tend to stay only two to three years and then move on to another (preferably larger) theatre. The average contract duration of ensemble members thus equals roughly half the length of the average employment relationship in Germany. Moreover, whereas employees in industries and services are often able to find a new workplace within their town of residency, for actors, a change of employers usually means moving cities. As an actor's career is defined by moves from smaller to larger theatres, actors have to be mobile in terms of place at least during the first 20 years of their career. Short-term mobility is required when actors work in several projects at the same time: Busy actors may shoot a film or rehearse for a guest role during the day several hundred kilometres from the place of their nightly show.

Additionally, the tight time schedule requires high degrees of temporal flexibility. Actors have to adjust to monthly programmes and weekly rehearsal schedules which are often changed on a day-to-day basis. The planning department will announce the daily schedule via notice board postings and the actors either have to check the notice board themselves or call the theatre porter to confirm their rehearsal times. Even if they are not scheduled for a play or rehearsal on a certain day, they have to be available for short-term changes until 5 pm. Only after 5pm can the theatre manager not demand their *ad hoc* attendance, for instance to substitute for a sick colleague.

Our study shows that actors react in many different ways to these requirements regarding mobility and flexibility and in doing so indeed apply work-related logics to private life. Renting instead of buying property is one common practice to ensure spatial mobility and is presented as a choice rooted in career trajectories. Two respondents reported buying only furniture it was easy to move house with: 'The rigid backs of IKEA's Billy bookcases make them too inflexible if you move house frequently' (actor). The focus on spontaneity and flexibility is so strong that one actress terminated her life insurance contract because 'I just couldn't get my head around such long-time planning.' She preferred to invest the money into childcare facilities that allowed her to be flexible at work: 'Giving my child to the international school costs me a lot of money, but, on the other hand, since school does not end before 5 pm, spares me *the cost of a babysitter and the trouble of organising one when rehearsals are not finished early enough'*[4] (actress and single mother). The same reasoning is applied to exercise, which actors recounted to conduct *'in order to keep in shape for the stage'* (actor) rather than as a source of recreation.

As described earlier, personal relationships are also subject to the economic logic of work. Firstly, friendships always have a latent economic value, of which actors are very conscious. Secondly, love and family relationships are ruled by the requirements of theatre work. *'So, once again, all four of us were sat in the car crying when we left our former city of residency. But that's life.'* (dramaturge about moving house with the family) Failure in private life is measured up against career success: *'One reason for breaking up with my wife was that I had to change cities so many times. Still I do not regret moving around that much'* (actor). While some of these themes may be found in other employment systems as well, the explicit commitment to theatre with which they were recounted in the interviews was remarkable. Many interviewees complained about contradicting self-expectations of themselves as girlfriends or fathers on the one hand and of actors on the other. Nevertheless, if push comes to shove they understand themselves as actors first and will prioritise their career over private life. Assessing her own career, an elderly actress summed up: *'You live for theatre only and in the end you are alone. Friends and relations have died or live far away. Living in and for the theatre is only non-problematic while you are young.'*

Most of the time, however, actors do not employ explicitly economic vocabulary when considering private activities. But the question of the effects of the considered activity on the job is the first thought they come up with. How common such calculations are becomes evident when colleagues interpret liaisons between young actresses and directors or theatre managers as business-motivated in the first place – only in exceptional cases is romance considered the reason for those relationships once they become known in the occupational community.

Voß and Pongratz also point out that economisation of life is accompanied by blurring boundaries between work and life. Self-employed employees do not separate work and life with respect to, for instance, time, place or partners, but tend to mix or integrate both spheres (see also Warhurst *et al*, 2008). With theatre actors, this phenomenon can be observed especially in two aspects: their self-understanding as an artist and their attitude to life outside theatre. Our interviews showed that actors understand themselves primarily as actors and artists. They categorise their profession as a *vocation* rather than an occupation. Most of our interviewees had always wanted to become theatre artists, enact a bohemian lifestyle and regard their work as their life and vice versa (see also Eikhof and Haunschild, 2006). This self-understanding is mirrored in the way our interviewees related to the world outside their occupational community. One actor stated that *'During the two years that I've been working at this theatre and in the new city now I got to know nobody outside the theatre'* (actor). Most actors recounted feeling detached from *'the world outside'* and having few friendships and little social life beyond *'the theatre family'*.

Partly this enclosure is due to practical reasons: actors usually have to work when friends outside theatre are off work. Secondly, the intensive work relations in cultural production have a much more private character than usual business relations in industry or services. Since a much bigger part of one's personality is involved in work anyway, the step from a business relationship to a friendship is easily and often not even intentionally taken. Thirdly, fellow theatre artists show more understanding for one's attitude towards friendship. Actors do not have to explain to other actors that nothing is more important than the nightly show and that even an important birthday party can not be attended if one spontaneously has to substitute a sick colleague at night. How exclusively theatre actors keep to themselves can be illustrated by the case of one actor who proudly emphasised that, in contrast to all his colleagues, he had a girlfriend from a totally different profession. She was an orchestra musician.

Some theorists diagnose an invasion of private life by economic logic (Voß and Pongratz, 1998; Sennett, 1998; Hochschild, 1997) and others argue that economic logic has always been the underlying principle of social practices but had to be disguised or at least not made explicit in non-economical spheres (Bourdieu, 1983; Haunschild, 2004a; Eikhof and Haunschild, 2007). Whichever of these may be true, our analysis of theatre actors shows an economisation of life as described by Voß and Pongratz for self-employed employees.

Conclusions

This paper has characterised theatre as a project-focused industry and theatre artists as self-employed employees (*Arbeitskraftunternehmer*). Voß and Pongratz's concept of *Arbeitskraftunternehmer* has been used to show that these forms of work require workers to be self-controlled and self-economised as well as to economise large parts of life (which results in blurring boundaries between work and private life).

In contrast to most studies dealing with project-based work or work-related issues in the creative industries, this chapter has concentrated on the individual level. The individual perspective employed in our analysis can be linked to a broader development on the macro-level, described for instance by Foucault (1983, 1992; see also Deleuze, 1993; Gorz, 1999; Bröckling *et al.*, 2000; Hardt and Negri, 2000; Opitz, 2004) and Boltanski and Chiapello

(2005). Boltanski and Chiapello, in particular, argue that as capitalism integrates the arguments and values of its critics, project-focused organisation of production becomes the dominant paradigm. They show how the economic system increasingly enacts the vision of a *cité par projets*, promoting values like entrepreneurship, networking and flexibility instead of company careers and long-term commitment. Following this analysis projects will be the main organisational form of production especially in knowledge-intensive industries. This idea is in line with Brooks (2000) and Florida (2002) who analysed lifestyles in the US and detected the rise of a 'creative class', i.e. a social class working in creative jobs often organised as projects. Thus, our work studying theatre actors as self-employed employees provides fruitful starting points for discussing consequences of working in dynamic relationship and project-based industries in general (see also Eikhof and Haunschild, 2004).

In addition to the individual coping strategies we have analysed in this chapter, the example of theatre actors as self-employed employees sheds some light on the labour process and human resource management practices in creative and knowledge-intensive industries. Self-control, the internalisation of market rules and the economisation of life induce a specific perception of human resource practices. Intrinsically motivated, self-controlled and self-economised workers are likely to be loyal to their profession or to individuals they work for rather than to a certain employer or organisation. Due to their continuous exposure to (internal and external) market forces, these workers evaluate and compare contractual options with respect to their potential to open up new prospects of succeeding projects. The example of theatre has shown that this can include learning opportunities (main roles, experienced colleagues), opportunities to engage in jobs outside the organisation (film productions, guest roles at other theatres), and opportunities to work together with influential players within the industrial community (directors, theatre managers).

Accordingly, Voß and Pongratz's ideal type of labour supply hints at forms of control, and thus human resource management practices, that differ from traditional forms of control over the transformation of labour potential into real labour. In contrast to external control and explicit human resource policies and schemes, in theatre intrinsic motivation, blurred boundaries between (transorganisational) work relationships and friendships as well as idiosyncratic, informal and personalised HRM practices are more prevalent. All these features of the theatrical employment system question attempts to locate the labour process at the organisational level only. Rather, transorganisational communities and networks, the enactment of organisational boundaries, and workers' lifestyle and intrinsic motivation need to be considered when trying to understand control structures and workers' motivations and strategies in project-based work environments.

Two recent developments support the thesis that an increasing number of workers will have to deal with the tensions between market-related and economised social relations on the one and (a profession-based) intrinsic motivation on the other side (Eikhof and Haunschild, 2007). Firstly, there is a growing economic pressure on and within the creative industries themselves. This leads to a higher degree of self-reflection beyond 'art for art's sake' and creativity. Secondly, the number of workers pursuing creative and knowledge-intensive jobs appears to be expanding (cf. Florida, 2002; Brooks, 2000) and this should lead to an increase in project-based work and market-mediated employment. Living a bohemian, artist-like life becomes a more common aspiration, which at the same time leads an economisation of life. The example of theatre actors as self-employed employees can help to identify and analyse problems individuals, organisations, industries or fields as well as societies might have to face when project-based work and employment become more widespread.

Notes

1 Pongratz and Voß (2003) use the term 'entreployee' as an English translation of 'Arbeitskraftunternehmer'.
2 Within the German-speaking theatre world, *dramaturges* act as artistic consultants with very idiosyncratic job definitions, but are key players in staffing and recruiting decisions in every theatre.
3 Unlike, for instance, in the UK, Germans tend to buy property only for long-term periods of residency, i.e. if they expect to live in the area for ten years or more. Externalising childcare, especially for babies and toddlers, is far less widespread than in other European countries.
4 German state schools are free, but finish at lunch time.

REFERENCES

Baumann, A. (2002) 'Informal labour market governance: The case of the British and German media production industries', *Work, Employment and Society*, 16: 27–46.

Benhamou, F. (2000) 'The opposition between two models of labour market adjustment: The case of audiovisual and performing arts activities in France and Great Britain over a ten year period', *Journal of Cultural Economics*, 24: 301–19.

Blair, H. (2001) '"You're only as good as your last job": the labour process and labour market in the British film industry', *Work, Employment and Society*, 125: 149–69.

▶

▶

Blair, H., Grey, S. and Randle, K. (2001) 'Working in film. Employment in a project based industry', *Personnel Review*, 30: 170–85.

Boltanski, L. and Chiapello, E. (2005) *The New Spirit of Capitalism*. London: Verso. (originally in French 1999).

Bourdieu, P. (1983) 'Ökonomisches Kapital, kulturelles Kapital, soziales Kapital', in R. Kreckel (ed.) *Soziale Ungleichheiten*, 2: 183–98. Göttingen: Soziale Welt, Sonderband.

Bourdieu, P. (1984) *Distinction: A Social Critique of the Judgement of Taste*. London: Routledge and Kegan Paul (originally in French 1979).

Bröckling, U., Krasmann, S. and Lemke, T. (2000) (eds) *Gouvernementalität der Gegenwart. Studien zur Ökonomie des Sozialen*. Frankfurt/M.: Suhrkamp.

Brooks, D. (2000) *Bobos in Paradise*. New York: Simon & Schuster.

Caves, R.E. (2000) *Creative Industries: Contracts between Arts and Business*. Cambridge: Harvard University Press.

DeFillippi, R.J. and Arthur, M.B. (1998) 'Paradox in project-based enterprise. The case of film making', *California Management Review*, 40: 125–39.

Deleuze, G. (1993) 'Postskriptum über die Kontrollgesellschaften', in G. Deleuze *Unterhandlungen, 1972–1990*, 254–62. Frankfurt/M.: Suhrkamp.

Dex, S., Willis, J., Paterson, R. and Sheppard, E. (2000) 'Freelance workers and contract uncertainty: the effects of contractual changes in the television industry', *Work, Employment and Society*, 14: 283–305.

Eikhof, D.R. (2006) 'Transorganisationale Arbeit am Theater: Eine empirische Untersuchung vermarktlichter Arbeitsformen', in Stiftung Körber (ed.) *Mythos Markt? Die ökonomische, soziale und rechtliche Gestaltung der Arbeitswelt*, 131–55. Wiesbaden: VS Verlag.

Eikhof, D.R. and Haunschild, A. (2004) 'Arbeitskraftunternehmer in der Kulturindustrie. Ein Forschungsbericht über die Arbeitswelt Theater', in H.J. Pongratz and G.G. Voß (eds), *Typisch Arbeitskraftunternehmer? Befunde der empirischen Arbeitsforschung*, 93–113. Berlin 2004: Sigma.

Eikhof, D.R. and Haunschild, A. (2006) 'Lifestyle meets market. Bohemian entrepreneurs in creative industries', *Creativity and Innovation Management*, 13(3): 234–41.

Eikhof, D.R. and Haunschild, A. (2007) 'For art's sake! Artistic and economic logics in creative production', *Journal of Organizational Behavior*, 28(5): 523–38.

Faulkner, R.R. and Anderson, A.B. (1987) 'Short-term projects and emergent careers: Evidence from Hollywood', *American Journal of Sociology*, 92: 879–909.

Florida, R. (2002) *The Rise of the Creative Class and How It's Transforming Work, Leisure, Community and Everyday Life*. New York: Basic Books.

Foucault, M. (1983) 'The subject and power', in H.L. Dreyfus and P. Rabinow: *Michel Foucault: Beyond Structuralism and Hermeneutics*, 2nd edition, 208–26. Chicago: University of Chicago Press.

Foucault, M. (1992) *Was ist Kritik?* Berlin: Merve Verlag.

Fraser, J. and Gold, M. (2001) '"Portfolio workers": Autonomy and control amongst freelance translators', *Work, Employment and Society*, 15: 679–97.

▶

Gorz, A. (1999) *Reclaiming Work. Beyond the Wage-based Society*. Cambridge: Polity Press.

Hardt, A. and Negri, M. (2000) *Empire*. Cambridge, Mass. & London: Harvard University Press.

Haak, C. and Schmid, G. (1999) *Arbeitsmärkte für Künstler und Publizisten – Modelle einer zukünftigen Arbeitswelt?* Research Report, P99–506, WZB Berlin.

Haunschild, A. (2003) 'Managing employment relationships in flexible labour markets: The case of German repertory theatres', *Human Relations*, 56: 899–929.

Haunschild, A. (2004a) 'Contingent work: The problem of disembeddedness and economic reembeddedness', *Management Revue*, 15: 74–88.

Haunschild, A. (2004b) 'Employment rules in German theatres. An application and evaluation of the theory of employment systems', *British Journal of Industrial Relations*, 42: 685–703.

Heilbrun, J. and Gray, C.M. (1993) *The Economics of Art and Culture*. Cambridge: Cambridge University Press.

Hochschild, A.R. (1997) *The Time Bind*. New York: Metropolitan Books.

Jones, C. (1996) 'Careers in project networks: The case of the film industry', in M.B. Arthur and D.M. Rousseau (eds) *The Boundaryless Career. A New Employment Principle for a New Organizational Era*, 58–75. New York: Oxford University Press.

Jones, C. and Walsh, K. (1997) 'Boundaryless careers in the US film industry: Understanding labor market dynamics of network organizations', *Industrielle Beziehungen*, 4: 58–73.

Marsden, D. (2004) 'The "network economy" and models of the employment contract', *British Journal of Industrial Relations*, 42: 659–84.

Menger, P.-M. (1999) 'Artistic labor markets and careers', *Annual Review of Sociology*, 25: 541–74.

Opitz, S. (2004) *Gouvernementalität im Postfordismus. Macht, Wissen und Techniken des Selbst im Feld unternehmerischer Rationalität*. Hamburg: Argument.

Pongratz, H.J. and Voß, G.G. (2000) 'Vom Arbeitnehmer zum Arbeitskraftunternehmer – Zur Entgrenzung der Ware Arbeitskraft', in H. Minssen (ed.) *Begrenzte Entgrenzungen. Wandlungen von Organisation und Arbeit*. Berlin: Sigma, 225–47.

Pongratz, H.J. and Voß, G.G. (2003) 'From employee to "entreployee": Towards a "self-entrepreneurial" work force?', *Concepts and Transformation*, 8(3): 239–54.

Raider, H.J. and Burt, R.S. (1996) 'Boundaryless career and social capital', in M.B. Arthur and D.M. Rousseau (eds), *The Boundaryless Career. A New Employment Principle for a New Organizational Era*, 187–200. New York: Oxford University Press.

Sennett, R. (1998) *Corrosion of Character: The Personal Consequences of Work in the New Capitalism*. New York: W.W. Norton.

Sydow, J. and Staber, U. (2002) 'The institutional embeddedness of project networks: The case of content production in German television', *Regional Studies*, 36: 215–27.

▶

Throsby, D. (2001) *Economics and Culture*. Cambridge: Cambridge University Press.

Tolbert, P.S. (1996) 'Occupations, organizations, and boundaryless careers', in M.B. Arthur and D.M. Rousseau (eds), *The Boundaryless Career. A New Employment Principle for a New Organizational Era*, 331–49. New York: Oxford University Press.

Voß, G.G. and Pongratz, H.J. (1998) 'Der Arbeitskraftunternehmer. Eine neue Grundform der Ware Arbeitskraft?', *Kölner Zeitschrift für Soziologie und Sozialpsychologie*, 50: 131–58.

Warhurst, C., Eikhof, D.R. and Haunschild, A. (2008) 'Out of balance or just out of bounds? Analysing the relationship between work and life', in C. Warhurst, D.R. Eikhof and A. Haunschild (eds) *Work Less, Live More? Critical Analysis of the Work-Life Boundary*. Basingstoke: Palgrave.

Making 'The Bits Between the Adverts': Management, Accounting, Collective Bargaining and Work in UK Commercial Television, 1979–2005

Alan McKinlay

Introduction

This chapter examines the long-run dynamics of collective bargaining, management control and the labour process in British commercial television. The chapter is based on archival research, interviews and non-participant observation inside broadcast organisations and television studios. From its inception, British commercial television was highly unionised, all production tasks were tightly defined, and subject to formal state regulations reaffirmed once every decade. Every aspect of commercial broadcasting was thoroughly regulated: from how the broadcasting firms cooperated in a national network; the duration and range of programming; the balance of, for example, regional and national content; the types, costs and targets of advertising; the pace of technological change, work organisation, and career paths. All of this was overseen by a range of state and non-state actors, including a range of powerful craft trade unions. The Independent Television (ITV) Network was based on fifteen companies and centred on two large corporations with smaller broadcast companies. All ITV companies had regional broadcasting responsibilities and produced content for an integrated, national system. ITV lobbied the state regulator as a single body, collectively negotiated all advertising rates, which were distributed between the companies according to an agreed formula, with little effective oversight. This highly regulated system proved hugely profitable for all the ITV companies. The Network system remained intact for almost thirty years until a series of changes from the mid-1980s presaged wholesale restructuring after 1988. The chapter begins by outlining the dynamics of industrial relations and work organisation before 1988, a watershed for British commercial broadcasting. In 1988, the British commercial television employers unilaterally ended national collective bargaining. Before 1988, it was impossible to understand the commercial television labour process without acknowledging how profoundly work was regulated by collective bargaining. From 1988, television companies began to disentangle work organisation from collective bargaining and for the first time developed detailed cost profiles and alternative patterns of labour deployment. In part, this was triggered by the Thatcherite attack on trade unionism. But, more importantly, British commercial television employers had been developing their collective organisation and a strategy to demolish the unions' workplace power base since the bitter national dispute of 1978. These processes are considered in the second section. Section three considers the fate of trade unionism in commercial television. In particular, trade union representation was increasingly restricted to maintaining the *possibility* of collective bargaining about contracts and accepted that they had little purchase left within the workplace. Finally, we apply Michael Polanyi's notion of tacit knowledge to the experience of a television crew moving between a low-budget, 'live' broadcast and the making of 'formula telly', 'Wheel of Fortune'. The crew's studio experience is used to examine how the deregulated, post-1988 industrial relations system has impacted upon the labour process.

Competition, regulation and the workplace

For almost three decades, UK commercial television stations were insulated from competitive pressure. The industry was regulated by state-controlled franchises issued every decade. Multi-channel, cable and satellite competition remained in their infancy until the 1990s. Commercial television franchises established detailed regulations governing programming, capital equipment, training, and staffing, effectively standardising cost structures. By negotiating advertising rates nationally, and maintaining their internal systems of revenue allocation, the ITV companies constructed a robust, highly profitable system. The so-called 'White Book' of binding national agreements with the unions specified – in fine detail – work organisation and technology, eliminating them as competitive factors. The cost of predictability was an acceptance of union job controls around the conference table and in the studio. Employers were intimately involved in the construction of this highly regulated work regime (Brown, 1972). National bargaining established the floor for local bargaining. The Association of Cinematograph, Television and Allied Technicians (ACTT) was a highly centralised, craft union that pursued an uncompromising bargaining strategy based on a pre-entry closed shop: *only* existing union members could work in television, and new memberships were strictly rationed. ACTT's experience in the post-1945 film industry was fundamental in shaping its bargaining strategy. For ACTT, maintaining job security and high wages in the inherently uncertain, project-based film industry was wholly dependent upon restricting entry to the labour market and maintaining tight control over task definitions and technological change. Maintaining such wide-ranging controls was predicated on all levels of the union adopting a highly combative, uncompromising bargaining strategy. The film industry, including film processing, was dominated by London and ACTT had a similar metropolitan focus. Outside London, local bargaining was not coordinated by the ACTT nationally. The assumption was that no local union would tolerate any deviation from the 'White Book'. In practice, the national agreement set the basis for opportunistic local bargaining. At station-level, collective bargaining was a 'free for all' fuelled by 'the power and bottle of individual stewards and shop committees', a system that generated significant contractual diversity (Interview, former ACTT, Father of Chapel, July 2004). In Granada, one of the two dominant firms in the ITV Network, producers/directors, for example, were awarded a 15 per cent rise in 1982 to buy-out their right to claim overtime payments. Within a year, in *all* stations the 15 per cent tariff for buying-out overtime rates was established as a *minimum*. In Scottish Television (STV), aggressive local bargaining secured the 15 per cent rise *and* retained the right to claim overtime, *plus* lieu days for week-end work for producer-directors (more generally, Campling, 1992; McKinlay and Quinn, 1999). Local bargaining was opportunistic and unpredictable, save for one characteristic: the unions *always* gained, and management incurred costs and lost authority.

The 'White Book' specified each craft's tasks, tools and materials and when and under what conditions tasks could be temporarily switched between trades. There could be no encroachment by one trade on another's jurisdiction. Unlike other craft-regulated industries, there was no serious inter-trade rivalry over boundaries or new technologies. The sequential nature of the labour process of other craft-based industries meant that any technical change almost inevitably impacted on more than one occupation, the simultaneity of television meant that production – for instance, camera and sound engineers – and ancillary trades – electricians – largely worked side-by-side. For managements and unions, incremental technical change was most easily absorbed into existing job roles. There were no inter-union rivalries that management could exploit, and no great financial incentives for management to pursue radical technical change. Quite the reverse: the heavy costs of production over-runs and the extreme perishability of lost advertising slots, placed a heavy premium on production management *always* seeking compromise. Should any manager attempt to insist that any task be completed by one trade rather than another, this would infringe the rights of both trades. By violating the *principle* of craft regulation, managers would incur the wrath of *all* trades. All managers exercised extreme caution to safeguard their production. The tactics of job control and the myths celebrating worker autonomy would have been familiar to any Victorian craftsman.

> It got to the ridiculous stage. There is the story of a chap who bumped into a lamp stand and the lamp was falling over, so he grabbed it and put it upright. That caused major problems with the electricians – not because he bumped into the lamp but because he grabbed it and put it back up (Interview, Stage Manager, 1998).

No wholesale shift in work organisation was triggered by technical change. ACTT successfully assimilated technical change into existing occupational boundaries. The unions' power of veto limited new technology's appeal. The parallel experience of the newspaper industry further discouraged television management (see Martin, 1981). Beneath the stability of formal collective agreements, there were forays across the frontier of control but these were local, episodic and conditional. In Granada, a primitive computerised system to cue adverts was used for a listings programme based on images from different media. Integrating several media required cumbersome manual editing. Manual editing and mechanical cuing set long lead-times, sapping the listing programme's immediacy. Computerised cuing accelerated the editing process and allowed diverse media to be integrated virtually to the moment of broadcast. For programme-makers, this cannibalised technology promised greater immediacy and improved production values. However, a local agreement limited the cuing technology's operation to a *maximum* of four cued inserts per hour. Most engineers abided by the agreement; others simply ignored the restriction. The programme's director would know if he 'was dealing with someone who would play ball, allow a little give-and-take'. Such concessions never occurred in Network programming but were restricted to local productions. Such concessions were invisible after the fact and could not be used by management as a precedent. The wariness over workforce reactions to new technologies was paralleled by an awareness of the effectiveness of low-cost industrial action. One Granada manager recalled watching the studio monitors with mounting horror as a live show missed its start time. Just before broadcast, the ACTT steward had confronted the programme's freelance Director about his overdue union fees and demanded immediate payment. The Director's humiliation – and the delay to the broadcast – was a warning about the use of freelancers (Interview, Granada Producer/Director, October 2006). Such guerrilla tactics were unpredictable, incurred no cost in terms of lost wages, but had an immediate and irrecoverable impact on advertising revenues.

Through the mid-1980s individual stations won significant victories over the unions, notably Thames in 1984. In particular, the employers ramped-up the strength of their Association (ITVA) and pursued a clear strategy first, to reduce the centrality of national bargaining and, secondly, to support any individual station engaged in an industrial dispute. This did not just eliminate the unions' most potent bargaining weapon – the capacity to escalate any local dispute into a national strike – but turned it on the unions. That is, through the use of the first Thatcher government's employment legislation, the ITVA redefined any local dispute as a 'secondary' action and so exposed trade union funds to loss without limit (McKinlay and Quinn, 2007). *Any* local dispute now held the potential to bankrupt the union. ACTT, the main television union, failed to respond to this threat and was plunged into a strategic and organisational collapse after 1988, a tailspin that was not halted until the mid-1990s.

Company strategies and performance measures

The launch of Channel 4 in 1982 legally required that 25 per cent of broadcast commissions would be allocated to the nascent independent sector. This altered regulatory and competitive landscape did not trigger a rapid shift towards greater management control of production costs. There was, however, a burst of innovation in management information systems. Essentially, the new independent companies developed a standard accounting package. This standard accounting package produced rate cards that rendered labour costs transparent. Crucially, this transferred the 'indies' cost structures into mainstream commercial broadcasting. The ITV companies were given access to their rivals' detailed cost data which informed – and accelerated – their pursuit of a deeper understanding of their own production costs. Consultants established cost profiles for different programme types and fine-grained analyses of the independent sector's labour costs. This process lasted for between three and five years to 1993. This signalled the start of a race to the bottom in terms of production costs. Inside the ITV Network, programme-making was no longer cross-subsidised and every budget was benchmarked against the market-chasing costs of the independent sector.

Initially, commercial stations developed in-house software to track programme costs. This 'lashed together' software permitted only high-level budgetary analysis. Despite their primitive nature, this was the first time detailed accounting controls had penetrated into the routines of television production. Capital budgets, for instance, were no longer simply attributed as a corporate cost but to specific programmes. While management constructed these information systems they also struggled to develop analytical practices: how to *use* these systems: 'it was very rough and ready in the early days – we just followed the cash costs'. Labour costs were allocated to programme budgets in weeks, not hours; financial control remained retrospective, not real-time. Accounting control remained porous. Directors easily evaded budgetary control:

> We were like burglars who 'stole' carpenters, sparks, or whatever and who fenced them to other burglars who were 'stealing' resources from their projects. This was under the noses of the accountants. Maybe they were turning a blind eye, or maybe they just didn't see it. Whatever: that couldn't last long. And it didn't (Interview, Producer/Director, D, 2000; Lury, 1993).

Informal coping strategies were eliminated as the television studio was ever more tightly policed by programme accountants (Interview, Producer/ Director C, 2003; Taylor, 2003: 215). In-house software gave way to standardised systems that generated real-time reporting in ever finer detail. Studio rostering became more fine-grained and the management of labour utilisation statistics was reported to corporate boards. Budgets proved increasingly impervious to the practical logic of programme-makers:

> You can't argue with a spreadsheet. It doesn't *know* anything except numbers. Once upon a time, you could negotiate with the accountants based on the realities of the shoot. Now that's impossible: they simply wave the spreadsheet in front of you, *that's* the contract (Interview, Producer/Director, B, 2005).

One programme accountant insisted:

> Our numbers are robust: they tell us how long and how much it costs to make a programme, *any* programme. My job is to remind producers of the numbers that *they* have agreed. It's not personal, it's a contract (Interview, Programme Accountant, 2005).

Importantly, despite their increasing sophistication, management control systems stopped well short of any attempt to monitor crew performance: to do so would have violated the intimacy and flexibility essential to the television labour process (Bowker and Starr, 2000: 231–3).

By the early 1990s, the relationship between company executives and work organisation was changing. Cost pressures on production were no longer part of a conversation between programme makers. Rather, budgetary cuts were being imposed by executives *without* programme-making experience. The relationship between the studio and the executive became exclusively financial. The paradox was that this increase in management's power to reshape work organisation was achieved without any increased managerial visibility in the studio. The regulated television studio was based on a highly socialised form of order in which decision-making was mediated by long-standing, personal relationships. The development of computerised management information systems destroyed this negotiated order. Management operated at a distance from the studio, mediated by spreadsheets rather than inter-personal exchange (Miller and Rose, 1990: 7; Lash, 2002: 75, 216).

The impact of financialisation on the social relations of production was evident in a 2001 workforce survey conducted by the regional commercial broadcaster, STV. Ninety per cent of all staff agreed that the company 'too often sacrifices the quality of our product in order to cut costs', a perception that was universal for production staff working on high budget network programming. Between 42–58 per cent of respondents in the television production divisions reported that they experienced 'excessive pressure' at work. More than half of all television crew 'found it difficult to balance work and life outside work'. Crew working on higher-specification Network programming were more than twice as satisfied as those assigned to local productions with the calibre of their managers. Two-thirds of Network crew reported that their line managers encouraged individual initiative and innovation and 80 per cent felt that their skills were understood, valued and developed. While studio management received the workforce's broad endorsement, this pattern was reversed for the executive level. Two-thirds of respondents affirmed the organisation was pursuing a clear strategy, but only one-third was satisfied that this was complemented by effective planning. The workforce perceived a disjunction between corporate strategy and implementation. While almost three-quarters of respondents 'were willing to change the way they work in order to progress the business', only half of this group were confident that the company would 'recognise and respond' to this willingness. The break-down of union representation and the organisation's failure to create alternative communications systems was paralleled by a widespread erosion of individual's trust in management integrity. Eighty-four per cent of technical staff working on Network productions and 58 per cent of those producing local television reported that they were 'seriously considering leaving the organisation'.

'Stick with the union'

> Occasionally I'll be copied into an email or pass a notice-board announcing a union meeting. *Shock*: they're *still* here; they *still* have meetings (Interview, STV, Producer, 2007).

In commercial television there was no union derecognition or any frontal assault on lay organisation: basic time allowances for union duties remained intact. The collapse of the pre-entry closed shop signalled an end to any barrier to entry to the labour market (Skillset, 1996). Between 1989 and 1994, freelance staff in commercial television increased from 9–13 per cent to at least 45 per cent per station (Saundry and Nolan, 1998: 9). Between 1995 and 2000 the informal system of collective bargaining all but collapsed. Particularly in ITV regions, HR managers closed off all back-door communications: the unions' only remedy was employment law, not collective bargaining. Paradoxically, this had the effect of raising the unions' profile. Union density was slowly rebuilt from a low of 30 per cent until 2000 when it had returned to its historic norm of between 75–80 per cent (Interview, BECTU regional official, August 2006). This process was paralleled by developing a core of around twenty activists who focused on health and safety issues. For the Broadcasting, Entertainment, Cinematographic and Theatre Union (BECTU), a desperate merger of failing unions across the media and entertainment industries, this tactic rebuilt activists' negotiating skills, delivered visible results for core staff *and* freelancers, and restored some life to the informal system of collective bargaining. This remarkable turnaround was, however, almost entirely defensive. Above all, BECTU sought to ensure some degree of union voice during any lay-offs, to maintain basic procedures for individual grievances, rather than any collective push for improved contracts or restoration of bargaining power inside the studio.

The performance measures that were painstakingly refined from the late 1980s proved critical to a renewal of collective bargaining. Labour utilisation statistics enhanced management cost control and were a precondition to flexible rostering. Before 1988 the unions' tight control of working time regulations was a critical bargaining weapon. This had been completely disarmed by the early 1990s. By 1995 labour utilisation statistics were no longer a tool to monitor middle management performance. Rather, comparative utilisation percentages identified individuals for redundancy. The unions articulated the workforce's unease about the accuracy and purpose of the performance statistics. This undermined the legitimacy of management information systems. Many studies portray performance management regimes which *necessarily* ensnare and enfeeble workers while rendering managerial power opaque (Rose, 1991). Conversely, labour utilisation statistics were used by the unions to make the arbitrary nature of the performance technologies visible. Collective bargaining reversed the logic of performance measurement to *close* the distance between the workplace and the technology, an engagement that rendered management, not just workers, *visible*. Benchmarking established that around one third of staff of one regional station was paid above the rates of other commercial stations or of the freelance market. A wage freeze, coupled with voluntary redundancies, would allow the company to re-establish its rate-card margin of 22 per cent. Tense negotiations were dominated by national officials desperate to win tactical concessions over the timetable for salary cuts that would maintain their legitimacy as negotiators, and no less anxious to avoid a strike that ran the risk of demonstrating the organisation's weakness with no chance of altering the course of negotiations. In 2000 a new House Agreement was imposed on the workforce without negotiation and minimal consultation. Restoring a significant union presence in terms of membership and individual representation was insufficient for any equivalent gain in union bargaining power.

In 2000 and 2001 the threat of a further wave of redundancies across the commercial network provoked a series of local strikes (see Saundry and Nolan, 2001: 32). For local union stewards, maintaining the fabric of collective bargaining was 'more important than the redundancies. If the Agreement goes then we might as well [fold the union]'. The senior lay union representative – the Father of the Chapel – told a mass meeting, 'People might as well give themselves a 1 per cent pay rise and stop paying their dues. The new House Agreement means the end of negotiations; it might mean the end of the union' (Father of Chapel, March 2000). Management's proposed House Agreement no longer covered terms and conditions but was restricted to bargaining procedure. Salaries were to match the freelance market. Contracts would be individual and entirely at management discretion: 'blue eyes yes; brown eyes no' (BECTU steward, House meeting, March 2000). Job security would hinge upon individuals' labour utilisation percentage. In a sense, management was merely seeking to formalise the experience of the past five years. New technology had been introduced without consultation, far less negotiation; the previous two annual wage settlements had been imposed, not negotiated. The journalists' Father of Chapel acknowledged the continued salience of the distinction between staff and freelancers but insisted that this was an increasingly false contrast: 'we are all freelancers now'.

Union officials did not hold out the prospect of staving off redundancies or salary cuts. Rather, the objective was to maintain the union as a presence in a negotiated process that regulated contracts and redundancies 'We can't black screens', although without unionised journalists the quality of the main news broadcast was severely compromised: 'at least we can have a laugh at a sweaty, terrified manager mumbling and stumbling his way through the news' (Interview, BECTU steward, August 2007). The 2000 one-day strike was largely symbolic: 'We're still here. We might have to accept what you're doing to us, but don't think that we agree with this'. If this was not to be a demonstration of the unions' impossibly weak bargaining position, then the rationale for the dispute was in terms of strengthening the negotiators' hand: 'we're still solid – we still have a voice and we're saying that we may be forced to accept your offer but don't imagine we're satisfied'.

For BECTU, the success of the one-day strike, within its limits, re-established the union as a realistic bargaining partner and confirmed the necessity of formal negotiations to the company.

'Make every shot count'

The second half of the 1980s was marked by the deregulation of the work-place and the labour market. This was paralleled by the disintegration of day-to-day production routines such as the marking of time codes that eases post-production. That practice has fallen into disrepair, particularly where loosely connected freelance crews have only the faintest connection with fading craft practices. This has contributed to the reshaping of the television labour process, pushing ever-more tasks onto post-production editing. The compression of budgets and the time allocated for filming has curtailed pre-production technical scripting. Together with a general shift towards a style that emphasised movement, dynamism through fast-cuts and chop-shots, there is a willingness to accept, even pursue, momentary loss of focus or poorly framed shots. All of this, whether artifice or not, shifts time and task into the highly individualised post-production editing suite in which the director works closely with one or two editors. The highly socialised studio setting gives way to the solitude of the editing suite, a process which is characterised by long hours, tight deadlines and lost to any trade union oversight, far less regulation. In this section we consider the impact of de-regulation on the commercial television labour process. Specifically, we trace the experience of one small crew's working day as they move from shooting a regional politics programme to the elaborate set of a long-running Network game-show. The live broadcast is the limit case of broadcasting in which there is *necessarily* a complete reliance upon the crew's improvisational cap-acity. With no room for error, no scope for retaking shots, and deprived of the possibility of post-production editing, the live broadcast requires a balance between economy of style and the maintenance of production values. By contrast, the recording of the relatively high-end game show, 'Wheel of For-tune', was driven by a highly standardised format that demanded complete uniformity in terms of image, pace and sound. The test of the crew's indi-vidual and collective skill was not improvisation but complete compliance to the programme's standard format.

As we entered the building the stony-faced commissionaire greeted us ironically with a hearty, theatrical, 'Work, work, damn you, work'. The crew assembled in the studio, exchanged greetings, and wandered around check-ing the set and equipment. The programme was a political talk-show, a relaxed Sunday morning conversation in which politicians ruminated, inter-spersed by whimsical pre-shot items. The experienced Director had worked across all genres, including complex, multi-camera, live environments. This was his first shoot on this programme, and probably his last. Dropping onto the couch that was the set's centre-piece, he commented: 'Cheap sofa, cheap set, cheap programme'. The programme's limited budget was skewed towards research, ensuring high-profile guests, not high-end production values. Or, as the programme accountant put it, 'spectacle costs money'.

The crew comprised three camera operators and a lighting engineer. During the perfunctory run-through, the Director lamented the lack of a sound engineer as they struggled to eliminate off-stage noise. As the Director and vision mixer assessed the script for the main camera moves, the PA arrived with some oil for a squeaky studio door. She smiled as the crew laughingly wondered whether she was now multi-skilled, a carpenter and an engineer. She scowled, and replied that she was off to iron the presenter's shirt. 'Three jobs in ten minutes', the engineer smiled ruefully. 'But only one pay packet', replied a camera operator. Two huge lamps were being gently nudged into position by the lighting engineer, checked by eye. The engineer then *confirmed* his sensory judgement with a light meter (more generally, see Mitchell, 2006: 85–90). A camera operator – there was no set dresser – adjusted the slats to ensure the symmetry of the Venetian blinds that completed the set. The same camera operator – there was no stage hand – then helped the lighting engineer shift one of the lighting rigs. Until the mid-1990s this programme would have had a full function crew for two days, supplemented by background, archive film, and offline editing: in 2005 the programme was shot live with a skeleton crew and no post-production 'sweetening'. There was no stage manager to ensure that all the technical and preparatory tasks were completed. 'That's why I'm here so early', explained the Producer, in an affected posh accent: 'Once upon a time I'd come in with my white gloves on and ask: "Everything ready? Then let us proceed". Not now: I'm chief cook *and* bottle washer. But hey, we're having fun' (Reed, 1996). Experienced crew perceived the gradual, absorption of important ancillary tasks into their roles. It is difficult to argue that this represents significant labour intensification. Certainly, there has been informal job enlargement, but the impact of this process has not been primarily physical but it has eroded downtime, the moments during which crew relaxed or prepared their next shots.

Props framed shots and provided focal points for zoom and crab shots. The aim was to avoid static images. Slow, measured camera movements conveyed the relaxed exchanges on screen. Lingering on particular shots gave the crew and Director longer to move and to establish successive shots, reducing the risk of poor framing or lost focus. All this was done immediately before transmission: there was no rehearsal. Minimising risk is essential in a live broadcast: there is no opportunity to rectify errors in post-production. The Director instructed one of the camera operators to try out different angles to vary the three or four stock positions. A couple of over the shoulder shots looked promising but were dismissed as too risky, exposed to unexpected movements by the interviewee. These judgements were communal, based on gestures or short conversations. The Director's conversation with the crew was interrogative and open-ended, leaving ample scope for collective sense-making and judgement. The conversation served as a reminder and as a series of prompts of their shared tacit knowledge and how this was to be mobilised during the broadcast (Polanyi, 1957: 98–9). This was *not* a rehearsal of fixed moves. Rather, this short interlude permitted the Director and crew to invoke their collective imagination: to rapidly integrate the perceptual clues that are indefinable in advance but which gain coherence as they unfold in real-time (Polanyi, 1969a: 66–7). None of this was discussed explicitly. Indeed, very little of such exchanges *could* be articulated, even to other film-crews (Dreyfus and Dreyfus, 1986: 30–5; Turner, 1994: 120).

During the shoot, the Director's key task was to sequence images, to ensure the programme's integrity, and maintain the series' signature look. As each frame was broadcast, he instructed the other two camera operators to assume their next positions. This was an intense process but calm and orderly. To the Director's side, the vision mixer synchronised the shots. The Director moved the crew and chose shots while listening to the interview's flow and watching the body language: who was leaning forward for emphasis or backwards while pondering an answer. This was fine-grained judgement and relied on the entire crew moving at the same speed, giving – and taking – precise, but gentle, instructions. There was little conversation during the filming. Instructions were almost whispered, brisk – never rude – and unambiguous: the camera operators were completely silent, any uncertainties were signalled through minute changes in their postures or the merest of sideways glances (Glevarec, 1999). These all but imperceptible signals constitute the discourse of tacit knowledge. These gestures conveyed context-specific meanings *and* registered the communal nature of tacit knowledge (Gill, 2000: 44–50). The camera operators' movements were rapid, but unhurried. Their graceful swoops complemented and underscored the relaxed ebb and flow of the on-screen conversation. There were none of the abrupt shifts in camera angles or quick edits used to punctuate faster-moving genres. All of this was shared, tacit knowledge of the demands of the format and extensive experience of working together.

> We've worked together many times over the years. I *know* which camera guys can move quickly, who can *really* think on his feet; who is the best technically ...in terms of framing shots; who's a little bit slower because he's got a sore back; who's likely to use his imagination and give me a

different kind of shot. Now, when you're working with a freelance guy, you don't *know* any of that. (The freelancer) might know his lenses, his focal distances, but he might not *know* what we need today, right now. The other guys, they *know* because they've worked with me on all sorts of programmes.

The crew's familiarity with each other, even if by reputation rather than personal experience, was critical to the social shorthand they used so easily on the set. But this was not the whole story. The slimmed-down, multi-skilled crew and tight time constraints enabled, perhaps generated, the tacit knowledge essential to effective production. The more formal, hierarchical organisation of the pre-1988 regulated television studio impeded the expression of this type of tacit knowledge. The Director had an intimate knowledge of the crew: a sense of their individual repertoires, willingness and ability to improvise, accept a restricted – or extended – role in aesthetic decision-making: when to move, which angle to choose. In turn, the crew understood the conventions of the genre, the constraints of this programme and the likely preferences of *this* Director operating under *these* conditions. The vision mixer explained one of the subliminal signals in the Director's posture. If the Director gripped the desk with his left hand while shifting his weight to the right, this betrayed anxiety over the next sequence of shots; if he leant back in his chair this signalled that he had a clear sequence of shots settled in his mind. Each shot, each whispered direction and exchange of glances were cues in a shared, complex deployment of tacit knowledge that unfolded through the production process (Polanyi, 1958: 59–61; 1969b: 152; Ruzsits Jha, 2002: 52–3). It is not that tacit knowledge is context-specific, rather it is contextually relative and only partially consistent (Grunfeld, 2000: 158). Tacit knowledge can, therefore, be deployed beyond the moment, but this requires integration. For Polanyi, integration is a defining characteristic of tacit knowledge. Polanyi's most famous metaphor for tacit knowledge illustrates the processual, integrative nature of tacit knowledge. The resonance of the metaphor hinges on the reader's use of *their* tacit knowledge to grasp his meaning, intellectually, sensually and corporeally. Perhaps only someone who has driven in a nail, however inexpertly, can fully appreciate his meaning.

When we use a hammer to drive in a nail, we attend to both nail and hammer, *but in a different way*. We *watch* the effect of our strokes on the nail and try to wield the hammer so as to hit the nail most effectively. When we bring down the hammer ...we are certainly alert to the feelings in our palm and the fingers that hold the hammer. They guide us in handling it effectively, and the degree of attention that we give to the nail is given to the same extent but in a different way to these feelings. The difference may be stated by saying that the latter are not, like the nail, objects of our attention, but instruments of it. They are not watched in themselves; we watch something else while keeping intensely aware of them. I have a *subsidiary awareness* of the feeling in the palm of my hand which is merged into my *focal awareness* of my driving in the nail. (Polanyi, 1958: 55)

Just as the relative importance of the senses switches throughout this skilled act, so the sharp distinction between tool and object blurs. This blurring of tool, task and object is all the greater in collective labour. There was no clear separation between hand and brain, task and tool, as the camera operators shifted their positions in anticipation of the coming shots. Here, Polanyi is very close to Bourdieu's habitus, a way of being or mastery of a given social space, as a taken-for-granted, implicit, anticipatory ease. The individual 'takes it for granted, precisely because he is caught up in it, bound up with it; he inhabits it like a garment or a familiar habitat. He feels at home in the world because the world is also in him, in the form of habitus', an ease that permits effective action without calculation (Bourdieu, 2000: 141–2). Nor did the Director have the only complete overview of the production process: *every* crew member has a clear appreciation of the programme's aesthetic, technical and budgetary demands. At best, any attempt to interrogate the use of tacit knowledge in purely analytical terms will be incomplete, and any attempt to decompose such tasks will be counter-productive.

For the crew, this studio experience represented a moment when they were released, however temporarily, from anxiety about precarious employment, and compliance with targets and budgets. The live shoot was a moment of coordination without control, a moment in which the Director channelled their collective tacit knowledge. This was a moment during which the crew were sublimated to their collective identity. Following Polanyi, this specific collective existed *only* in the moment of its making. This was not, however, a moment in which their performance was based on dull compliance. Rather, this was an experience that confirmed their identities as skilled programme-makers, sharply distinguished from the firm's financial imperatives and claustrophobic management systems (similarly, Fleming and Spicer, 2003: 160). Paradoxically, as management control systems were became increasingly alien so the understanding of the studio and work as a temporary refuge from control became more intense.

Crew were not necessarily allocated exclusively to specific programmes but were rostered for several programmes on a given day. Where the minimum crewing agreements of the pre-1988 era left little need for detailed manpower planning, individual rostering required fine-grained allocation of technical staff to particular parts of the day. By 1997 all British commercial television companies had moved to three monthly crewing schedules: 'So they would cram it in, jam it, force it – do whatever they liked. It wasn't a case of you worked for so many days and get some days off. It was you worked continually and get a lot of days off. They were basically destroying your life. It is an existence, not a life. Your only purpose in life is to be here when they want you: if they say go home, then home you go. [pause] And all to make the factory work' (Interview, Sound Engineer, 1997). The crew was allocated to two productions, a thirty-minute regional programme, 'Politics', which was filmed in the 'blank' – the period used to test equipment and prepare contestants – inside 'Wheel'. The crew had to move from the improvised production of 'Politics' to 'Wheel', but also quickly fit into their job roles in the game-show's larger crew.

'Wheel's' set was simple: a three contestant panel faced by an ad-libbing compere working without a script but around a standardised format; an assistant spinning the wheel and responding to the compere's wisecracks; and a display of the prizes to be won, complete with cheesy voice-over. The programme had been made for more than a decade. From its early prime-time period, 'Wheel' had slipped into a less prestigious late afternoon slot. But, while the prizes and the presenter became less expensive, production values were protected. Endless repetition had established the format and allowed management, with the multinational franchise-holder, to squeeze out costs. There were three live cameras and one locked-in to the panel of contestants. The set was managed by the floor manager with occasional glances up to the Director in the glass control booth. The set was relatively relaxed: the crew had been recording the programme for almost five weeks and knew the format intimately. This was a programme produced for the Network. It was a Sunday and the aim was to record seven 28 minute programmes: the norm was five per day. A white board stood at the side of the set. There were three notices: the number of editions left to the end of the run; suggestions for the wrap party; and, in a telling parody of the game-show itself, complete with hand-drawn stars, the current record for completing five episodes, 7 hours 42 minutes was the time to beat.

The crew all knew their places, and almost took their cues directly from the presenter, seldom waiting for the Director's instructions. There were loud groans, and occasional curses from the crew when the presenter's ad-libs fell flat or were too risqué. Such missteps resulted not just in the specific moment being reshot, but could jeopardise an entire sequence. This risked the loss of precious time: cast and crew could lose the programme's pace, or a contestant unnerved. The crew was infinitely more tolerant of the nervous contestants than the host's outré humour. The crew's familiarity with 'Wheel' called on none of the improvisational skills of 'Politics'. Where the production of 'Politics' relied upon the mobilisation of tacit knowledge,

'Wheel' demanded that the crew be completely subordinated to the format. 'This is formula telly. Industrial telly – this *is* a machine' (Interview, Floor Manager, 'Wheel', 2003). Management remained indirect. There was no management presence driving the pace of production. There were no overt targets or performance indicators. Rather, employment, for core and freelance staff, was project-based. The 'cost' of any slippage in production schedules was borne entirely by cast and crew. Management had all but eliminated uncertainties over budgets and fully externalised risks of over-runs onto crew. Tacit knowledge was geared towards maintaining the pace of production, avoiding any time slippages. There was little need for expertise and no call for improvisation.

The television labour process is not impervious to management pressure. There has been a major reduction in technical and ancillary staff attached to particular programmes. The elimination of ancillary staff has been masked by the absorption of many small, routine tasks by technical crew. Management accounting controls establish the context for programme-making but they do not intrude into social relationships on the studio floor. This reflects both the practical limitations of management control techniques and their questionable legitimacy among crew. Paradoxically, the importance of tacit knowledge was particularly pronounced in the low budget programme, 'Politics', where live broadcast left no opportunity for any real-time management intervention into the details of the labour process. In this live, low-budget setting the gap between management control structures and processes and the experience of work was maximised. The experience of commercial television confirms that there is no *necessary* relationship between the financialisation of the corporation and the experience of work. Nor is there any straightforward relationship between corporate pressure on programme budgets and the experience of work. Contrast the demanding, inclusive experience of the crew on the low-budget 'Politics' with the highly routinised work process on high-budget 'Wheel'. That is not to say that the productive space of 'Politics' was unmanaged but, rather, that it was regulated by quite different principles: the pressures from budgets and performance indicators were temporarily suspended. The work process was almost all-consuming, a space in which formal hierarchy was temporarily abandoned and in which aesthetic and technical decision-making became collective responsibilities. The workplace became a sanctuary in which individuals and workgroups deployed and displayed their skills and reaffirmed their identity as creative labour.

Conclusion

The financialisation of corporate organisation has thinned out, if not severed, the links between executive decision-making and the workplace. All forms of social compacts between capital and labour – empowerment, teamworking or partnership – have proved difficult to sustain. There is, however, another side to this. In commercial television until the late-1980s, work organisation was largely defined by negotiated rules. Formal rules were buttressed by the unions' aggressive defence of job boundaries. Nor was shopfloor bargaining power solely shaped by union strategies. Rather, fragile, often idiosyncratic, production technologies generated widespread and essential pockets of tacit knowledge and huge uncertainty for management. Any managerial violation of formal or informal work rules was likely to incur a significant financial cost, either in the shape of *ad hoc* payments or, in extreme cases, blank screens and lost – irrecoverable – advertising revenues. Equally, when job controls *were* relaxed, this was always a tactical, temporary and sometimes whimsical, concession that was paralleled by the tightening of other union rules governing contracts or work organisation. Management could not assume that *any* concession was permanent or signified a weakening of union job controls. By the mid-1990s work organisation and collective bargaining were completely disconnected. Further, there was no clear relationship between work roles and union identities. The bargaining power of unions and technical crew to levy a punitive toll for any breach of custom and practice was as important to occupational identities as the tools and equipment they used. The collective defence of contracts and work roles was an essential part of the everyday experience of television production. This is no longer the case, and not simply because of the end of the closed shop. Just as financialisation has distanced corporate strategy from the workplace, so too union representation has lost its intimate connection with the workplace. This is not to say that BECTU did not represent its members on contract and work issues. Rather, such issues are voiced formally without any necessary workplace equivalent. Where the union has sought to rebuild its workplace voice, notably around working time and health and safety, this has been more about re-establishing the union's visibility and credibility than renewing informal job controls. The television unions' representational activities are now at one remove from the workplace.

The marginalisation of collective bargaining and union voice in the workplace has not, however, standardised the experience of television production. Here we have contrasted the experiences of one television crew, working in the same organisation, across two productions on the same day. The contrast between 'Politics' and 'Wheel' suggest that there is no necessary link between programme budget or production values and the experience of work. For crew, the high-end 'Wheel' was so heavily formatted that their creative input was all but eliminated, while the success of low-budget 'Politics' was completely dependent on their total immersion in all aspects of the production. Nor could this contrasting experience be attributed to differing directorial styles: the same Director was in charge of both productions.

The contrasting experience of this crew suggests that the concept of *creative labour* has to be grounded in the specificities of production and cannot be ascribed wholesale to types of labour or organisations, far less to entire economic sectors.

REFERENCES

Bourdieu, P. (2000) *Pascalian Meditations*. Cambridge: Polity Press.

Bowker, G. and Starr, S. (2000) *Sorting Things Out: Classification and its Consequences*. Boston, Mass.: MIT Press.

Brown, W. (1972) 'A Consideration of "Custom and Practice"', *British Journal of Industrial Relations*, Vol. 10, No. 1, 42–61.

Campling, J. (1992) 'Competitive Shock and the Employment Relationship: A Study of Employee Relations in Commercial Television, 1985 to 1991', University of Cambridge, unpublished DPhil. Thesis.

Dreyfus, H. and Dreyfus, S. (1986) *Mind over Machine: The Power of Human Intuition and Expertise in the Era of the Computer*. New York: Free Press.

Fleming, P. and Spicer, A. (2003) 'Working at a Cynical Distance: Implications for Power, Subjectivity and Resistance', *Organization*, 10/1: 157–79.

Glevarec, H. (1999) 'Le Travail a France Culture Comme Actione Situee: Sociology de la Production Radiophonique', *Sociologie du Travail*, 41: 275–93.

Gill, J. (2000) *The Tacit Mode: Michael Polanyi's Postmodern Philosophy*. Albany, NY: Suny Press.

Grunfeld, J. (2000) *Soft Logic: The Epistemic Role of Aesthetic Criteria*. Lanham, MD: University Press of America.

Lash, S. (2002) *Critique of Information*. London: Sage.

Lury, C. (1993) *Cultural Rights: Technology, Legality and Personality*. London: Routledge.

McKinlay, A. and Quinn, B. (1999) 'Management, Technology and Work in Commercial Broadcasting, c. 1979–98', *New Technology, Work and Employment*, 14/1: 2–17.

McKinlay, A. and Quinn, B. (2007) 'Remaking Management, Work and Industrial Relations: British Commercial Television, c. 1979–2000', *Historical Studies in Industrial Relations*, 23/24: 155–80.

Martin, R. (1981) *New Technology and Industrial Relations in Fleet Street*. Oxford: Clarendon.

Miller, P. and Rose, N. (1990) 'Governing Economic Life', *Economy & Society*, 19: 1–31.

Mitchell, M. (2006) *Michael Polanyi: The Art of Knowing*. Wilmington, DE: ISI.

Polanyi, M. (1957) 'Problem Solving', *British Journal for the Philosophy of Science*, 8: 89–103.

Polanyi, M. (1958) *Personal Knowledge: Towards a Post-Critical Philosophy*. London: Routledge & Kegan Paul.

Polanyi, M. (1969a) 'The Creative Imagination', *Psychological Issues*, 6/1: 52–70.

▶

Polanyi, M. (1969b) 'The Logic of Tacit Inference', *Knowing and Being*. Chicago, IL: Chicago University Press.

Reed, M. (1996) 'Expert Power and Control in Late Modernity: An Empirical Review and Theoretical Synthesis', *Organization Studies,* 17/4: 573–97.

Rose, N. (1991) 'Governing by Numbers: Figuring out Democracy', *Accounting, Organizations and Society,* 16: 673–92.

Ruzsits Jha, S. (2002) *Recovering Michael Polanyi's Philosophy*. Pittsburgh, PA: University of Pittsburgh Press.

Saundry, R. (2001) 'The Limits of Flexibility: The Case of British Television – Regulation, Fragmentation and Flexibility', *Industrial Relations Journal,* 32/1: 22–36.

Saundry, R. and Nolan, P. (1998) 'Regulatory Change and Performance in TV Production', *Media, Culture and Society,* 20: 409–26.

Saundry, R. and Nolan, P. (2001) 'Employee Relations in British Television: Regulation, Fragmentation and Flexibility', *Industrial Relations Journal,* 32/1: 22–36.

Skillset (1996) *Labour Force Surveys*. London: Skillset.

Taylor, A. (2003) 'Not all roses', in J. Finch (ed.) *Granada Television: The First Generation*. Manchester: Manchester University Press.

Turner, S. (1994) *The Social Theory of Practices: Tradition, Tacit Knowledge and Presuppositions*. Oxford: Polity Press.

Part III
New Media

Situating the Production of New Media: The Case of San Francisco (1995–2000)

10

Andy C. Pratt

Introduction

This chapter is concerned with that nature of work in the new media industry. Specifically, this paper explores three questions. It examines the emergent organisation of work in new media companies. Related to this point two further issues are explored. Second, it looks at how 'material' or 'virtual' the industry is; in short does it have a connection to place, and why? Third, I consider the validity of the generalisations produced by 'new economy' theorists when applied to new media, and visa versa. This chapter is divided into two major parts; the first part locates the discussion of new media in the literature of economic change, the second part reports on research interviews with new media companies in San Francisco between 1998–2000. Other aspects of this research are reported elsewhere (Jarvis and Pratt, 2006; Pratt, 2006; Pratt, 2002; Pratt, 2000).

The chapter takes as its subject the new media industry in San Francisco. Located at one end of Silicon Valley in California, and considered by many to be one of the most 'creative cities' in the world (Florida, 2002) it is not surprising that the new media industry began there, based upon nascent internet technologies. One part of the city, the one or two blocks adjacent to South Park, located in a (then) run down area of town called South of the Market (SoMa), was the epicentre for development: it gained the moniker 'multimedia gulch'. The paper covers the period 1995–2000 (the 'first age' of the internet). The dot.com slump (Cassidy, 2002) marks the end of this period; it was not the end of the new media industry, but it did stimulate a new round of re-structuring and re-location within the city that is not covered here. As implied by this location-specific focus, I want to challenge the trend for dis-embedded analyses of the new media industry.

For an industry commonly not recognised as a job creator new media had an impact on San Francisco, an impact more keenly felt as the city was recovering from recession. In 1995 there were 21,000 persons employed in new media in the City; by 1997 the figure had risen to 35,000 and totalled some 400 companies (Coopers and Lybrand, 1998), by 2000 this was 40,000 (San Francisco Partnership, 2000). Average company size has been growing over time in 1995 on 6 per cent employed more than 100 persons; in 2000 it was 16 per cent (San Francisco Partnership, 2000). Thus, even at this macro-scale location is salient.

It is a surprising fact that most analyses of new media have concerned themselves with the interface of new media and the rest of the economy (consumption). Matters of distribution, and the control and regulation of products (many of which are stubbornly made of atoms), and most critically, of production, are commonly either passed over or assumed away. A classic case in hand is the debate about the 'weightless economy' which posits zero distribution and reproduction costs of digital goods, and concludes that this will lead to the 'death of distance' as a factor of location (Coyle, 1998; Cairncross, 1998; Quah, 1999). Although not made explicit, the authors imply a death of production too. However, auto-production, software producing its own software, let alone physical products, is still in the realm of science fiction. Even within a cost-free reproduction and distribution model an initial investment in software production has to take place; commonly it is costly, labour intensive, and localised. Accordingly, production still takes place, and it involves people doing jobs. As I will point out in this chapter, when and where they do those jobs matters. In fact, rather than place not mattering any more, it might be suggested that place and location, in the sense that they facilitate a variety of face-to-face interactions, are more important than ever.

Much has been claimed for the changes wrought in economy and society by the internet (Feng *et al*, 2001; Kelly, 1998; Department of Commerce, 2002); this paper takes a sceptical view of the new economy 'revolution'. The two drivers of such change are commonly argued to be the efficiency gains of the application of new technologies, and, the potential role of consumer choice mobilised by digital delivery systems. On the first of these points, there is now a body of work that offers a serious challenge to the assertion that the use of technology, especially computers, leads to greater business efficiency (David, 1999; Gordon, 2000; Jorgensen and Stiroh, 2000; Temple, 2002). Second, as writers such as Reich (2000) argue, the 'age of the terrific deal' was brought about by pain free switching between alternate suppliers. Reich's 'terrific deal' is reasonable in theory; however, anyone who has tried to switch utility suppliers, banks or insurance companies will know that it is not quite as seamless as it is often portrayed. Reich does highlight a substantive point that I want to return to later, namely the implications for workers who are in jobs one day and out the next, and the intensification, and as I will note later extensification, of work has commonly come with new technologies (Thompson, 1983). Finally, as will be clear, I am concerned here about the specifics of new media, and not to generalise to the whole economy. I will point out that there are some distinct differences within and between companies and industries in the 'new economy', and different impacts on potential outcomes.

Situating new media

The definition of new media can be problematic, not in the least because it is an emergent and fast changing industry. Initially it was called multi-media, and then new media became the preferred term. Analytically, both terms help to point to the convergence of different media (image, text, and sound) via digitalisation, and that this is different to old, or analogue, media. Second, the new media industry used the internet as the means of communication and/or distribution of information, goods and services, (superseding CDs which had previously been the main medium). There has been much debate about how the internet changes media, the notion of many to many, or peer to peer, communications is a break from both the one to many model of the mass media and the many to one mode of direct marketing.

Structure

The previous paragraph sets out the technological possibilities; and the impact and extent of these changes that extends by the day as more people spend time online.[1] However, what we are concerned with in this paper is the use that people have made of these possibilities to create new business activities. A much talked about distinction is whether it is businesses talking to one another for intermediate sales (B2B), or businesses selling to customers (B2C), or the emergent customer to customer (C2C) it is not surprising to note that the first uses of new media was by logistics companies who developed real-time tracking of packages. Of course, as with all technologies the most effective changes build upon existing structures, and in so doing transform them. Likewise, the company that builds the 'front end' – the customer facing web site – often drove back new media into the supply chain and logistics. Indeed, the most commercially successful areas of new media such as online shopping exploit these possibilities. Current developments of peer to peer (and what is termed Web 2.0 (O'Reilly, 2005)) are being taken up most actively by advertisers who have long seen the limitations of mass market penetration (getting your message broadcast on a majority of all TVs) in favour of eyeball counts (the number of people who actually read the advert). The latest experiments here are 'viral adverts' where audiences themselves circulate adverts via friendship networks thereby creating messages from trusted senders that are more likely to be read.

Space

The field of logistics was already populated by technically literate workers before new media came along, a more significant challenge was to incorporate markets (business or consumers) into these supply chains. This is the role of design, advertising and web sites: effectively the shop front and store. These technologies opened up new possibilities of linking producers and consumers. However, we should not forget that underpinning the vast majority of this activity was physical products being made, and trucked, from factory to warehouse and home (Dodge, 1999). Generally, people have <u>not</u> shifted to an exclusively digital product. However, they can now use new media to <u>buy</u> products from a variety of sources/suppliers. The upshot is that we do not live online; rather, that there is a complex mix of digital and physical goods and services, or as some have characterised it: 'bricks and clicks'.

There is a geography of new media production, as there is of distribution. Retail facilities may evaporate for some goods, for others they will exist alongside virtual ones – performing different functions, or serving different market segments. The area of customer service has almost exclusively been separated out to remote and specialised facilities such as call centres (Frenkel et al, 1998; Bennet, 2004). These are subject to their own economic logic that has seen relocation to peripheral regions of the world based upon the rate of pay, and time shifting (for 24 hour service).

As I will note later in this chapter, the geography of new media production is very localised. In part this is due to its craft or specialised nature; here we can contrast it with the Fordist factories producing standardised software (Cusumano, 1991; Cusumano and Selby, 1996). We can also contrast it with the different disciplines and organisation of new media activity in the film industry or computer games. Both activities use new media, but the role that it performs, and the nature of the market, that is quite different in each case. Again, this is a reminder that the nature of production and work in new media is highly differentiated by segment of the industry, let alone the same across the whole 'new economy'.

Transitions

Theorists of the new economy point to a range of outcomes and explanations for the changes in economic life in recent years. The main outcome identified concerns flexibility of businesses: this is usually characterised as an ability to switch suppliers at short notice, however a more extreme version is the short life, or project enterprise. For workers the implications are the growing preponderance of casualisation or freelance status jobs. The driving force is primarily economic, cost reduction via out-sourcing and competitive subcontracting (Lipietz, 1992; Piore and Sabel, 1984; Amin, 1994). The general lines of this argument are well rehearsed and cannot be reduced to the technology of the new economy, as they have been identified as strategies since the mid-1970s. However, it is conceivable that they have intensified in recent years.

Sociologists have sought to develop analyses of the consequences of this economic organisation for the social realm; perhaps the most powerful accounts deploy the notion of the allocation of risk (Beck, 2000; Sennett, 1998) and precarity (see Gill and Pratt, 2008). As people must continue their lives they develop strategies to make the best of such a situation. One example of this is the notion of a portfolio career. Some have argued that the portfolio career is a positive choice for some rather than a position forced upon them. Finally, Reich (2000), points to the consequences of the instability of switching as reflected in the household (as a direct result of unstable incomes and employment conditions), a situation that can lead to a degree of stress and wider social instability.

Returning to the realm of work organisation, there is a body of work that explores how firms adapt and cope with these new conditions of flexibility. Whilst writers, such as Castells (1996), highlight the emergence of network modes of interaction others have focused on projects that are situated within networks. Castells stresses a number of examples that gives support to the notion of the distributed firm; where ICTs are used to co-ordinate activities and there is no 'location' to the firm; or, there is no firm. Others have suggested that the consequences of this type of transition will mean that cities, as generally high cost locations, will lose their attraction (Cairncross, 1998). Mediated interactions can, it is argued replace, face to face ones; and, digital, or weightless, goods are not required to be close to market in order to minimise transportation costs (in fact as they are argued to be zero cost, they can be anywhere).

The network and ICT dis-embedding of the economy is challenged by an older literature based on the nature of project working, an activity characterised by the construction industry, and of film and television (Jones, 1996; Blair et al, 2001). Here workers are allocated to teams to work on a single project for a limited time; at the end of the project the team is dispersed to other projects. More recently, Grabher (2001a, 2001b, 2002a, 2002b, 2002c, 2004) has suggested that projects within, and sometimes across, organisations are a characteristic of the advertising industry too. Moreover, project working tends to embed workers and firms in places. Allied to this several authors have pointed to the importance of the 'buzz' or informal and tacit knowledge that further embeds firms (in selected industries) in particular places (Storper and Venables, 2004; Bathelt et al, 2004). The research findings that follow take up, explore and extend these notions.

The new media industry in San Francisco

The central question that I want to explore in this chapter is that of how is the production of new media is organised. Before that, it is helpful to provide a little context. The emergence of the new media cluster in San Francisco can be dated to 1992/3. By the turn of the century, when nobody used the term multimedia anymore, it was estimated that one third of all US internet business were located in this cluster (Bay Area Economic Forum, 1996). The precise location was the buildings surrounding South Park, a small open park in a run down part of the city comprising warehouses and rooming houses, plus a few bars and nightclubs, which had been neglected by many attempts to regenerate it. One floor of a warehouse facing South Park became the headquarters of *Wired* magazine. *Wired* became the epicentre of political and quasi-economic lobbying throughout the 1990s. Macromedia, the seminal web tools authoring company, also set up shop near South Park. Just a few miles into Silicon Valley a company that eventually became Netscape was developing the first Graphic User Interface (GUI) browser for the internet. Marcomedia provided the tools, Wired the hype, and Netscape the means to browse; collectively a precondition for new media company start-ups.

The key change in the structure and organisation of economic activity facilitated by new media is a possibility of a dis-intermediation (usually from the retailer) and the re-intermediation via the web portal. Such a reconfiguration opened up major possibilities for restructuring of economic relationships. Producers for example could deal direct with customers and customers could deal directly with suppliers. These possibilities are further meshed with corporate power and market domination as in the film industry. The notable exception is music. The key point is that whilst many products could be rendered in digital form, consumers like to possess some physical part of the product. Whilst there could be more digital consumption of film, for example, the industry has sought to block it, ostensibly on the basis of copyright issues, but also to defend its structural domination of distribution that is secured via physical means. As can be noted in the case of music, downloading has the possibility of undermining structural domination of the corporations. In the early years of new media larger companies were happy to outsource new media to small independents. Hence, the structure of the industry was unusual.[2]

New media companies sought to make a profit, however, they were not clear exactly what could be used to make a profit: commission on a service, an interface, or a new product. Many companies were experimental in the sense that they had a product, but were not sure either how to take it to market or how to make money out of it (Pratt, 2000). On the other hand, the hype created by the media about the revolutionary potential of the internet attracted investors to part with large sums of money invested in very risky, or ill-conceived ventures. The effect was that start-up companies could continue for quite a time without making a profit, it was this cycle that created the bubble economy (Wolff, 1998) that crashed in 2000 (not the fundamental weakness of new media as a new techno-economic formation). In the next section I will elaborate four key dimensions of new media organisation found in San Francisco new media companies at this time.

Project organisation

The notion of the *project-based enterprise* sounds deceptively simple: a limited life project is taken on, planned and tasks are assigned and managed. However, the organisational challenges of 'creative businesses' extend beyond the purely logistical to include such vague notions as creativity and excellence. Our findings suggested that there were at least two dimensions along which respondents reported organisational focus: managing in, and managing across, projects.

In the former case a new industry (with new technologies, and new skill sets such as new media) faces many unique challenges as to how best to manage itself. Interviewees reported uncertainty and a lack of confidence about how to organise, let alone plan for, future growth. Most companies were small and had grown out of, or were, small projects in which there was a large degree of equality in work practice: everyone does everybody else's job. In part, employees were trying to figure out what actually needed to be done on a project and to improvise. They were literally making it up as they went along. The challenge was most keenly felt when working across projects, as businesses grew (in new media this can be over a number of days or weeks), or, when a larger project was taken on, at which point the lines of responsibility became unclear. Many respondents also referred to the tensions involved in the maintenance of a creative team when the firm grows from a small (often friendship-based) group to a larger firm.

Some respondents talked of the need for more formal lines of control and management at this stage. Interestingly, some reported that their organisation was not a problem *per se*, but when funders or clients discovered what seemed like anarchic organisation they were put off. Firms discussed the adoption of an organisational form commonly found in advertising, art studios, and film production; what they called the 'studio model'. This model is characterised by the key role of the director, who has to have the 'vision' and who has to meld different sets of interests (technical and artistic), and keep an eye on, or delegate control of, budgets, as well as being responsible for keeping the 'creative juices flowing' and morale, high. The studio model was discussed as a response to the perceived compromise of a hierarchical 'chain of command' and a more collective, professional equality that many principals aspired to. Within such a model there is commonly a core team into which extra employees or freelancers were temporarily recruited. However contracting was not used in a simple numerical expansion or contraction manner. In this context many firms mix and match specific skill-sets to particular projects by using freelance labour.

A substantive finding from the research interviews was that there was little evidence of the ideal typical case of the 'project-based enterprise'. It was seldom the case that the firm ceased to exist on project completion. In the majority of cases it would be more accurate to characterise these entities as 'serial project-based enterprises'; that is, enterprises constructed for a project that involved a number of freelancers added to an already existing core group. Thus, the core of these enterprises was commonly two or three key persons around which the 'firm' would concertina with work flow. This form of organisation means that companies have to regularly recruit specialists who will be able to work in the team/project already constructed.

The social burden of contracting is that not only has trust to be built and maintained but also reputation. There is clearly a social market for reputation and skill at particular tasks: principals seek to position themselves in this market; the means to do this is by the communication of previous successes.

The serial project-based enterprise seeks to morph itself at every possible opportunity until it secures a market niche. It may seem a paradox for a temporary phenomenon such as the project-based firm, but the strategic development of many new media companies has to be viewed in a long-term perspective. Firm histories read like a cross section through recent technological change. What these companies were involved in was continual migration to 'the new thing'; each change might involve lay-offs and hiring new personnel. Some firms stumbled upon a reflexive moment when they realise what they are good at is not products but processes; in particular heuristic processes. Such situations commonly stimulate a migration up the production chain.[3] Indeed, it might be argued that the logical conclusion of a knowledge-based/learning company is to be a 'consultant' offering knowledge services to 're-engineer' companies to the norms of the leading edge practices.

Reputation

Reputation played a significant part in the organisation and functioning of many industries (Pratt, in press), the new media industry is no exception. It had two interlocking dimensions: firm reputation and employee reputation. The notion of firm reputation is an essential aspect of a project-based economy: a prime contractor has to have a track record and a reputation that they can draw upon to tender for future contracts. This fact was keenly felt by many informants.

Several made comments along the lines that 'you're only as good as your last piece of work'; making the point that a firms' portfolio of previous work is recursively also part of the pitch for subsequent work. This is formalised by some who have consciously placed their work in the public domain in order to 'pitch' for work to attract interest (or reputation). In fact some argued that these strategies were in effect loss-leaders to attract business. Another way of putting this is that firms often sought to over-engineer or over-produce to 'push the envelope', on each project to grab the attention of future clients.

Employers, or directors of teams, had not only to employ a variety of people who could fulfil a changing roster of functions, but, critically, would also be able to work with the other team members. Here, employees had to use considerable personal knowledge and draw upon gossip (situated, informed knowledge) to help to make a decision on creating a project team. Clearly, such a situation was not likely to deliver a satisfactory equality of opportunity (Gill, 2002).

The recruitment of people for the job was commonly difficult because, at the time, many people with skills could work freelance. In part the computer coding, and design, community had a significant counter-culture attitude to working for somebody else. Thus an aspirant employer had to attract employees by the promise of future riches (stock options), or more likely just a 'cool' place to work (Pratt, 2002). This fact further generated tensions when companies sought to organise themselves in a more hierarchical fashion.

Another reason for building a reputation might be to attract workers by being 'the best', or 'the most interesting'. In the new media industry the labour market was tight, and to a large extent an unknown quantity as many skills were being developed *in situ*. As is commonly discussed in the notion of portfolio careers, people choose their next job as much on the basis of the career development or challenge that it presents as much as it simply is a job that pays. This strategy is rather underlined as necessity rather than choice when one considers reports of the almost complete lack of training offered by employers. There is a very strong culture of self-training, commonly at the employers' expense and in their time (Christopherson, 2002). The premium for employees of getting an interesting employer who was doing cool projects generated (and vice versa) a huge rumour mill that employees were connected to. In part this was linked to online email lists, and to a large extent exchanged on a word of mouth basis.

Place

Contrary to the notion of new media workers all sitting at computers at home, ideally in a beach-front house, all of those interviewed worked both in a small part of the city, and predominantly in open plan offices. In part, the open plan, converted warehouse, was the 'raw space' aesthetic that res-onated with the bohemian pretensions, or simply the preferred style, of new media workers at that time. As noted above, it was important for employers to get this right, as it was one of the components that attracted workers to work for a firm. Second, the open plan structure reflected the fluid organisational structure of many companies, and allowed them to re-configure workplaces as projects changed. Finally, the open-plan structure was preferred as project teams liked to solve problems via 'the shout' (Pratt, 2002). A person asks the group how to solve a problem and then several will come and huddle round the screen and animatedly look and point and suggest a solution. This seems to be the very antithesis of the online stereotype of new media.

It would be incorrect to simply see the boundaryless or portfolio career as a perfect market where people were bouncing from job to job. In SoMa there was a vital infrastructure, one that is embodied and strongly embedded in place. Gossip was a vital means of communication, one that is underpinned by trust and confidence: topics ranged from who is working well or not, who has the best or most exciting project, or who messed up on their last job, as well as discussions about the latest technology and software, and what the latest jobs were. The gossip from the local café, or in the next firm, or building can be vitally important.

Gossip, or what others have termed 'buzz', occurs in both informal settings, especially in and around the cafes of South Park, and the 'sandboxes' or relaxation areas of firms. There is an online dimension too. One such email job list – Craig's list (www.craigslist.org) – grew out of a group of workers all laid off when an early firm failed. They kept in touch and created a small job-seeking and gossip network that others hooked up to. So, the gossip and information network relied upon both on, and offline sources. In many senses this was also a curse, arguably a more developed mode of 'presentism'[4] than that commonly experienced in US workplaces.

Extensification

Much of the discussion of flexibility is dis-embedded from place, time or social structures. My interviewees' responses were indicative of this embedding and the tensions that it generated (see Jarvis and Pratt, 2006). The spatial dimension of flexibility is the fact that it requires workers and firms to interact with others; there is clearly an action space. I have already noted the importance for some of working in an open plan office, however, workers spent much time if not actually between jobs but thinking and exploring what and where there next job would be; likewise for firms (notionally for a freelancer they we one and the same). New media, like many other cultural industries, is sustained in part by circulation of fuzzy market information. The nature of this information may be trivial or serious (although it can be difficult to separate the two from one another, it may be context dependent) but it feeds into an ongoing 'processing' that every workers and firm is involved in. It is a requirement to be 'in the loop'. So, new media workers experienced a particular sort of presentisim: the need to be constantly around others working in the industry and to keep 'in the loop' of knowledge and related gossip. Hence, the much discussed positive vibe of 'buzz' that is perceived to make work exciting and almost like play can be seen as work intruding on play, or home life. In fact, it required individuals to continually make an investment in networking, being at the right bars and cafes and speaking to the right people. This activity is not without cost, as I have noted elsewhere; it is far easier for the unattached single person than for those with caring responsibilities.

Extensification is a locational issue (being in the right place), but it has a temporal dimension too. The nature of project working, experimental deadlines and untried technologies commonly led to projects over-running or workers having to 'pull all-nighters' on multiple occasions to get projects in on time. In some cases this was seen as a willing choice, in fact an excitement of the job, to be compensated by the longueurs of 'downtime'. For those with responsibilities outside the workplace (to others, partners, pets and children) it created a significant burden. Rather than a choice to work longer hours, or so socialise, it was a requirement, or a necessity required of those who sought to remain in the industry. In this sense we can see that the flexibility is won at considerable cost, not simply in the form of freelancing and portfolio careers, but at a cost of a life outside the requirements of the industry. As such, the flexibility was 'paid for', or sustained, by partners and children, and manifest in the chaos of 'flexible work times' on their schedules, and the enforced socialisation that takes carers out of the home.

Discussion

The aim of this chapter has been to explore the organisation of work in the new media industry. I began by relating the dominant literature in the field that highlighted a tendency to generalise the processes that were presumed to constitute the 'new economy' and infer new media practices from them. Given that new media is the archetypical new economy activity, the findings in this paper should cause us to pause. In exploring new media production I have pointed to the tendency to overlook production in favour of consumption issues; clearly, both are important. I have shown that, in the San Francisco new media industry at least, contrary to expectations new media production relies upon material and face-to-face relations organised in very loose organisational configurations. To a large extent this organisational form was a result of a focus on novel products and processes. It is clear that in the dedicated software industries a large scale, rationalised, Fordist model obtains; however, we can also note that there are differences again in the computer games industry. This leads to the conclusion that organisation is associated with the product, market and dominant institutions rather than technology *per se*.

Moreover, the literature pointed to the emergence of 'project-based enterprises' in some cultural industries. Whilst new media did exhibit this broad form, the interviews lead to a revised view that might be better characterised as morphing firms. Morphing firms re-configure themselves and even their products and market position between projects. This general character of 'projectification' led, as others have pointed out, to an embedding in place. This embedding is associated with labour markets comprised of freelancers and those employed on projects: it is a labour pool effect. But more than this it is about buzz, that is the embedding of both labour markets and firm operation in a social and communicative environment. Again, the more general commentaries on new media and the new economy would lead one to expect such communication to have migrated online; this study pointed to the contrary.

Finally, this chapter pointed to further ramifications of what might be termed the 'tyranny of buzz' where the endless networking, and all-night working, has a social impact on the rest of society; most particularly friends and family. I pointed out that the bravely flexible new media industry was perhaps simply exporting its costs from the production to the social reproduction sphere.

There are a number of areas that would repay further work. Clearly, having pointed to the variations in work practices within industries I would call for more studies of production in both new media and the rest of the 'new economy' industries. As noted above, the notion that technology creates savings has been questioned, what is suggested by the research reported on here is that savings are being gained at the expense of social reproduction. Second, my core point in this paper has been to stress not only the social and economic embeddedness but also how that embeds place in the 'new economy'. Further place specific studies of new media production would be useful to test this argument further (for indicative work see (Indergaard, 2004; Braczyk *et al*, 1999; Scott, 2000).

Notes

1 Not all people either choose to, or are able to, spend time online as debates about the digital divide underline.

2 Only in the post-2000 period have new media functions begun to be incorporated within larger companies rather than be the source of contract services.

3 It can generate the migration down the production chain too; for example some new media companies became more concerned with logistics.

4 Presentism is a term that refers to people being at their desk to show that they are 'at work', even when they are not. It is a sort of disciplinary

control that undermines effective working for many workers. Another variant on this is 'presenteeism', which is where people turn up for work but are ill, and hence do not work effectively, and/or may take longer to recover Warner, J. (2004) '"Presenteeism" Hurts Employees and Employers: Sluggish Employees Cost Companies More Than Sick Days'.

REFERENCES

Amin, A. (ed.) (1994) *Post-Fordism: A Reader*. Oxford: Blackwell.

Bathelt, H., Malmberg, A. and Maskell, P. (2004) Clusters and Knowledge: Local Buzz, Global Pipelines and the Process of Knowledge Creation. *Progress in Human Geography*, 28: 31–56.

Bay Area Economic Forum (1996) The Bay area: leading the transition to a knowledge based economy. San Francisco, Bay Area Economic Forum.

Beck, U. (2000) *The Brave New World of Work*. Cambridge: Polity.

Bennet, O. (2004) A new chapter in publishing. *The Independent*. London.

Blair, H., Grey, S. and Randle, K. (2001) Working in film – Employment in a project based industry. *Personnel Review*, 30: 170–85.

Braczyk, H.J., Fuchs, G. and Wolf, H.-G. (eds) (1999) *Multimedia and Regional Economic Restructuring*. London: Routledge.

Cairncross, F. (1998) *The Death of Distance: How the Communications Revolution will Change Our Lives*. Boston: Harvard Business School Press.

Cassidy, J. (2002) *Dot.con: The Greatest Story Ever Sold*. London: Allen Lane.

Castells, M. (1996) *The Rise of the Network Society*. Cambridge, MA: Blackwell Publishers.

Christopherson, S. (2002) Project work in context: regulatory change and the new geography of media. *Environment and Planning A*, 34: 2003–15.

Coopers and Lybrand (1998) *The Interactive Media Industry Survey*. San Francisco: Coopers and Lybrand.

Coyle, D. (1998) *The Weightless Economy*. London: Capstone.

Cusumano, M. (1991) Factory concepts and practices in software development. *Annals of the History of Computing*, 13: 3–32.

Cusumano, M. and Selby, R. (1996) *Microsoft Secrets*. London: Macmillan.

David, P. (1999) Digital technology and the productivity paradox: After ten years what has been learned. Washington DC: Department of Commerce.

Department of Commerce (2002) Digital economy 2002. Washington DC: Department of Commerce, USA.

Dodge, M. (1999) Finding the source of the Amazon.com: examining the hype of the earth's biggest bookstore. London, Centre for Advanced Spatial Analysis, University College London.

Feng, H.Y., Froud, J., Johal, S., Haslam, C. and Williams, K. (2001) A new business model? The capital market and the new economy. *Economy and Society*, 30: 467–503.

Florida, R.L. (2002) *The Rise of the Creative Class: And How It's Transforming Work, Leisure, Community and Everyday Life*. New York, NY: Basic Books.

▶

▶

Frenkel, S.J., Tam, M., Korczynski, M. and Shire, K. (1998) Beyond bureaucracy? Work organization in call centres. *International Journal of Human Resource Management*, 9: 957–79.

Gill, R. (2002) Cool creative and egalitarian? Exploring gender in project-based new media work in Europe. *Information, Communication and Society*, 5: 70–89.

Gill, R.C. and Pratt, A.C. (2008) In the social factory? Immaterial labour, precariousness and cultural work. *Theory, Culture & Society*, 25: 1–20).

Gordon, R. (2000) Does the new economy measure up to the great innovations of the past? *Journal of Economic Perspectives*, 14: 48–74.

Grabher, G. (2001a) Ecologies of creativity: the Village, the Group, and the heterarchic organisation of the British advertising industry. *Environment and Planning A*, 33: 351–74.

Grabher, G. (2001b) Locating economic action: projects, networks, localities, institutions. *Environment and Planning A*, 33: 1329–31.

Grabher, G. (2002a) Cool projects, boring institutions: Temporary collaboration in social context. *Regional Studies*, 36: 205–14.

Grabher, G. (2002b) Fragile sector, robust practice: project ecologies in new media. *Environment and Planning A*, 34: 1911–26.

Grabher, G. (2002c) The project ecology of advertising: Tasks, talents and teams. *Regional Studies*, 36: 245–62.

Grabher, G. (2004) Learning in projects, remembering in networks? Communality, sociality, and connectivity in project ecologies. *European Urban and Regional Studies*, 11: 103–23.

Indergaard, M. (2004) *Silicon Alley: The Rise and Fall of a New Media District*. New York: Routledge.

Jarvis, H. and Pratt, A.C. (2006) Bringing it all back home: the extensification and 'overflowing' of work. The case of San Francisco's new media households. *Geoforum*, 37: 331–9.

Jones, C. (1996) Careers in project networks: the case of the film industry, in Arthur, M.B. and Rousseau, D.M. (eds) *The Boundaryless Career*. New York: Oxford University Press.

Jorgensen, D. and Stiroh, K. (2000) Raising the speed limit: US economic growth in the information age. *Brookings Papers on Economic Activity*, 31: 125–211.

Kelly, K. (1998) *New Rules for the New Economy*. London: Fourth estate.

Lipietz, A. (1992) *Towards a New Economic Order: Postfordism, Ecology and Democracy*. Cambridge: Polity.

O'Reilly, T. (2005) What Is Web 2.0? Design Patterns and Business Models for the Next Generation of Software.

Piore, M.J. and Sabel, C.F. (1984) *The Second Industrial Divide: Possibilities for Prosperity*. New York: Basic Books.

Pratt, A.C. (2000) New media, the new economy and new spaces. *Geoforum*, 31: 425–36.

Pratt, A.C. (2002) Hot jobs in cool places. The material cultures of new media product spaces: the case of the south of market, San Francisco. *Information, Communication and Society*, 5: 27–50.

▶

▶

Pratt, A.C. (2006) New Economy: A Cool Look at the Hot Economy, in Daniels, P., Beaverstock, J., Bradshaw, M. and Leyshon, A. (eds) *Geographies of the New Economy*. London: Routledge.

Pratt, A.C. (in press) Advertising and creativity, a governance approach: a case study of creative agencies in London. *Environment and Planning A*.

Quah, D. (1999) *The Weightless Economy in Economic Development*. London: London School of Economics and Political Science Centre for Economic Performance.

Reich, R.B. (2000) *The Future of Success*. New York: A. Knopf.

San Francisco Partnership (2000) Digital Industry 2000. San Francisco: San Francisco Partnership.

Scott, A.J. (2000) *The Cultural Economy of Cities: Essays on the Geography of Image-Producing Industries*. London: Sage.

Sennett, R. (1998) *The Corrosion of Character*. New York: Norton.

Storper, M. and Venables, A.J. (2004) Buzz: face-to-face contact and the urban economy. *J Econ Geogr*, 4: 351–70.

Temple, J. (2002) The Assessment: The New Economy. *Oxford Review of Economic Policy*, 18: 241–64.

Thompson, P. (1983) *The Nature of Work: An Introduction to Debates on the Labour Process*. London: Macmillan.

Warner, J. (2004) '"Presenteeism" Hurts Employees and Employers: Sluggish Employees Cost Companies More Than Sick Days', WebMD Medical News 2004, April 23, http://www.webmd.com/content/article/86/98895.htm?action=related_link (accessed October 2008).

Wolff, M. (1998) *Burn Rate: How I Survived the Gold Rush Years on the Internet*. London: Weidenfeld and Nicholson.

Beyond the Hype: Working in the German Internet Industry*

11

Nicole Mayer-Ahuja and Harald Wolf

Introduction

The discussion about the present shape and future prospects of work is characterised by a wide variety of novelty-speak. Among the most influential contributions are concepts of an 'information society', ranging from 'network
society' (Castells, 1996) to 'knowledge capitalism' (Burton-Jones, 1999). Such
notions are closely associated with the assumption of a paradigm break, implying the emergence of 'post-fordist' forms of organisation, employment, and
work. These are supposed to be informed by a 'new spirit' of capitalist organisation, basically substituting vertical domination (hierarchy) with horizontal
co-ordination (project-work) (Boltanski and Chiapello, 1999).

According to these concepts, fundamental changes in organisations' relationship to their environment are to be expected, among them a growing
'financialisation' (i.e., dependency on the stock market) and a general 'marketisation' of organisational structures (implying workers' more immediate
confrontation with market pressure and customer demand). Moreover, the
importance of small organisation units and enterprise networks is argued
to be increasing. At the same time, a changing relation of organisations to
work and workforce is assumed, supposedly expressed in a radical flexibilisation of employment relationships as well as in a 'liberation' and 'empowerment' of workers by means of de-bureaucratised 'projectification'. Generally,
workers are considered to acquire more autonomy in determining their work
process and employment-relationships, causing new problems of employers'
control and workers' commitment. The fact that employment-conditions
are usually determined by companies rather than workers, and that discontin-
uous job biographies threaten long-term social security (especially in the
German insurance-based system), however, are hardly mentioned in these
discussions.

Strictly speaking, most of these characterisations and assumptions belong to the sphere of management discourses and models, however, which obviously influence the orientation of actors, but whose relation to 'real' work, let alone to the vast variety of working and organisation practices is often anything but clear. Still, in some seemingly new or increasingly important fields of high-tech or cultural economic activity (like IT, biotech, multimedia), new forms of work organisation are thought to have materialised already, thus displaying some of the trends and attributes mentioned above. The Internet-industry has been discussed as one of the most prominent forerunners of 'new work', since it has emerged in the US constellation of the 'roaring nineties' with its neo-liberal apotheosis of market hegemony, emphasis on shareholder-value and 'new economy'-speak, particularly nourished by the new kind of economic activity and work centred around the World Wide Web. As the hype associated with 'web-services' is now history, it may prove possible and useful to take a closer look at the prosaic working realities in this industry, shedding some light on the chances these trends and concepts might have to materialise on a more general scale in future.

The empirical findings presented below are results of the research project 'Varieties of Organising 'Knowledge Work' between Autonomy and Binding' (see, for details of the research context, Gottschall and Wolf, 2007). In order to analyse the wide (and still emerging) range of companies and patterns of work organisation in the Internet industry, we draw upon intensive case studies based on qualitative interviews in 12 companies, including older as well as start-up firms specialising in web design, programming, e-learning or e-business applications (for details of the sample see Tables 11.1 and 11.2, pp. 76–7). Roughly 50 semi-structured interviews have been conducted with workers, 30 with managers and 10 with industry experts from unions, associations and research institutes since the fall of 2002. The collection of data proceeded until the summer of 2004 (see, for further details, Mayer-Ahuja and Wolf, 2005).

The main focus of this chapter is directed towards methods of control and their consequences for workers' chances to determine their work autonomously (in the literal sense of setting their own rules). In order to discuss these issues, some features of the emerging organisational field 'Internet industry' in Germany need to be sketched first, providing information on its size, structure and financial resources. We will then turn to the organisation of work in this industry, presenting an overview of central tasks, jobs and skills, and commenting on the impact of 'projectification' as observed in the companies of our sample. The main section deals with some aspects of hierarchy and control, searching for traces of 'marketisation', de-bureaucratised control and self-determined work. Finally, the main results will be summarised, arguing that work organisation in the German Internet industry is

Table 11.1 Number of staff from the company's foundation to 2003*

Company	A	B	C	D	E	F	G	H	I	J	K	L
Orig. staff	60	3–4	3	60	120	2	5	4	4	800	4	n.k.
(year)	(1996)	(1996)	(1996)	(1996)	(2000)	(1970)	(1993)	(1995)	(1998)	(1998)	(1996)	(1992)
Staff 2000/01	180	16	n.k.	230	120	120	35	17	9	110	26	180
Staff 2003	62	22	30	45/230	100	100/79	15	12/2	7	75	19/13	60

*'n.k.' indicates that this information is 'not known', i.e., not provided by the firm. Company D had 45 employees in 2003, but was experiencing a merger, which was about to raise the employment figures. Company F had 79 employees in 2003, with an additional group of 21 persons working for a subsidiary company, and companies H and K reduced their staff around the time when interviews were performed in 2003.

Source: Authors.

Table 11.2 Character of employment relationships (2003/04)

Company	A	B	C	D	E	F	G	H	I	J	K	L
Staff 2003	62	22	30	45/230	100	79	15	12	7	75	19	60
Part-Time*	3	1	1	n.k.	–	3–4	2	2	7	1	2	–
Time-Contracts	–	–	1	n.k.	–	1	–	–	–	–	–	–
Standard Employment (in %)	95.2	95.5	93.3	n.k.	100	94.3	8.7	83.3	0	98.7	89.5	100

*'n.k.' indicates that this information is 'not known', i.e., not provided by the firm. Company D had 45 employees in 2003, but was experiencing a merger, which was about to raise the employment figures. Company F had 79 employees in 2003, with an additional group of 21 persons working for a subsidiary company, and companies H and K reduced their staff around the time when interviews were performed in 2003.

Source: Authors.

characterised by conflicting methods of control, oscillating between many employers' attempts to regulate the labour process more hierarchically and the necessity to co-ordinate creative work in a more egalitarian manner, although the latter still seems to be considered the ideal organising principle by employers and employees alike.

Internet- and multimedia-companies: an industry in the making

The emergence of Internet- and Multimedia-companies can be traced back to the early 1990s, when the World Wide Web took its present shape (Zerdick, 1999). Labelled 'Internet industry' by some and 'New Media' by others, their activity is defined as combining 'elements of computing technology, telecommunications, and content to create products and services which can be used interactively by consumers and business users' (Batt *et al*, 2001: 7). Although the emergence of this industry (and especially the increase of 'start-ups' in this area) seemed to prove the assumption that a 'New Economy' would put an end to economic crisis and create 'mass employment', its quantitative development is far from clear: there are no official statistics, and available data are scattered, incomplete and not representative. One major problem in judging the Internet- and Multimedia-industry's size is due to the fact that, in the late 1990s, computer access and an IT-infrastructure's connection to customers or subcontractors were sufficient to apply the label 'Multimedia' to a company and to consider it part of an 'Internet-Economy' (Schnorr-Bäcker, 2001). Still, this haziness is not just a statistical artefact, as Internet-services are in fact often performed in-house by companies, rendering it difficult to make out a specialised 'core industry' – for Sweden, it has even been argued that 'in-house interactive media operations are just as large, and most likely larger, than the ... sector of specialised interactive media producers' (Augustsson and Sandberg, 2004: 13). Moreover, many specialised service providers are closely connected to and influenced by older and more traditional companies, especially from a small number of 'founding sectors'. In Hamburg, for example, 34 per cent of all founders of Multimedia enterprises came from classical media (Print- and AVMedia), another 32 per cent from the IT-sector, 26 per cent from advertising and 10 per cent from telecommunications (Läpple and Thiel, 2002: 20). Doubtlessly, however, there is a 'core' of specialised service providers, which were largely founded in the second half of the 1990s and are focusing on e-business, Web-Design, Hosting, e-learning or other Internet-related services as their main business. This chapter's focus will be directed towards these 'dotcom-enablers' (Kanter, 2001: 2), or rather, towards a decisive sub-group of them: not towards technology providers (like Sun, Cisco etc.), but towards

'Internet-service providers' (*Internet-Dienstleister*), understood as individuals or companies specialised in assisting others (mainly via software production and consultancy) to make use of the World Wide Web. This definition explicitly does not cover, then, the famous 'dotcoms' like eBay, Amazon or Yahoo, operating online businesses, nor does it include companies performing Internet-services in-house for their own purposes (like, e.g., a radio station or a retail company producing its own website).

As the Internet- and Multimedia industry's boundaries are thus blurred, the number of employees has been estimated to have increased from 14,500 in 1997 to 72,000 in 2001 according to one survey (Michel, 2002: 32), and from 70,000 employees in 1999 to 151,000 in 2001, not including about 67,000 freelancers, according to another (Krafft, 2000: 13; Krafft, 2001a: 5). These figures may at least indicate the rough size of employment, however, which does not seem to have expanded as massively as expected. After the industry had been hit by a profound crisis in the years 2000/01, employment data are even harder to find, but it seems clear that founding activities receded (for the 1990s: Michel, 2002: 30, 32; for Hamburg: Läpple and Thiel, 2002: 20). As to business size, the average number of employees per firm had increased from nine in 1995 to 13 in 1998 (Michel, 1999: 13), and one year later, especially companies with more than 15 employees, were experiencing an expansion of staff (Michel and others, 2000: 13). Although there were some companies with several hundreds of employees, the industry always remained dominated by small and middle-sized enterprises. According to Krafft (2001b), there were 15,000 'Internet and E-Commerce' startups in the year 2000, out of which 10,000 had less than 10 employees, another 4,000 had 10–50 employees, and only 160 companies employed more than 50 persons. After the breaking point of 2001, this dominance of small enterprises seems to have persisted: according to surveys of 2003, 50 per cent of the 'web-entrepreneurs' interviewed by Oertel and others, (2003: 52–3) had no employees at all, and 57 per cent of the 'new media'-employees participating in a trade union survey worked in companies employing up to 50 persons, among them 10 per cent in companies with up to five employees, after every second company had reduced staff (Brasse, 2003: 14).[1] Even if these surveys are not representative in a statistical sense, it may still be argued that founding activities declined after 2001, and that the German Internet- and Multimedia-industry is dominated by small-scale enterprises, which were likely to expand in the late 1990s and to lay off staff when the crisis began. This structure should be kept in mind, as it obviously influences the way in which work is organised.

Even though the focus of economic activity in this sector still seems diffuse and companies are offering a wide range of services, it can still be considered a specific industry in the making: first of all, the representatives of Internet- and Multimedia-companies are quite decisive about their belonging to a new and distinguishable industry. For example, 43 per cent of those interviewed for the 'I-Business Executive Summary 8/2003' (6) considered themselves part of the 'Internet- and Multimedia-sector', which is quite an impressive share as 'individuality' and 'being different' are generally perceived as synonyms for 'quality' and 'innovation' in this industry. Moreover, the activities of organisations like the German Multimedia Association (*Deutscher Multimediaverband: dmmv*)[2] may have strengthened this self-perception, for instance, by defining a certain 'in-group' of competing Internet- and Multimedia-companies in the annual '*dmmv*-Service Ranking'.

Our sample of 12 companies is, then, quite typical for this 'industry in the making' in several aspects: the companies are all part of this 'inner circle', and they are small enterprises, today employing between six and 79 persons (usually after a reduction of staff, see Table 1). Moreover, although this can only be mentioned briefly, they are typical in *not* displaying any tendency towards 'financialisation'. In 2001, only 2,000 out of nearly 15,000 German 'E- Startups' had access to venture capital, capital of business angels or strategic investors (Krafft, 2001b: 3–4), whereas *none* of the companies in our sample used such shareholdings. Instead, all relied upon (partly private) bank loans, and none went public, although this had been seriously considered by two joint-stock companies (A, D), before the German 'New Market Index' (*Nemax*) collapsed.

It may thus be argued that the late 20th century has indeed seen the making of a distinguishable Internet- and Multimedia-industry. As Internet-Services are constituting a new blend of IT, telecommunications, advertising and media, however, companies need to assemble different competencies, thus employing programmers, designers, project managers and sometimes even content specialists. It is their tasks and skills to which we will now turn.

Making internet services work: tasks, processes, job profiles

Although this may seem quite obvious, a general feature of work in the Internet industry requires emphasis: the fact that it implies working *with* the Internet *for* the Internet, being based on and orientated towards this information technology. For employees, the Internet is the 'element' in which they are moving, rather than a working tool which they are using. Hence, the difference between 'means' and 'ends' becomes blurred, as almost all tasks are performed in the channels of computer systems.

Moreover, even if the analytical value of the term 'knowledge work' may be doubted, high-skill creative work in Internet companies does display a certain peculiarity, as it is shaped by a common organisational feature: the *project form* of almost all work flows and activities. This results from the proximity to customers and the high specificity of most solutions elaborated here. Within this organisational framework, five task complexes can be identified: first of all, there are the tasks of *customer contact* (co-ordination with the client) and of *planning and organisation functions* (distribution of financial, time and personnel resources and controlling). Then there are *conception* tasks, among them the definition of key ideas, of a communication strategy for the client's product or service and of its textual shape and information structure. In short, it has to be decided, what content should be conveyed by means of which text and in which structure. Prominent among *design* tasks is the elaboration of the visual and graphic key ideas as well as of the information structure (interface, logo, image, usability). Finally, *programming and technical implementation* comprise a broad range of software-creating and computer-related activities (like front-end programming, application programming, source code documentation and testing).

Theoretically, the process of a website's production as defined in the manuals of many Internet companies contains three distinct phases: definition, conception and implementation. The *definition* process starts with a customer's request or an invitation of tenders, followed by a presentation of a rough outline of the site, by feedback and re-definition loops, which result in the drawing up of an offer and the final order. After that, *conception* implies the elaboration of a rough concept (including the fixing of a communication strategy, of contents, functional features, basic visual ideas and technical framework) and its presentation. If accepted by the client, a process of detailed conceptualising follows: material for contents is collected, interaction, design and technical features are conceptualised, an extranet for the customer may be established and a prototype constructed. *Implementation*, finally, constitutes the most time-consuming and decisive phase of the process: it contains the drawing-up of texts, front-end and application programming, source code documentation, testing, corrections by the customer, training activities, and the final documentation of results.

This sequence of production phases is only an ideal-type construction, however. Under conditions of a usually very tight time budget and incompleteness of information, the handling of projects may vary, according, for instance, to their size and complexity. Moreover, project work is generally characterised by permanent iteration and backward loops to former stages, and there is a tendency towards reducing the time spent on definition and conception, as efforts are increasingly concentrated on implementation. This is, at least partly, due to the growing importance of old and steady (rather than new) customers, whose demands are already known, even if their own Internet competencies are increasing, which often results in a stricter external pre-definition of tasks.

Taking a closer look at how these tasks are usually bundled into job definitions, three main job areas can be distinguished: the so-called creation area (content conception, graphical conception, and design), software development, and project management. The common task of the *creation* workers is to determine what should be 'said' (via a website) and how it should be said. In some firms, this task is ascribed to one job, in others it is distributed between a *conceiver* and a *designer*. The former generates the core ideas and outlines the content (partly also composing texts), whereas the latter elaborates the graphic concept (layout, colors, images). Both jobs require basic knowledge of marketing/advertising and, of course, of the Internet itself, but these skills need to be combined with imaginary and creative intuition, as more often than not, new solutions have to be found in the course of daily work. Obviously, improvisation is not a new work requirement, but it could be argued to be the rule rather than the exception in Internet-companies (van Treeck, 2002). Creation workers, then, have to combine improvisation with an analytical and conceptual approach and partly (in the case of designers) also with graphical skills. Moreover, quasi-artistic attitudes as well as a strong orientation towards aesthetic or technical norms, values and fashions are shaping conceivers', designers' and, in a similar way, even software developers' (see below) relation to their work. This applies, even if there seems to be an overall tendency to emphasise 'structuration' and analytical thinking in this job area, thereby 'channelling' creative abilities and orientations.

Software development is a broader and, numerically speaking, the biggest task area in the Internet companies of our sample, and the number as well as the importance of software-developers still seems to be growing. In accordance with varying job differentiations, we found *systems architects, lead developers* and *programmers* with different specialisations, among them Java programming, front-end or HTML programming, and the development of data bases and content management systems. Technological complexity has increased enormously in this software realm of our sample, not least because solutions need to be more and more integrated in the customers' work-flow and information infrastructure, generating problems of compatibility and adaptation to specific processes. Software developers' skills and knowledge vary considerably, and some jobs imply more routine than others. However, analytical skills and knowledge of rapidly changing programming languages seem to be essential for their relatively complex task of solving technical problems, whereas the importance of social skills for these jobs is usually downplayed by experts and programmers alike.

Finally, the extensive planning and control functions required for coordinating these different jobs are increasingly ascribed to unit leaders or to whole units (like quality management), thus taking over management tasks. Although there is a clear tendency to promote such a division of labour (see below), it meets with limits, given the high uncertainty and complexity of the work environment. For this reason, planning and control functions partly remain integrated in the operative workflow itself, even if they are formally concentrated in the position of so-called *project managers*. This denomination is quite misleading as these workers usually have no real management position or directive authority. Hence, they are called 'customer adviser' (*Kundenbetreuer*) in some companies, which describes their core tasks much more precisely. Project management is a kind of boundary job, then, combining sales functions with functions of internal organisation. In those companies of our sample which have taken to employing 'PMs' at all, they represent 10 to 20 per cent of the workforce. A project manager may be responsible for certain customers or for all customers from a specific industry segment, as most firms try to concentrate customer contacts and relations in this job definition in order to turn only 'one face to the customer'. The skills required of these 'managers' comprise knowledge of the customer's business, of commercialising and controlling basics as well as of the Internet's potential and limits. Moreover, social skills are of major importance for coordinating customer relations and the work of project-teams. Let us now turn to the question of how these social relations are regulated in Internet companies, focusing on the (changing) importance of hierarchy and control.

Making employees work: limits of self-determination in internet-companies

One of the most debated aspects of new forms of work is the extent to which employees are enabled to organise their work more autonomously, autonomy here being understood (in the literal sense) as the (individual or collective) capacity to set one's own rules. In the late 1990s, mass-media have indeed cultivated a picture of autonomous labour in Internet- and Multimedia-companies: founders and employees, the story ran, were often friends, who quit university in their twenties and set up their own lucrative business. These youngsters were presented as creative and independent incarnations of entrepreneurship, who could not be bound by ordinary labour contracts and squeezed into formal hierarchies, but preferred to be freelancers, cooperating in virtual networks. If they worked for a company at all, it had to be an egalitarian organisation, offering freebees to those who spent day and night in the office, motivated by their enthusiasm about Internet-technology and their highly productive and hip scene (for a critical account see Meschnig and Stuhr, 2001). In some of our interviews, such accounts are referred to as reflecting the atmosphere of the late 1990s, although it is hard to tell to what extent they invoke a (former) self-perception or a (former) reality. The manager of company A, for instance, remembers the late 1990s, when there was 'money left ' for such 'goodies' as free weekend trips, body-massages and breakfasts for all employees: 'We did that because we were making profit and because we like to share', he said (A, M, 7).[3] In other companies, 'corporate identity' was promoted less spectacularly even in the period of expansion, and none of them seems to have displayed a systematically designed or 'engineered' organisational culture as described by Kunda (1992). After the turning point of 2001, however, work organisation seems to have changed everywhere. The following paragraphs provide some hints on the development of employment relationships, of horizontal as well as vertical differentiation and of methods of controlling working-time and labour-process. These results may add to qualifying some assumptions about self-determined work in Internet-companies.

Searching for part-timers and freelancers

Most of the 12 Internet-Companies in our sample have experienced a severe reduction of staff since 2001. Only company C seems to have expanded regularly, as this year is not mentioned as a turning point.

The reduction of 'regular' staff, which shaped the whole industry (see Table 11.1), is apparently not compensated for by freelance-arrangements, however. According to Läpple and Thiel (2002: 25–6), the share of freelancers in Hamburg's Internet- and Multimedia-companies only amounted to 11 per cent in 2002. It has even been argued that four regular employees faced one single freelancer in multimedia companies, whereas 'classical' media displayed almost the opposite ratio of 1:3 (Michel, 2002: 31). In our sample, freelancer-numbers are also small: two companies (B, J) do not cooperate with freelancers at all, and four smaller companies draw upon a marginal number (C:2, G:6, I:4; K:1).[4] Only three (bigger) companies (D, E, F) maintain a whole 'pool' of around 100 freelance partners, partly in order to avoid dependency on individual competencies. As reason for this hesitant approach, one manager mentioned his

> ... aim to do as much as possible internally, i.e., without freelancers, as far as possible. Because the freelancers do actually never have time when you need them and always call, when you don't need them. As they live on many agencies, it is always a bit difficult to coordinate, but you can't evade them in order to cushion peaks. (C, M2, 6)

Another manager states that some customers provided 'very sensitive data', which 'could only be entrusted to a core team' (F, M2, 7), and according to the head of a coding department, outsourcing threatened quality and the development of in-house skills:

> If I give something to somebody outside and he returns a complete module, this sounds fine, but there are usually changes required or we

have to be careful to understand it ourselves in order to be able to re-use it. Every piece of software emerging with us is an investment which makes the calculation of new projects easier and more correct. For this reason, outsourcing is disadvantageous for us, because I can't control it. I need to have know-how here. (G, E1, 11)

Hence, problems of quality management, coordination and lack of trust seem to make companies rely on regular employment relationships. Among those, the German 'standard employment pattern' (*Normalarbeitsverhältnis*), i.e., full-time employment with a permanent contract, is strongly preferred. Part-time work is uncommon in companies of our sample – where it is found, this can be due to individual employees' wishes (C, K, M), but also to a shortage of orders (A, M, 16). Only in one company, working hours have been reduced collectively because of family duties (I, M, 13, 19), which might indicate a more self-determined coordination of work and private life, but this is the proverbial exception which proves the rule. Time-contracts seem to be even more exceptional, apart from apprentices and trainees. The German 'standard employment pattern', which still accounts for more than 60 per cent[5] of all jobs in Germany despite increasing 'atypical' arrangements (Bosch and others, 2001: 29), thus appears to be almost ubiquitous in our sample. This marks a sharp difference, for instance, to the New Media industry of New York, where almost half of all employees were part-time or temporary workers or independent contractors in 1997 (see Batt and others, 2001: 8).

Segregation between 'standard employees' on one side and a flexible, part-time-, fixed-term- or freelance-workforce drawn upon to compensate for changing customer demands on the other side, does not seem to be of major importance in our sample, then. Whereas it may well be argued that the lack of fixed-term contracts does in fact improve workers' bargaining position, they can hardly opt for part-time work or freelancing at the moment. It reduces the chance to organise their work-life-balance individually, even if these forms of 'atypical employment' imply their own risks as far as working-times, employment stability, and social security are concerned.

Horizontal and vertical differentiation

In the small-scale enterprises of our sample, one would of course not expect a multi-levelled vertical differentiation, and in most of them there are indeed no elaborated formal hierarchies. According to the founder and manager of company B, hierarchies are neither functional for his enterprise nor for the Internet-industry in general. 'We do cooperate', he told us, in a way 'which does not necessarily work with hierarchies and sanctions, but rather with motivation and responsibility'. Relations within his company were 'very comradely', 'friendly', even constituting a 'kind of family':

> We have a common goal, we have a common idea, and I do think, we also have a common vision, and that's where we want to go. And all of us contribute, so to speak, the same to this. I am one of the 22 parts of this story. (B, M, 8)

A closer look at our sample may reveal, however, that work organisation is in fact shaped by increasing vertical differentiation (as expressed in hierarchies) as well as horizontal differentiation (as expressed in the internal division of labour). As far as hierarchies are concerned, even the smaller Internet-companies (B, C, G, H, I, K), all of which were founded by private individuals and display strongly personalised relations, fall short of the egalitarian ideals invoked in the above quotation.[6] After all, there is (at least) a decisive line of division between founders and managers on one hand and rank-and-file-employees on the other. In company B, for instance, only one person functions as founder, manager and investor of the initial capital, providing him with an outstanding position, even if no formal hierarchies are introduced. In the 'bigger' companies of our sample (mostly employing more than 30 employees), the gap between management and employees is even deeper, as all of them have been founded by larger enterprises like advertising agencies (A, D), IT- (E) and telecommunication companies (J) or other 'old economy' enterprises (L). Managers were appointed from the mother enterprise's staff, and persisting close relations (based, for instance, on financial dependencies; D) reinforce the manager(s) standing as the only person(s) with a 'direct link'.

Even apart from the divide between management and employees, the internal hierarchy of Internet companies is far from uniformly egalitarian. In bigger companies, several levels of hierarchy have already been introduced in the period of expansion: one manager remembers that he engaged a 'whole school class' (i.e., 20–30 persons) each month, appointing '24-year-olds superiors of 22-year-olds, and you don't know either of them' (A, M, 17). Such 'spontaneous' hierarchies do obviously not indicate a strategic decentralisation of responsibility, which could have enhanced employees' chances to self-determined work, especially as one manager even stresses that titles were mainly used to impress customers:

> People are hot on titles, they don't want to know that a designer works on their thing, but [expect] at least an art director. And they also want to know 'who's the creative director?' If somebody would ask: Which creative director is responsible for my project, I could tell him, who it is. But

nobody would ever dream of calling this person by this title [internally], and this person would never dream of using this title himself. (C, M1, 16)

Although the late 1990s inflation of spectacular titles has often been ridiculed, these titles do function as symbols of recognition for employees and as reassurance for customers: after all, the growing number of customers could no longer be attended to by the manager personally, but would at least demand contact with somebody in a leading position. Most importantly, however, this initial introduction of formal (though practically insignificant) hierarchies paved the way for a more substantial restructuring after 2001, when competition increased and staff had to be reduced.

In most of the small companies of our sample (B, C, H, I, K), restructuring only implied horizontal differentiation: formal fields of specialisation were identified and a more consequent division of labour introduced, separating the spheres of designers and programmers and strengthening the position of the latter within these companies, as IT-complexity of services and products is growing. In slightly bigger companies, however, even vertical different-iation increased, as formal departments were installed and heads of depart-ment appointed (A, D, E, L), implying new (and this time real) career options. In two older enterprises (F, J), finally, existing departments were now re- structured several times, rendering it difficult for many interviewees to name their position or department correctly. This horizontal and vertical differentiation seems to have been forced upon many Internet-companies from outside, i.e., by customers' pressure to appoint superiors and to raise productivity: as customer demands became more complex and Internet-budgets were cut around 2001, founders and managers, even of small com-panies, started concentrating on the acquisition of new projects and could not function as responsible programmers or designers anymore. Hence, they 'delegated responsibility' (A, M, 9), which had enormous impact on the internal distribution of power, as some employees were ascribed authority over others. At the same time, employees had to specialise in certain tasks, increasing their routine and productivity. This tendency to replace collective muddling-through by a clearer distribution of functions is presently cul-minating in the emergence of project managers responsible for customer relations and the internal organisation of project work. This more con-sequent division of labour is apparently welcomed by many employees as indicating professionalisation and stability, although it implies a loss of com-petencies, increases the need to cooperate and thus reduces employees' chances to organise their work independently. Moreover, at least the introduction of formal hierarchies is a double-sided process: when some employees are pro-moted, others are left behind, causing disappointment and ambivalences as to ideal structures of work organisation. In some interviews, then, egalitarian ideals still inspire employees' claims for 'transparency', and hierarchical 'command and control' is rejected as being incompatible with the independent work required of them. At the same time, however, hierarchies are explicitly accepted and 'more leadership, actually more structure' demanded (K, E1, 20). According to a programmer in company K, managers could not say:

> ... 'I [am] the boss, you [are] a co-worker, I tell you what you have to do, then things will work out'. I can't demand of people to cooperate respons- ibly on the one hand and to take over many tasks and not to bother me with questions, and on the other hand I want to lead them very, very strictly and do not do this in the end. At some point, there will be a crash then. (K, E2, 25)

Many employees' ambivalence towards hierarchies could not be expressed more clearly: the management is accused of strict leadership which conflicted with creative tasks, but is expected to effectively exert the leadership it claims.

Remembering one manager's assumption that 'his' Internet-company resem- bled a family rather than an hierarchical enterprise, it may thus be argued that this account always fell short of the work reality in our sample, given the prominent position of founders and managers. In the period of consolidation, however, new hierarchies have been introduced and the division of labour increased in response to customer demand and growing competition. This opened career options for some employees, reduced the influence of others, and generally set narrower limits to self-determination at work. Under these conditions, the 'family-comparison' does obviously not reflect egalitarian rela- tions between brothers and sisters, as insinuated by the above quotation and wished for by many employees. Instead, the 'family enterprise' is increasingly based on hierarchies, even if they are still perceived as 'natural' rather than 'formal' by many managers. In company D, for example, the manager con- stantly compares his tasks to the education of children, culminating in the wish to take his 'co-workers' to a traditional enterprise, just like he would take his children to Africa in order to make them appreciate their standard of living (D, M, 3). The Internet-companies of our sample, then, display an explosive mixture of egalitarian ideals, patriarchal managerial attitudes and a wide range of informal as well as formal hierarchies, based on a generally increasing div- ision of labour. Which aspects will prove dominant in different organisational settings is open to future discussion.

Methods of control

In scientific debate, it is widely accepted that high-skill creative work cannot be decreed by superiors in the same detailed manner as practised in Taylorist industrial enterprises (see Heidenreich, 2002). Hence web-workers could also be expected to organise their work more autonomously, collectively or individually determining its time, place, pace, and content. A brief glance at our sample displays a broad variety of formal as well as informal methods of control, however. These controls are usually not only exerted by superiors, but also by colleagues and customers, considering that working 'on the frontline' with the customer generates additional control problems:

> Relations between front-line workers and customers tend to be contradictory since the workers are required, on the one hand, to satisfy individual customer's requirements ..., while, on the other hand, to project a positive image of the organization. The former invites less management control, while the latter encourages closer management attention. (Frenkel *et al*, 1999: 25)

As far as working-times are concerned, many managers and employees consider it advantageous that hours of presence are not controlled formally in Internet-companies, for instance by way of attendance recorders. In company F (as in many other places) we were told that 'it is kind of individual, if somebody rather works early or later' (F, M2, 11). This view seems to be shared by many employees, as the overwhelming majority of 'New Media'-workers participating in a trade union survey described themselves as 'very content' (21 per cent) or 'content' (50 per cent) with working-times (Brasse, 2003: 18). In many companies of our sample, however, the regulation of hours is disputed, even if not always discussed openly. In company D, for instance, the manager keeps emphasising the renunciation of an attendance recorder, whereas graffiti in the elevator says: '12:36 – went for lunch'. Obviously, the absence of formal controls has not reduced at least one employee's feeling of being under supervision. Conflicts like these are likely to have occurred after 2001, when enthusiasm faded, the reduction of staff increased work-pressure in many companies, as they 'suddenly managed to achieve the same turnover with half our troops' (A, M, 2), and formal hierarchies were established (see above), disappointing many employees' belief in egalitarian structures and collective responsibility. It is hard to tell whether this has reduced employees' willingness to work overtime, or whether a lack of customers made working-hours decrease, but there is some evidence that working-times have approached the standards defined by collective agreements in other sectors. According to a trade-union survey, most labour contracts of 'New Media'-employees (85 per cent) today decree 35–40 hours per week. Even if 48 per cent of the participants state they work much longer in fact (Brasse, 2003: 15–18), this seems to indicate some kind of 'normalisation'. The *location* of working hours does not resemble the late 1990s' stories either, about offices virtually turned into living-communities.

In our sample, night-work as well as weekend-shifts are rather uncommon, and regular working-hours last from Monday to Friday, starting between 8 and 10 a.m. and terminating between 4 and 7 p.m. This coincidence with German standard office hours is mainly ascribed to the close cooperation with customers, requiring 'that every team ... has to be present to an extent enabling us to give qualified answers if a customer calls' (B, M, 12). This reduces employees' chances to determine their 'work-life-balance' individually, and the same is true for the *distribution* of working-hours. Although most employees emphasise that overtime-work could be compensated for by leaving earlier on other days, the balance usually appears unequal. One technical employee, for instance, tells himself:

> Well, I was here for three additional hours yesterday, I'll quit one hour earlier or one-and-a-half hours earlier today. We try, I would guess, ... always to keep the balance in favour of [company] K. (K, E1, 13)

This widespread acceptance of unpaid work may be argued to indicate that 'control by self-control', which is supposed to gain importance in 'post-bureaucratic' work organisation, still plays a certain role in Internet-companies of our sample, despite disenchantment with 'corporate identity' in times of economic crisis. It needs to be discussed, though, if this way of regulating one's own work can meaningfully be described as 'autonomous', considering that duration, location and distribution of working-times are usually not determined by individual employees, but by customers, project teams, and superiors.

The necessity to be available for customers, for instance, does not only result in conventional office hours, but also in frequent overtime-work. According to one programmer,

> ... it often happens, then, that customers call at 7 pm saying: 'Damn, I've got a presentation tomorrow, and we have to get this going somehow.' And I would be a bad service provider if I said: 'I'll go home'. (G, E1, 16)

Cooperation with colleagues also requires shared office-hours, as project tasks are usually distributed among team members who are often involved in several projects at a time, and tasks have to be completed in hours rather than days. Theoretically, this cooperation could enhance collective autonomy, but as customers' office-hours need to be respected and work-pressure is high, team work seems rather to be guaranteeing mutual control. The management of company F, for instance, told us:

> The team will complain if somebody is letting the team down, so to speak. And if somebody is only there at 10 o'clock instead of half past

nine or half past eight (core time), this does not turn into a problem, so to speak, until the team makes it a problem. But it is not the boss standing there and saying: 'You are half an hour late today!' (M2, 11)

'It is not the boss' controlling working-times – statements like this abound in our interviews. In fact, at least computer-based control and knowledge management systems, which could be expected in this IT-based industry, are hardly used in our sample so far. Nevertheless, managements obviously determine working-hours indirectly (by composing teams etc.), and some managers even control them personally, as they do not trust in the disciplinary power of customer relations and peer pressure. In such cases, employees complain about the discrepancy between their superiors' emphasis on 'management by objectives' and the strict control of working-hours they actually exert. One programmer, who faces difficulties ensuring extended lunch-breaks or an earlier parting now and then, stated ironically that she thought of purchasing an attendance recorder for her manager at an eBay-auction (K, E2, 20). In spite of such tensions, however, many employees still emphasise individual decision, customer demand, and pratical constraints inherent in project-work as most important determinants of working-hours. Hence, being independent workers constitutes a decisive part of their self-perception, although it is hard to trace in the actual organisation of work, which is closely scrutinised by omnipresent managers.

Finally, high-skill creative employees like programmers and designers are generally supposed to be most productive if it is left up to them to define the contents and pace of their work more or less autonomously, as long as they generate certain results. Instead of relying on direct supervision, employers are advised, they should negotiate target agreements with their employees, thus exerting indirect control. Again, the actual work-organisation in Internet-companies of our sample is kind of disillusioning, however. Just like working-times, concrete task performance is strongly influenced by the need to cooperate with customers, colleagues and superiors, the speed and intensity of work being determined by tight project deadlines and frequent demands for immediate assistance. This *ad hoc* character of work apparently results not least from the spatial situation of many companies. More than half of them (A, D, E, G, H, I, K) are situated in old factories or warehouses with wide halls and open-plan offices, resounding with ringing telephones and the conversation between colleagues. Mutual control is inevitable here, because moving through these halls, superiors as well as colleagues automatically look over shoulders at monitors, noticing not only who arrives late or leaves early, but also supervising the progress of each individual's work. This easy way of exerting direct personal control is explicitly appreciated by many managers, which may explain why 'home-office' arrangements are virtually not found in the companies of our sample, although the Internet- and Multimedia- sector is supposed to pioneer tele-cooperation. Only company E has strongly promoted 'home-office' work so far, by reducing the number of personal desks and thus forcing 50 per cent of the employees to work at home. In all other companies, 'home-office' is resented because of the necessity of close cooperation and security problems. One programmer explained:

> It is not only about talking to the customer, it is also about querying data directly. This means, a dedicated line would have to be installed, causing costs and risks because of 'hackers'... [Moreover,] I have my colleagues here, whom I can address directly if I don't know how to proceed. It is not feasible as far as the working process is concerned. (K, E1, 16)

Another programmer in the same company, however, insists on home-office if her tasks require concentration, although the manager is suspicious about her 'shutting herself away':

> If somebody is working at home, and you call him and you hear that the telephone call is forwarded and he is sitting in the garden – then I think: What's the point? I think it doesn't make a difference where he works, in the garden or at night. (K, E2, 9–10)

Obviously, this programmer would have preferred to choose her place and time of work more autonomously, and she expects her superior's acceptance as long as she meets her deadlines. Even this very basic concept of 'management by objectives' does not seem to persuade many managers in our sample to refrain from direct control, however, although most of them draw a far more complex picture of their regulating methods. In the end, only companies E, J and L rely on more or less elaborated target agreements, and it may not be accidental that all of them are (or were) part of large enterprises where management by objectives is generally pursued. Apart from that, only very basic target agreements can be found in our sample, defining turnover-objectives for the company or mainly qualitative targets for teams or individual employees. In some companies, bonuses are paid to all employees at the end of year if turnover-targets are met or surpassed, and in others (H; I), there is no management by objectives at all, which may be due to their small staff size. In most companies of our sample, then, managerial emphasis on 'target agreements' appears overstated, considering that there seems to be hardly any long-term strategic planning, neither with respect to the acquisition of projects nor to the development of skills. When one manager was asked to give an example for 'qualitative targets', he hesitantly mentioned the agreement to improve qualification by 'reading a book now and then' – 'problem being', he added, 'that nobody ever did it' as no sanctions were applied (C, M, 22). This answer is quite typical, implying that under present conditions of severe economic crisis, the labour-process is most strongly influenced by the necessity of *ad hoc* reaction to demands of customers, followed by those of colleagues and superiors. This may be argued to enhance autonomy, as there is obviously not much ground for 'Taylorist' planning. At the same time, this kind of work organisation leaves hardly any scope for strategic development of knowledge and qualification by management or by employees, however, which could enable the latter to determine the rules of their own work.

Conclusion: grounding concepts of 'new work' in internet-companies

The starting point of this chapter was the widespread notion of a paradigm break regarding organisation, employment and work, as well as the assumption that future forms of work organisation could already be studied in certain especially innovative parts of the economy. Our findings may provide useful empirical grounding for these debates which are often dominated by generalising theoretical speculation, out of touch with developments even in pioneering sectors. According to our results, then, currently debated trends and concepts only seem to have materialised to a minor degree in the Internet and Multimedia industry, although it is usually considered to be a forerunner (in Germany as elsewhere). Undoubtedly, this industry is dominated by small units, characterised by project work (as the term 'projectification' indicates) and by a rather direct confrontation of employees with market forces and customers' demands, which has been labelled 'marketisation'. Apart from that, however, work organisation in Internet companies is neither shaped by a 'financialisation' of organisational activity nor by a radical flexibilisation of employment relationships. Moreover, control is far from being abandoned or 'de-bureaucratised' – instead, a distinctive mixture of 'simple', 'bureaucratic', and 'technological' strategies (as described by Edwards, 1979) is emerging, combined with features currently discussed (with or without neo-liberal impetus) as 'post-bureaucratic' (Heckscher, 1994).

Most strikingly, work organisation in Internet-companies resembles the practices prevalent in traditional small businesses, which have always applied less elaborated strategies of control than bigger-scale industrial enterprises. The fact that superiors' 'simple' personal control is re-invented in the small firms of a 'once-New Economy', may well appear as an irony, given the high expectations related to 'new work'. At the same time, however, some elements of 'bureaucratic' control as defined by Edwards have been established – controls which are based on hierarchical social relations and on a set of systemic rational-legal rules, designed to reward compliance and to sanction non-compliance. This type of control, which had spread from industrial production to other parts of the German economy after the 2nd World War, is presently losing importance according to those who promote a 'post-bureaucratic paradigm'. In the Internet companies of our sample, however, at least some features usually associated with old-fashioned 'bureaucratic enterprises' even seem to experience a revival. The most striking example is the dominance of German 'standard employment patterns' which have outlasted the much-discussed freelance arrangements of the expansion period. Moreover, the division of labour is currently increased, responsibility (for customer relations etc.) is centralised, and formal hierarchies are established in many companies, transferring authority and planning functions to project managers, heads of department or the management. This does not (necessarily) imply deskilling and micro-control of tasks, but nevertheless, the collective muddling-through of the late 1990s, which may have implied some potential for self-determined labour, is losing ground to an amazing extent. Finally, standardised working-hours seem to be emerging, which are usually associated with Fordist times, but accepted by employees in order to adapt to customers' office hours, to cooperate with colleagues and to match superiors' preferences. As far as technological control is concerned, computerised surveillance of working-time and progress does not play a decisive role in our sample (yet), and one of the most discussed 'post-bureaucratic' strategies is even harder to find: indirect control by means of target agreements is only applied in a very basic shape in some companies of our sample, whereas control by self-control or 'concertive control' (Barker, 1993), which characterises (almost) all varieties of work organisation, may indeed be of special importance in the Internet industry.

The main aspect distinguishing Internet companies from more traditional small-scale enterprises, then, is the fact that organisational structures and concepts are still in the making, and that the founding myth of a juvenile, innovative and egalitarian part of the economy has survived the industry's crisis. This myth nourishes the statements of managers, who claim that hierarchy and control were just formal compromises necessary to satisfy customers, as well as the self-perception of employees. After all, many of them demand autonomous and creative work – an impulse which is *required* for high-skill project-based tasks, but *restricted* and channelled at the same time by newly established hierarchies, stricter controls and the subsumption under economic imperatives. Hence, employees' wishes often collide with every-day work-experience, which may cause disappointment as they 'can no longer practise their hobby, which they turned into their job, as a hobby in this job' (A, M5, 5). It is an open question, whether this widespread frustration will fuel more explicit forms of conflict and resistance at the workplace or whether creative compensations will be sought beyond firm and employment. However, the fact that hierarchy and alienated work are still not considered, self-explaining and natural by many Internet- and Multimedia employees, may be the real innovative potential of this young industry.

Notes

*This study was sponsored by the German Federal Ministry of Education and Research from 2002 to 2005. The authors would like to thank the reviewers of *Critical Sociology* where this article first appeared as well as Fredrik Movitz, Åke Sandberg, Paul Thompson and Chris Warhurst for critical and helpful remarks on earlier versions of this article.

1 This is even more impressive, as the interviewing of individuals (rather than of companies) renders it likely that firms with more workers are over-represented in the survey.

2 Recently this name has changed to Federal Association of the Digital Economy (*Bundesverband der Digitalen Wirtschaft*).

3 All quotations marked in this way are taken from (German) interviews with managers (M) and employees (E). First capital letter refers to the company (see Table 1), page numbers refer to the transcript. Translation by the authors.

4 Like in companies A, K, L, that counted freelancers as part of their regular staff, freelancing simply seems to imply that certain persons are employed on a less permanent basis than others, but still considered as 'employees' in principal.

5 In 1988, 67.4 per cent of all persons in gainful employment had a full-time job without time-limitation. In 1998, this share had decreased to 62.1 per cent.

6 It is probably not accidental that the smallest company in our sample (company I with seven persons) comes closest to egalitarian ideals: the four founders have only been joined by one apprentice, one 'proper' employee and the mother of one founder; but even here, the dividing line is marked by the fact that the founders have signed the original bank loan, still function as company owners and are liable with their private assets.

REFERENCES

Augustsson, F. and Sandberg, Å. (2004) *Interactive Media in Swedish Organizations. In-house Production and Purchase of Internet and Multimedia Solutions in Swedish Firms and Government Agencies.* Stockholm: Arbetslivsinstitutet.

Barker, J. (1993) 'Tightening the Iron Cage: Concertive Control in Self-Managing Teams,' *Administrative Science Quarterly*, 38: 408–37.

Batt, R., Christopherson, S., Rightor, N. and Jaarsveld, V. (2001) *Networking. Work Patterns and Workforce Policies for the New Media Industry.* Washington: Economic Policy Institute.

Bosch, G. and others (2001) Zur Zukunft der Erwerbsarbeit. Arbeitspapier 43 der Hans-Böckler-Stift ung. Düsseldorf: Böckler.

Brasse, C. (2003) *Junge Branche, alte Muster. Vom Arbeiten und Leben in den Neuen Medien. Daten und Analysen zur Arbeitssituation der Beschäft igten in der Multimediabranche. Ergebnisse der bundesweiten Umfrage von connexx.av.* Berlin.

Boltanski, L. and Chiapello, È. (1999) *Le Nouvel Esprit du Capitalisme.* Paris: Gallimard.

Burton-Jones, A. (1999) *Knowledge Capitalism. Business, Work and Learning in the New Economy.* Oxford/New York: Oxford University Press.

Castells, M. (1996) *The Rise of the Network Society. The Information Age*, Vol. I. Cambridge: Oxford: Blackwell.

Edwards, R. (1979) *Contested Terrain.* New York: Basic Books.

Frenkel, S.J. and others (1999) *On the Front Line. Organization of Work in the Information Economy.* Ithaca/London: Cornell University Press.

Heckscher, C. (1994) Defining the Post-Bureaucratic Type, in Charles, C. Heckscher and Anne Donnellon (eds) *The Post-Bureaucratic Organization*, 14–62. Thousand Oaks: Sage.

Heidenreich, M. (2002) Merkmale der Wissensgesellschaft, http://www.uni-bamberg. de/sowi/europastudien/dokumente/blk.pdf (accessed 01.03.2002).

Kanter, R.M. (2001) *Evolve! Succeeding in the Digital Culture of Tomorrow.* Boston, Mass.: Harvard Business School Press.

Krafft, L. (2000) Bestandsaufnahme und Perspektiven der Internet-Gründerland-schaft in Deutschland. Paper presented Nov. 17 (all Krafft -papers quoted in this paper are available at http://www.e-startup.org/ergebnis.htm).

———. (2001a) Aktuelle Beschäftigung und Mitarbeiterbedarf bei Internet/E-Commerce-Gründungen in Deutschland. Paper presented Feb. 2001.

———. (2001b) Internet/E-Commerce Gründungen in Deutschland. Segment-analyse: Multimedia-Agenturen. Paper presented Feb. 2001.

Kunda, G. (1992) *Engineering Culture: Control and Commitment in a High-Tech Corporation.* Philadelphia: Temple University Press.

Läpple, D. and Thiel, J. (2002) *Chancen und Risiken in neuen Arbeitsfeldern der Informationsgesellschaft: Das Beispiel der Multimedia-Branche.* Zwischen-bericht. Technische Universität Hamburg-Harburg, Arbeitsbereich Stadt und Regionalökonomie. November.

▶

▶

Mayer-Ahuja, N. and Wolf, H. (2005) Arbeit am Netz: Formen der Selbst-und Fremdbindung bei Internetdienstleistern, in Nicole Mayer-Ahuja and Harald Wolf (eds) *Entfesselte Arbeit – neue Bindungen. Grenzen der Entgrenzung in der Medien- und Kulturindustrie*, 61–108. Berlin: edition sigma.

Meschnig, A. and Stuhr, M. (2001) *www.revolution.de. Die Kultur der New Economy*. Hamburg: Rotbuch.

Michel, L. (1999) *Karrierewege in der Multimedia-Wirtschaft. Qualifikationsanforderungen und Arbeitsmarktentwicklung in einer Zukunftsbranche*. Essen.

———. (2002) '"Arbeitsmarkt für, flexible Spezialisten". Berufsbilder und Qualifikationsanforderungen in der Konvergenzbranche Multimedia'. *Medien & Kommunikationswissenschaft*, 50: 28–44.

Michel, L. and others (2000) Final report of the project 'Ausbildung für die InternetÖkonomie' [job training for the internet economy] carried out for the Bundesministeriums für Wirtschaft und Technologie (BMWi). Essen.

Oertel, B. and others (2003) Selbständig im Netz. WerkstattBericht Nr. 58. Institut für Zukunft sstudien und Technologiebewertung. Berlin.

Schnorr-Bäcker, S. (2001) 'Neue Ökonomie und amtliche Statistik'. *Wirtschaft und Statistik*, 3: 165–75.

van Treeck, W. (2002) 'Man kann nicht immer kreativ sein, ... man muss kreativ sein' – Verführungen der Internet-Arbeit. In Jutta Meyer-Siebert and others (eds) *Die Unruhe des Denkens nutzen*. Festschrift für Frigga Haug, 195–206 (Argument Sonderband, Neue Folge AS 290). Hamburg: Argument.

Zerdick, A. (1999) *Die Internet-Ökonomie. Strategien für die digitale Wirtschaft*. 2nd Edition. Berlin: European Communication Council.

The Organisation of Creativity: Content, Contracts and Control in Swedish Interactive Media Production

12

Fredrik Movitz and Åke Sandberg

Introduction: creative labour and interactive media production[1]

What is the role of creativity in the production of interactive media solutions? How is creative labour related to other aspects of the production process? How do managers try to ensure that workers produce commercially viable commodities rather than purely artistic artefacts with limited economic value? In contrast to free artistic activities, creative labour is after all based on employers' payment for the time workers spend on creating profits (even in cases where creative labourers are self-employed).[2] Unlike repetitive manual labour, creative, intellectual, innovative, etc. labour is often regarded as forms of labour that go beyond 'just' showing up and performing routine work. Braverman's (1974) distinction between hand and brain (with reference to Taylorist work) is insufficient to capture creative labour as workers are not only encouraged, but expected, to think and create something new, appropriate and at the same time profitable. Given this, a relevant question to ask is whether employers within interactive media production use other strategies, than those commonly found in repetitive production, in order to ensure that employees act in accordance with employer interests.

The purpose of this chapter is to describe issues of content, contracts and control in the production of interactive media solutions in Sweden. Furthermore, we analyse the role of creativity in the meeting between aesthetic, technological and economic aspects of production and how issues of content, contracts and control contribute to construct interactive media solutions that are commercial commodities, rather than artefacts of the free arts. Our results show that the three aspects of production can be ascribed to three different groups of workers focusing on aesthetic, technological, and economic and management tasks, respectively, although flexible specialisation means that there are no clear-cut boundaries between the three groups. Creative working tasks are most prominent among although not confined to aesthetic workers, whereas overall control over the labour process and outcome is largely in the hands of those handling business and management issues.

The terms creative labour and creative sectors are, like knowledge work and knowledge intensive sectors, vague and somewhat problematic since creativity – like knowledge – is an integrated part (albeit to differing degrees) in all work (cf. Smith and McKinlay, Chapter 1 of this volume, Alvesson, 1995). As with knowledge intensive sectors and work, it is easier to point to sectors and types of jobs that are creative than to give a strict definition or explain what makes them creative (cf. Ericsson, 2001; Unsworth, 2001). Following the debates on knowledge work (Powell and Snellman, 2004; Warhurst and Thompson, 2006), we might define creative sectors as those sectors where creativity is a central, integral and necessary aspect of the production process, a source of competitive advantage, a highly contributing or decisive factor in customers' choice of suppliers and consumption and thus a source of status and economic resources (cf. Augustsson, 2005b). From this follows that whether or not a sector is creative or not is a matter of degree rather than black or white.

Creativity itself can be defined as the ability to come up with something that is different from the previously existent, whether or not the new is perceived as interesting, progressive and even important.[3] When it comes to creative *labour*, perceived usefulness and appropriateness is however central (Aspers, 2006) and, among other things, an area where control might be enforced. As creativity to differing degrees is part of all work, one should in principle talk of creative *intensive* labour, which denotes work where external evaluation of appropriate creative capability (including knowing the right people, Burt, 2004) is central to the hiring, status and economic rewards of workers and firms. For matters of simplicity, we will however write creative labour.

From the above follows several implications of relevance for this chapter. First, creative labour – and even creative intensive labour – is not restricted to creative sectors, but can be found to differing degrees in all sectors. Second, not all labour within creative sectors is best viewed as creative. Like all companies, interactive media producing firms need to pay bills and salaries, fulfil government requirements, handle HRM, etc. Our empirical data show that 10 per cent of employees in firms that produce interactive media solutions are not engaged in the actual production at all. Third, even workers performing creative labour generally undertake working tasks that are not creative. Fourth – and more implicit – neither creative labour nor creative sectors are logically related to specific forms of organisation or labour processes (and are not something new that replaces other sectors). It is unfortunately rather common to conflate certain types of tasks (e.g. creativity) with specific forms of organisation (e.g. flexible specialisation or craftsmanship) and to contrast it to thought non-creative mass production. Empirically, it seems to be the case that creative labour and sectors are seldom organised according to Taylorism, but from this does not follow that creative labour must be organised as e.g. flexible specialisation. On the contrary, Disney, the production of Japanese Manga comic books and cartoons as well as Andy Warhol's Factory (sic!) resemble Taylorism.[4] Still, it is likely that certain forms of organisation encourages, nurtures and are able to benefit from creativity more than others (Manning and Sydow, 2007).

The conflation of tasks and forms of organisation in our view risks neglecting creative labour performed *outside* creative sectors and, perhaps more importantly, neglect differences in organisational and structural settings as well as workers' situation *between* different creative sectors and jobs. Our own studies of interactive media production in Sweden show that internal production in firms and government agencies is just as large and probably larger than in firms producing interactive media solutions for external customers (Augustsson and Sandberg, 2004a), although the former might be less creative in terms of progressive solutions (Augustsson, 2005a). Furthermore, the traditional state monopolies on TV broadcasting that has been common in Europe, with a large proportion of internal production, differ in many respects from e.g. the computer games, fashion and movie industries in the same countries.

We would argue that one of the aspects that makes creative labour and sectors particularly interesting to study is not creativity *per se*, but how creative aspects of the labour and production process interact with, and relate to other aspects, and how this shapes the sector and working conditions of those working there – as well as the solutions produced (on journalism and media content, cf. Benson and Neveu, 2005; Bourdieu, 1993; Norman and Sandberg, 2007). Of central importance here is of course economic aspects (Neff *et al*, 2005), which in most countries refer to capitalist modes of production under alternative institutional settings and types of welfare regimes (Hall and Soskice, 2001; Swenson, 2002). It is not until creativity becomes labour for income and potential profits that there is a need to consider several aspects of commercial production, i.e. aesthetics, technology and economics, and issues of control, content and contracts become urgent from the perspective of employers.

Creativity might however be harder to control, or at least require other *means* of managerial control and incentives, than e.g. repetitive manual labour. 'Excessive' creativity can be unwanted from the employers' perspective as it might result in expensive solutions that are too *avant garde* and only cater to small connoisseur audiences, in other words creative but inappropriate solutions (Augustsson, 2004). On the other hand, too much direct control might prove counterproductive, and not just because creative workers, much like experts and members of professions, tend to oppose control (cf. Abbott, 1988).[5] Still, employers do try to control creative labour within the Swedish interactive media sector to ensure, firstly, that employees work enough, i.e. provide wanted input, and secondly, to ensure that workers do the right thing, i.e. produce saleable solutions. In this sense, the basic *targets* of control in interactive media production (labour input and results) do not differ much from working life in general (Edwards, 1979; Marx, 1867/1990).

Studies, empirical material and methods

Interactive media solutions are here defined as digital, computer-based, online and offline solutions and artefacts that are interactive and multi-modal, like websites, computer games and information kiosks (cf. Sandberg and Augustsson, 2002). The production of interactive media solutions can be thought of as a practice made up of a series of activities that can be performed by the same worker or divided between workers and firms, including customers.

This chapter is based on a series of organisational level and individual level surveys carried out within the MITIOR research programme and directed to Swedish firms and workers involved in interactive media production. The firm level surveys used here were conducted in 2001 and 2003. The number and percentage of responses for the firms level surveys were 345 (44 per cent) in 2001 and 52 (91 per cent) in 2003. The individual level survey was conducted in 2003 and resulted in 370 responses (81 per cent). The surveys have been supplemented by an analysis of media coverage between 1990 and 2003, in total 8,000 articles were reviewed. More detailed information on the design of studies and empirical 'raw data' results are found in Augustsson (2005b), Sandberg and Augustsson (2002) and Sandberg *et al* (2005). The tables that follow are based upon this series of surveys.

The content of interactive media production

The content of interactive media as practice, social field and artefact is a contested terrain, the preliminary outcome of complex struggles between different groups of workers and firms centred around questions like what should be done, how should it be done and by whom (cf. Augustsson,

2005b). Whether there is an autonomous field that may be called interactive media is thus a fundamentally open issue – probably one might rather consider interactive media as dependent on and constrained by broader economic and technical fields, as well as fields of artistic creation, probably with the former two as the dominating ones.[6]

Suffice here to say that the work content for individual workers, i.e. the tasks they are involved in, is largely determined by the contents or parts of the production process of the firms they work in. What interactive media firms do is, in turn, determined by the necessary tasks that go into producing particular interactive media solutions, as well as ideas about what interactive media firms should and should not do. Here, we focus on work content depicted as the division and integration of working tasks, where working tasks are viewed as activities considered by those involved to be part of the practice of producing interactive media solutions.

Table 12.1 gives an overview of the extent to which employees and working owners in firms that produce interactive media solutions perform

Table 12.1 Workers' performance of activities included in interactive media production. n: 302–16

Activities	Yes, usually perform	Yes, sometimes perform	No, do not perform
Concept, storyboard,	24	38	38
Content research	15	42	42
Copy	9	36	55
Educating customers	15	35	51
Project management	28	32	40
Strategic advice	25	31	43
User-orientation	24	42	34
Graphics, web-design	26	37	37
Sound/music production	7	14	80
Video/film production	12	13	76
Photo	9	19	73
Animations	10	21	69
Illustrations, graphics	15	28	57
Providing actors for sound and vision	11	23	67
Programming (HTML, etc)	31	18	51
Systems development, databases, programming	24	10	67

different activities. From the perspective of creative labour, the activities that most intuitively are related to creativity are concept and storyboard, graphics and web-design, copy, sound and music production, video and film production, photo, animations, and illustrations and graphics; we will come back to advanced programming later. But these activities also contain routine and non-creative tasks. As can be seen from the table, workers are generally involved in more than one activity, meaning that there is not a complete internal horizontal division of labour. Furthermore, there is a huge proportion of workers that 'sometimes' perform several activities, indicating a certain degree of flexible specialisation, or at least variation in working tasks between projects.

Equivalent information on the firm-level reveals patterns that are consistent with those presented for individual workers: although firms tend to be more involved in some areas and less in others, no firms specialise in a single activity and most are involved in the majority of them. A large proportion of firms work both as subcontractors, outsource activities to other firms and have experience of customers handling activities themselves, and the activities performed within the firms, as subcontractor to other firms outsourced and handled by customers differ from project to project (see Augustsson, 2005a; Augustsson and Sandberg, 2004a; Sandberg and Augustsson, 2002).

The activities performed by workers – as by firms – are related (see Table 12.2). Those performing a certain activity are more likely to perform certain other activities and less likely to perform yet others. Using factor analysis, we can distinguish different groups of workers involved in interactive media production. On a more general level, using a shorter list of activities than the one presented in Table 12.1, employees and working owners are divided into those handling economy and management on the one hand and those handling systems development and graphic design/content on the other. Systems development and graphic design is actually not related, they are grouped together since they are both negatively related to the other cluster of activities. One can thus talk of three groups of workers, as shown by the more detailed specification of cluster of activities: overall concept and management (which we term economy), aesthetics and technology. Based on qualitative data, Neff *et al* (2005) find similar groups of workers in the New York new media industry, which they term 'creatives', 'techies' and 'suits'. The main difference between New York and Sweden is that the 'suits' take an active part in overall creative direction in the latter case. Since many workers are involved in most activities, it is more correct to talk of different clusters of activities (see Augustsson 2005b, for a discussion). Following this, the groups of workers are not professions or occupations. They are rather areas of expertise or experience related to particular parts of the production process.

Table 12.2 Clusters of activities on broad and detailed level among interactive media workers

Broad clusters of activities	
Economy and management	Production workers
Project management Marketing and sales HRM, economy, administration Business management	Systems development Graphic design/Content

Detailed clusters of activities		
Economy (Overall concept and management)	Aesthetics	Technology
Concept, storyboard Content research Copy Educating customers Project management Strategic advice Usability	Graphics, web-design Sound/music production Video/film production Photo Animations Illustrations Providing actors	Programming Systems development

Although creativity and creative labour is most closely linked to aesthetics, it is not fully confined to it. There are creative aspects to technology in the sense of finding creative ways of making computer hardware and software perform necessary computational operations to deliver desired results in term of e.g. graphics, sound and movement (Elsom-Cook, 2001; Kent, 2001; Manovich, 2001; Neff *et al*, 2005). This technological creativity is however usually referred to as innovative work. One can also talk of economic creativity – and not just in creative book-keeping and evaluation of some interactive media firms during the financialisation of the dotcom-bubble (Lindstedt, 2001; Perkins and Perkins, 2001; Ågerup, 2002) – but in developing new business models and ways to commercially exploit the new medium and the technological potentials of e.g. the Internet (Kelly, 1998; Tapscott, 1999). Creative economic labour is usually viewed as entrepreneurial activities, but there are no doubt creative elements involved. It is still possible to conclude that creative labour is most common among the group of workers engaged in the aesthetic cluster of activities, the creative aesthetic workers (cf. Aspers, 2006).

The three groups of workers or working tasks refer to the horizontal division of labour within firms. There is also a vertical division of labour within interactive media firms although the vast majority of firms are small and thus generally have few levels of management. In 2001, roughly 40 per cent of firms producing interactive media solutions had one level of management and another 50 per cent had two levels. The proportion of workers with managerial or supervisory tasks is large, 52 per cent. Managerial positions are not confined to owners, even though the majority of firms are rather small. Seventy-seven per cent of owners are managers, 39 per cent of managers are owners and 45 per cent of permanent employees have managerial tasks.

As implied by the findings presented in Table 12.2, the horizontal and vertical division of labour are related. By comparing the extent to which an individual is involved in a certain cluster of activities with his/her occupation of management and ownership positions, we find that involvement in economic activities is positively correlated to management and ownership positions, whereas involvement in aesthetics and technology is uncorrelated or even negatively correlated to such positions of power and authority.[7] In essence, this means that managers and owners in interactive media producing firms have *both* overall economic and creative control over the solutions produced. They are not just in charge of decisions related to running the firms, but also of technical and aesthetic decisions concerning the creative content of the solutions produced.

Contracts

Contracts are central for turning creativity into creative labour and for specifying the content and direction of firms' activities and workers' jobs. As argued by transaction cost economists (Coase, 1937; Williamson, 1985), the market contracts firms sign with their customers (as well as with subcontracting firms) and the employment contracts that employers sign with their employees are alternatives based on make-or-buy decisions. But it is often useful to analytically separate the two as they have different consequences for employees. Whereas market contracts usually are specified in great detail regarding content, obligations and time of deliverance, employment contracts tend to be open-ended (except for fixed-term employees) and less specified when it comes to content (Stinchcombe, 1990). The lack of specification in employment contracts means that employees' work content is largely determined by the market contracts firms make with customers and collaborating firms. In other words, employees' working conditions depend not only on their agreements with their employers, but on the agreements their employers make with third party external actors. With accelerating outsourcing these types of market agreements and networks between firms are growing in importance, and corresponding networks between employees and unions are not sufficiently developed in order to maintain and even less strengthen employee influence over production and working conditions.

During the dotcom bubble and in conjunction to debates about the coming of a new economy it was repeatedly held among IT gurus and to some extent also in the media that creative and cultural sectors are characterised by a high degree of itinerant workers such as temporary employees, freelancers and self-employed (Barley and Kunda, 2004; Batt *et al*, 2001). A survey of the New York New Media industry, for instance, reported that 50 per cent of workers were part-time, temporary or contract workers (Pricewaterhousecoopers, 2000). Teece (2003) and others have argued that firms need to change their organisation and relations to workers to take full advantage of expert talent. Furthermore, it was repeatedly stated in the media, and especially by employers' representatives and management gurus, that people *wanted* looser connections to their employers and no longer were interested in long-term employments. Instead, they were thought to be disloyal to their current employers, constantly on the move somewhere else, and urgent to become self-employed (DN 2000-08-17). The loose connections and high dynamics were thus presented as a *reality*, a *necessity* for firms and something welcomed by workers.

Our empirical results complicate this picture somewhat. Roughly 25 per cent of the firms that replied to our 2001 survey had no employees at all. Still, it is fair to say that the Swedish interactive media sector consists of a rather low level of self-employed compared to Swedish working life in general even though Swedish working life stands out internationally as having an extremely high proportion of workers employed by large firms and public sector organisations.[8]

The interactive media firms in our studies that *do* have employees on average have very few fixed-term employees and hired consultants. The vast majority of workers are either working owners/partners or permanent employees. Sixty-nine per cent are permanent employees and 26 per cent are owners or partners, leaving just five per cent fixed-term employees, free-lancers etc. We conclude that fixed-term employment and the insecurities connected to it are not characteristics of Swedish interactive media production. At the same time, we should be aware of the design of our survey. As the survey was directed to those currently working in firms (based on lists provided by managements), we were unable to reach people currently in between jobs. Nevertheless, we are quite certain that temporary employment has never been all that common in Swedish interactive media production. Either people are permanently employed, or they are hired as independent contractors for specific projects (compare Batt *et al*, 2001).

According to our data, roughly 95 per cent of owners worked in the same firm one year prior to the survey, as did 94 per cent of permanent employ-ees. Three years ago, 84 per cent of owners and 46 per cent of permanent employees worked in the same firm. Although owners generally have worked longer than permanent employees within the same firm, roughly half of workers have not changed job during the preceding three years. Further, one of the main reasons why the rest of workers were not employed in the same firm three years ago was simply that the firm did not exist or did not have any employees at the time. At the height of the dotcom boom and crash then, Swedish interactive media production was characterised by only moderate labour turnover.

How about workers' presumed desire for looser connections and high mobility then? According to our figures, nearly all interactive media workers want to be either permanent employees or owners, with a small proportion preferring to be freelancers. Fifty-one per cent of all interactive media workers would prefer to be permanent employees (as compared to the 69 per cent that currently are), 39 per cent would prefer to be owners or partners (as compared to the 26 per cent that currently are) and 7 per cent would prefer to be freelancers. Out of a total of 370 replies, not *one* interactive media worker would prefer to have a fixed-term contract (including the four people currently under such employment). Further, 71 per cent of all interactive media workers would prefer to continue within the same firm in the future, a figure which is higher than for Swedish workers in general, where 58 per cent would like to continue in the same firm (Aronsson *et al*, 2000). There is thus little support for the notion that interactive media workers have or would like to have loose connections to the firms where they work.

Interactive media firms neither seems to have had much problems with the existing Swedish labour market regulations concerning employment and lay-offs, or demanded looser connections between employees and the firms. In 2001, right after the dotcom crash when many firms laid off staff, managements in 65 per cent of firms saw labour market regulations as no hindrance at all for their firms development, 29 per cent saw them as somewhat of a hindrance and 6 per cent as a huge hindrance. By 2003, the proportion of managements that saw regulations as no hindrance at all had grown to 73 per cent and only 2 per cent of managements saw them as a huge hindrance.[9]

Controlling the production of creative solutions

As argued, there are limited possibilities of controlling creative processes and labour, at least in comparison to repetitive manual labour. How, then, do managers and owners attempt to control creative workers in order to ensure that they receive sought after labour input, and that workers contribute to producing useful (i.e. commercially profitable) solutions? Given the nature of creative work, we employ a broad definition of control: all direct and indirect means used by employers and owners to increase the likelihood of workers to act in their interests. Control, then, includes among other things design of labour and production processes, organisational structures (vertical and horizontal division of labour), direct control, access to relations, overall regulatory systems, professional standards, types and designs of contracts, incentives, values and norms, and visionary leadership.

Managers and owners within interactive media production use several strategies, both directly towards their own employees and indirectly in relation to the social field, workers and customers as a whole. In the latter cases, for instance regarding beliefs in rapid changes due to new technologies, globalisation and a new economy, managers and owners clearly do not have exclusive control over definitions of reality and to some extent are subject to the beliefs and fashions of the time (Augustsson, 2005b). But by contributing to the diffusion of such ideas in e.g. the media and pointing directly to them as motives for their decisions and the reasons for employees to act in certain ways, the ideas come to function as means of control.

Organisational structure

Swedish firms producing interactive media solutions are generally decentralised, in the sense that a large proportion of workers have managerial tasks. But those that are *not* managers usually have limited influence over

Table 12.3 Proportion of firms where different actors commonly participate in decision-making in alternative areas. More than one answer possible, most common in bold

Area	Individual worker	Project group	Project manager	Higher manager	Someone else
Daily planning	41	23	**48**	22	4
Weekly planning	18	26	**55**	30	4
Quality control	18	23	**55**	29	8
Results follow-up	7	11	52	**57**	3
Planning of competence development	23	13	27	**55**	4
Introduction of new employees	**38**	21	**38**	33	7
HRM, e.g. recruitment	7	8	20	**79**	7
Personnel administration	11	5	17	**56**	24
Maintenance of technical equipment	**59**	11	11	15	28

n = 230–241

the decision-making process concerning other areas than the daily planning and own job, according to firm level data from 2001 (Table 12.3). Project managers decide over daily and weekly planning and quality control, and higher managers follow up results, plan competence development and handle recruitment and other aspects of personnel administration. The two positions of project management and higher management are often held by one and the same person, due to the small size of most firms. At the same time, project and/or higher management positions are held by a large proportion of workers – nearly half.

Controlling external relations

Besides their dominance over internal decisions, project and higher managers most frequently have contact with external actors (Table 12.4). Project managers keep contact with subcontractors, customers and other companies, whereas higher managers most often have contact with universities and other government actors (if that occurs). Since work content is generally unspecified in employment contracts, managers' contact with external actors contributes to their control over employees working conditions. The dominance of project and higher managers does not mean that interactive media workers that are neither project nor higher managers lack any say in internal decision-making processes or external contacts. On the contrary, workers as individuals and collectives are quite often involved in the process. Still, by more often being involved in decision-making and external contacts and, not to forget, having more authority, project and higher managers have greater conceptual and operational control as well as control contracts.

Table 12.4   Proportion of firms where different groups of actors commonly have contact with alternative outside actors. More than one answer possible, most common in bold

Type of actor	Individual worker	Project group	Project manager	Higher manager	Someone else
Subcontractors	48	13	**63**	31	7
Customers	46	20	**72**	41	7
Other companies	40	20	**55**	54	9
Universities	20	8	34	**59**	9
Government actors	14	4	29	**67**	7

n = 234–239

Controlling creative content

Similar to other creative and knowledge intensive sectors, the status, economic rewards and future labour market prospects of interactive media workers are closely linked to their individual performance and the status of the projects they participate in, as well as the status of clients (Aspers, 2001b; Blair, 2001; Batt *et al*, 2001; Neff *et al*, 2005). Creative workers further often have personal creative 'agendas' and ideas about what constitutes good (i.e. usefully creative) interactive media solutions. As argued elsewhere (Augustsson, 2004, 2005b), workers' ideas concerning what constitutes good interactive media solutions are related to the cluster of activities within which they are active (cf. Aspers, 2001a; Bourdieu, 1996). More concretely, aesthetic workers will pay greater attention to aesthetic than technical or economic factors when evaluating the creative quality of interactive media solutions. Technical workers, on the other hand, will pay greater attention to the technical qualities (e.g. robustness and innovation) of solutions and economic workers to economic aspects (e.g. entrepreneurial and profit potentials).

Our results (e.g. Table 12.2) show that within Swedish interactive media production, control over creative content rests with the group of workers mainly engaged in the economic cluster of activities, 'the suits', who further to a greater extent occupy management and ownership positions. Managers and owners thereby retain a high degree of control over what is deemed useful and appropriate creativity, which they can be thought to generally base more on the economic than the aesthetic or technical qualities of solutions. By having more direct contact with customers and other external actors, they further have greater possibilities of diffusing their views of appropriate creativity and presenting external actors' ideas as in line with their own.

Economics incentives

During the hype years of the dotcom-bubble, there was a lot of media coverage of young (sometimes teenage) Swedish interactive media workers with obscenely high salaries and with options in often not yet publicly traded firms that made them 'multi-billionaires to be' once IPOs were completed. Particular attention was paid to founders and co-partners who were presented as billionaires on paper or, if they managed to sell parts or whole of their companies, simply as billionaires (even though payment often was issued as shares in the purchasing firm). A common image was that it was the presumed high salary levels and potentials to become rich that attracted interactive media workers and made them work hard.

Our data show that average salary levels within Swedish interactive media production were rather modest. In 2003, Swedish full-time interactive media workers on average earned 26,400 SEK/month (roughly 2,800 Euros). This is higher than for Swedish working life in general, were average salaries for full-time employees at the time was about 20,000 SEK/month (2,120 Euros), but given the average educational background and experience of interactive media workers, it was far from an exceptional salary compared to other sectors where they could have found jobs.

Our data further show that workers engaged in the economic cluster of activities, as well as those in managerial positions, generally earned more than aesthetic and technical workers. Neither was profit sharing or option programmes, at least not after the crash, as common as sometimes presented. Seventeen per cent of employees received profit sharing, as compared to 65 per cent of owners and partners. Forty-three per cent of owners and partners had stock-options, as compared to only 4 per cent of employees (Sandberg et al, 2005).

Salary levels were thus rather ordinary and profit sharing and options rather uncommon among employees. This does, of course, not mean that interactive media workers did not dream of becoming rich, or the possibility of such dreams to function as means of controlling workers. But it should, especially after the crash, be rather evident to workers that the possibilities of dreams of wealth coming true, were rather limited. It further ranks low on employees own reasons for wanting to stay in interactive media production. Twelve per cent of interactive media workers view wages as decisive and 59 per cent as very important for work motivation. Only career opportunities are viewed as less important in this respect (cf. CS 1997-09-02).

The desire for creativity as control

The idea of a possible unfoldment of one's creativity, as well as the perception that one was participating in a technical, economic and cultural revolution perhaps greater than the industrial revolution, were, and perhaps still are, important incentives for working in interactive media production. The perception of living in a revolutionary era in business was common, especially during the height of the new economy (Eckerstein et al, 2002; Girard and Stark, 2002; Holmberg et al, 2002; Staël von Holstein, 1999; Strannegård and Friberg, 2001; Willim, 2003).

Our empirical results show that in 2003, 35 per cent of interactive media workers viewed the possibilities to participate in innovative projects as decisive for their work motivation and another 54 per cent viewed it as very important. The aspects of their jobs that interactive media workers enjoy the most are those that least resembles 'normal' jobs and are closest to creative activities – both technology and aesthetics. Further, 42 per cent of interactive media workers view the quality of their own contribution in the solutions developed as decisive and another 54 per cent as very important for work motivation, and 91 per cent of workers in the sector claimed that they wanted to continue working with interactive media production in the future (Sandberg *et al*, 2005).

Many interactive media workers are thus highly devoted to the creative process and what they do. Their job is often also their personal interest, a vocation and a source of both work and personal identity (Himanen *et al*, 2001). This desire to participate in creativity has been used by interactive media owners and managers who offer workers the 'opportunity' to participate (at times for free) in interactive media production (thereby utilising the coolness as a means of control Neff *et al*, 2005), but the desire also functions as a basis for workers' self-control.[10]

Self-organisation

Findings from our survey directed to individual interactive media workers, coupled with analyses of media coverage, reveal that a central aspect of control in Swedish interactive media production is what Burawoy (1979) calls self-organisation. Here (and partially at odds with Burawoy),[11] we take the term to mean that workers push themselves hard and strive to rapidly deliver demanded results of high quality irrespectively of direct external (i.e. employer or customer) pressures. External pressures no doubt exist in terms of e.g. tight deadlines (see below), but workers control themselves beyond this as well. Many workers, and employees in particular, regularly work overtime without compensation, handle their own competence development outside working hours, refrain from staying home even when they ought to call in sick (based on their own judgements) and view their personal life as a hindrance to work and career. Still, a large proportion of workers are dissatisfied with both the quantity and quality of the job they perform (Augustsson and Sandberg, 2004b; Sandberg *et al*, 2005). One of the reasons for this self-control is the previously discussed desire to participate in creative work. Another reason is the competitive nature and high prevalence of performance-based self-esteem among interactive media workers. The latter concept, elaborated by e.g. Hallsten and colleagues (Hallsten, 2005; Hallsten *et al*, 2002), refers to individuals for whom what they perform at work and how others evaluate their performance is central for their self-esteem and perceived human worth. They are psychologically predestined to deliver to feel good about themselves.[12]

Visions as a means of enhancing desires and self-organisation

Visions and other forms of idea-based management strategies such as cultural and discursive influences are well-known means of trying to ensure management control (Alvesson, 2002; Czarniawska-Joerges, 1992; Sandberg, 2003). Here, we have limited first-hand knowledge on what interactive media managers and owners did and said within their own firms. We do, however, have access to information through the media and second hand information from employees, union representatives and other researchers. This information suggests that interactive media owners and managers far from hampered desires to work in the sector or dysfunctional aspects of self-control (which from a preventive work environment perspective would have been preferable). Instead, several managers and owners enhanced and intensified such tendencies through visions and behaviour, both directly in relation to their own employees and indirectly through the media and directed to practically all those who worked or wanted to work in the interactive media sector. For one thing, they pointed to the different and creative atmosphere of interactive media companies and how they often were brought about by employee demands (Strannegård, 2002; Willim, 2003). In articles about Icon Medialab, it was said that:

> We have no managers, but a lot of leaders. This is the most democratic place I have ever worked in (Staël von Holstein, in P&L 1997).[13]

> People here are creators. It is impossible to call them at eight in the morning and say you should come in (to the office) now and be creative for eight hours' (project manager in Du&Jobbet 1997-06-09).

> We would not have a single employee if we had a time clock and regular hours. We want to spread a rumour about how we work and that way be able to attract good personnel (manager in Du&Jobbet 1997-06-09).

The two most well-known interactive media entrepreneurs in Sweden by far, Jonas Birgersson of Framfab and Johan Staël von Holstein of Icon Medialab, argued that we (i.e. workers, firms, the sector and Sweden) had to work harder, smarter and be more creative or we would lose out to the global competition (a view shared by many other IT-gurus at the time; Augustsson and Sandberg, 2004b). Staël von Holstein, for instance, argued that:

> Sweden is today two to three years ahead of the rest of the world. The key is to use that advantage to build a whole new sector based on the Internet and modern communications technology (Staël von Holstein in SvD 97-02-24).

At another time, he said:

> My advice is to raise the bar, don't be so damn cute. Build cathedrals. They are vulgar and grotesque – never cute (Staël von Holstein in Vision 1997-02-26).

In opinion articles and interviews, Jonas Birgersson agreed, although with a welfare society twist, to the urgent need for Sweden to act quickly and shared Holstein's views on what this meant for recruitment and worker attitudes towards work:

> The advantages Sweden has built by skilful navigation during historical shifts (farming society and industrial society) have soon faded away ... the actors that reach the world market first can lay the foundation for a period of national wealth (Jonas Birgersson and prof. Bo Hedberg in SvD 1999-05-12)

> We are like the national team, we should be the best. Sweden needs a national team that can save the country. We will beat all top teams in the world and bring home money to our country ... one has to remember that it is hell to play in the national team. They are training dead hard when everybody else is out partying. It is totally unglamorous, sweat and hard work. And the players have no guarantees that they will get a place on the team. That is why it has to be worth the effort. [...] I am a competitive person and I hate to lose, but I have never had any ambition of becoming CEO. But I think it is my duty to build something for Sweden. [...] we want driven, different persons. We only have people who have done volunteer work before. To have worked for free shows that you are driven by something. The surface is not important for such people, it is the passion, the will to do something that means something (Jonas Birgersson, in Chef 1999-05-21).

Interactive media owners and managers further often pointed to their own behaviour as examples of what was needed and expected. The firm Spray was infamous for having kept bunk-beds in their office so that workers did not have to go home (Mattsson and Carrwik, 1998). Johan Staël von Holstein claimed that he constantly worked 24-7 and Jonas Birgersson was said to regularly sleep on a foldout bed in his office (Willim, 2002).

Labour and production process: project organisation as control

While visions contribute to making interactive media production desirable and to make employees devoted hard workers, it is the project organisation and tight deadlines of interactive media production that represents the most hands-on control of creative labour in the development of interactive media solutions. Client contracts and project plans direct, structure and restrict creativity in terms of what should be done, by whom, at what time and in what order, as well as the available resources for each task (while generally leaving it up to workers themselves to figure out *how* they should solve tasks). It further seems as if project plans and tight deadlines contribute to normalising high work loads. In our study, 72 per cent of interactive media workers report having deadlines that are hard to meet *at least* a couple of times a month, and the occurrence of tight deadlines that are hard to meet increases the more a worker is involved in aesthetic and technical working tasks. Seventy-four per cent of interactive media workers further have working tasks that are so complicated that they have to ask co-workers for assistance at least a couple of times a month, and 40 per cent of workers need to ask for such assistance at least once a week (Sandberg *et al*, 2005).

Following actor network theory, contracts and project plans further seem to blur management responsibilities by becoming entities or actors in themselves that workers and managers relate to and hold responsible (cf. Law and Hassard, 1999). While managers might agree that deadlines are tight and resources scarce, they can claim the situation is out of their control – it is what customers want and what the project plan dictates (even though they themselves generally have customer contact and have negotiated the terms of the contracts). Project organisation is thus on the one hand the most concrete form of control, on the other hand the most illusive as it leaves 'problem-solving' up to the employees' ambitions and their work-with-no-limits attitude, and so contributes to making managers and owners control and responsibility less visible.

Conclusion: the organisation of creativity

The purpose of this chapter has been to argue that creative labour even in creative sectors like interactive media production is not only determined by creative work itself, but has to be understood in relation to other less creative working tasks and as part of an overall process to turn creativity into appropriate commercial commodities (cf. Caves, 1998). In doing so, we have paid attention to the role played by content, contracts and control.

In terms of (work) content, our empirical findings show that it is possible to make a separation between three clusters of interactive media working tasks and groups of workers: economy, aesthetics and technology, although the boundaries between the three groups are not definite. All three clusters contain creative aspects, but creativity is most prominent among aesthetic interactive media workers. Our results further show that management and ownership positions are most closely related to the economic cluster of activities. Since those workers holding these positions generally also handle overall creative conceptualisation, they have control over both economic and creative aspects of interactive media production. This separation into three groups of workers mirrors similar separations found in several other technical and/or creative fields, i.e. on the one hand the suits (handling management and economics) and on the other the techies and/or aesthetic workers (Kidder, 1981; King and Borland, 2003; Kunda, 1992).

Regarding contracts, we see that a high proportion of self-employed, looser connections between employees and employers, and high labour turnover was neither a reality, nor a necessity for firms or sought after by interactive media workers. It does not, then, seem to be the case that Swedish interactive media producing firms are dependent on a large pool of short-term employees and freelancers to handle projects and reach flexibility. Given that interactive media and similar sectors were and to some extent still are viewed as models for future labour markets in general, how can this be understood? The common tendency of rhetoric (discussed by e.g. Ahrne and Papakostas, 2002; Augustsson and Sandberg, 2003a, 2003b) to exaggerate the speed and levels of change (which peaked during discussions of the new economy) aside, we would like to point to one often neglected factor of importance, namely Sweden's institutional system.

Swedish laws and regulations, taxation, social security, general welfare system, and so on, are built on the assumption of permanent full-time employment rather than short-term contracts and self-employment. Swedish workers' employment (as well as economic) security increases by the length of their current employment, which creates lock-in effects and disfavours high mobility (von Otter, 2004). For Swedish firms, it is further often beneficial to use other firms or self-employed, rather than short-term employees. Some Swedish firms use strategies to maintain competence and flexibility within the institutional system that are based on retaining a high proportion of permanently employed skilled workers and outsourcing production to other firms and freelancers, rather than using a system of hire and fire, i.e. numerical flexibility. What this tells us is that when it comes to contracts, there is no necessary or deterministic organisation of interactive media production or other forms of creative labour.

To the above factors, one should add more commonly referred to factors of importance for levels of permanent employees, self-employed and labour turnover: the relatively high level of technical and aesthetic skills necessary for producing interactive media solutions, the general shortage of such skills (often even during recessions), the average small size of firms and the family like relations and loyalties commonly found in smaller firms, the long-term relations fostering trust and (tacit) knowledge sharing that favour creative processes (which of course also can be organised in other forms than within the same firm), and so on.

We point to several strategies used by managers and owners to ensure the development of appropriate interactive media solutions. Owners and managers in particular retain much of the control over day-to-day decisions and external contacts. The managers, often more engaged in the economic cluster of activities, further retain control over the overall creative content of interactive media solutions and are thereby in a position to determine what counts as appropriate and useful creativity and to specify contracts and project plans together with customers. Through project organisation with tight deadlines, contracts and project plans are turned into objectified entities or even actors that directly control interactive media workers, normalise high work loads and blur management responsibility.

In general economic rewards within Swedish interactive media production are quite modest, and they seem to play a minor role as incentives. More important are workers' desire to be part of an emerging and cool sector, as well as innovative and creative projects, which together with a high prevalence of performance-based self-esteem contributes to workers' tendency to control and discipline themselves, and to push themselves hard. Our results further show that managers and owners have attempted to intensify feelings of desire and workers' self-organisation through the use of visions portraying the sector as different and creative with high demands in terms of work-load, working hours and performance.

The results we present at first glance seem to partially contradict the perceived high autonomy of interactive media work (Neff *et al*, 2005). It further goes against other empirical findings, which show that IT-consultants (including interactive media workers) along with researchers are the least regulated group of workers on the Swedish labour market.[14] We would however argue that there is no immediate contradiction here. Interactive media work is characterised by a high degree of autonomy and low levels of regulations, at least in comparison to many other parts of working life. But managers and owners retain much of the control over both the labour process and the output of creative labour, making the perceived autonomy and creative freedom of creative labour somewhat illusive. Workers are attracted by the creative aspects of their jobs, but repeatedly experience demands that limits the possibilities to engage in really creative processes: from other actors and other part of the production process, pressures from tight deadlines and the need to find time for competence development in order to be top performers and to build their portfolios to stay employable (Augustsson and Sandberg, 2004b). This is in line with several of the more ethnographic studies of work in the new economy (Barley and Kunda, 2004; Sennett, 2006; Smith, 2001). The desirable features of the creative class that Florida (2002) speaks of are far from fulfilled for all workers.

Notes

1 We are grateful for comments on earlier drafts from the editors and Thomas Florén.

2 See e.g. Karlsson (2004) on the problems of defining work and to separate it from other activities.

3 As the work of some artists, retro trends, 'adbusting' and ironic references within design and advertising show us, reuse of previously existing artefacts is also a form of creativity. But it still requires that something new is added – even if it is just a new setting – for it to be viewed as creative (Aspers *et al*, 2003). Some definitions of creativity include assumptions of usefulness and situational appropriateness (Woodman *et al*, 1993). Such external and partially *ex post* evaluations of creativity are however somewhat problematic as they contribute to bias (Unsworth, 2001).

4 To some extent, they also resemble old guilds with apprentices doing repetitive time consuming labour under the supervision of masters that function both as employers and creative directors. It does however seem to be the case that the upward mobility and possibility to gradually take on more advanced working tasks is in some cases lacking. The production of some US cartoons (like Simpsons) and many computer games rests on outsourcing of time consuming tasks to low wage countries in Asia and Eastern Europe similar to a creative labour version of the Babbage principle (Babbage, 1835/1971).

5 This is not to say that workers in repetitive manual labour can be easily controlled. On the contrary, there is much empirical evidence of workers' resistance to control under Taylorist and Fordist production regimes, and even under Panopticon-like control systems (Ackroyd and Thompson, 1999). Compare also Friedman (1977) on 'responsible autonomy' as an alternative to 'direct control', and Ehn and Sandberg (1979), Sandberg *et al* (1992) and Sandberg (1995) for discussions of employee and union resistance to Taylorist control and of Volvo's 'autonomous production groups'.

6 Cf here the discussion on the heteronomy of the journalistic field by Champagne (2005) and Bourdieu (2005).

7 The Pearson correlations between involvement in economics on the one hand and management and ownership positions on the other are .443** and .308**, respectively. Correlations between involvement in aesthetics and management and ownership are .008 and .123*, respectively, and for involvement in technology –.125* and .033, respectively. ** denotes significance at the .01 level and * significance at the .05 level.

8 A quarter of firms lacking employees obviously does not mean that the corresponding figure of the labour market is self-employed. Using figures on average number of employees in interactive media firms, we can estimate that self-employed make up less than 5 per cent of all those working with interactive media production.

9 In comparison, the proportion of managements that saw lack of venture capital, individual and firm taxation and lack of customer knowledge as

a huge hindrance to development was three times as high as for labour regulations both years.

10 Using unpaid workers with a desire to get experience and hopefully access to a creative sector by engaging them in cool projects that promise to give them contacts and reference work for their portfolios is not exclusive to interactive media production, it is a common feature in many cultural and creative sectors.

11 Burawoy mainly viewed self-organisation as 'playing a game' of making out following a relaxation of (direct) managerial control resulting in the manufacturing of consent (cf. du Gay, 1996). Even if Burawoy was correct in noting the obscuring of surplus value and creation of consent brought about by self-organisation, we view it less as a game more or less consciously played by workers and aimed at managers and co-workers. Instead, we would argue that it is brought about by the previously described desires among workers to participate in interactive media production – even if that desire is fuelled by e.g. visions (see more below).

12 Research from the now closed Swedish National Institute for Working Life further show that individuals with a high degree of performance-based self-esteem have increased risks of burnout and other stress-related psychosocial problems, especially if they are dissatisfied with the qualitative and quantitative results of their work performance (Hallsten, 2005; Hanson, 2004), as is often the case within interactive media production (Sandberg *et al*, 2005).

13 All quotations originally in Swedish. Translation by authors.

14 Based on not yet published analyses taken from a survey directed to a sample of 4,000 workers in Sweden, of which 2,731 (68 per cent) replied (cf. Allvin *et al*, 2006).

REFERENCES

Abbott, A. (1988) *The System of Professions: An Essay on the Division of Expert Labor*. Chicago: University of Chicago Press.

Ackroyd, S. and Thompson, P. (1999) *Organisational Misbehaviour*. London: Sage.

Ågerup, K. (2002) *Sagan om Adcore*. Stockholm: Stock Letter.

Ahrne, G. and Papakostas, A. (2002) *Organisationer, samhälle och globalisering. Tröghetens mekanismer och förnyelsens förutsättningar*. Lund: Studentlitteratur.

Allvin, M., Aronsson, G., Hagström, T., Johansson, G. and Lundberg, U. (2006) *Gränslöst Arbete-socialpsykologiska perspektiv på det nya arbetslivet*. Stockholm: Liber.

▶

▶

Alvesson, M. (1995) *Management of Knowledge-Intensive Companies*. Berlin and New York: De Gruyter.

——. (2002) *Understanding Organizational Culture*. London: Sage.

Aronsson, G., Dallner, M. and Gustafsson, K. (2000) *Yrkes- och arbetsplatsinlåsning. En empirisk studie av omfattning och hälsokonsekvenser. Arbete och Hälsa 2000: 5*. Stockholm: Arbetslivsinstitutet.

Aspers, P. (2001a) 'A Market in Vogue. Fashion Photography in Sweden', *European Societies*, 3: 1–22.

——. (2001b) *Markets in Fashion. A Phenomenological Approach*. Stockholm: City University Press.

——. (2006) 'Contextual Knowledge'. *Current Sociology*, 54: 745–63.

Aspers, P., Sverrison, A. and Fuerher, P. (eds) (2003) *Bilderna i samhället*. Lund: Studentlitteratur.

Asplund, J. (1968) *Sociala egenskapsrymder. En introduktion i formaliseringsteknik för sociologer*. Uppsala: Argos Förlags AB.

Augustsson, F. (2004) 'Webbsidor som visuella uttryck', pp. 139–59 in *Bild och samhälle. Visuell analys som vetenskaplig metod*, edited by Patrik Aspers, Paul Fuerher, and Arni Sverrison. Lund: Studentlitteratur.

——. (2005a) 'The Organization of Expertise. Swedish Organisations' Production, Subcontracting and Purchase of Interactive Media Solutions', pp. 112–31 in *Dealing With Confidence. The Construction of Need and Trust in Management Advice Services*, edited by Staffan Furusten and Anderas Werr. Copenhagen: Copenhagen Business School Press.

——. (2005b) *They Did IT. The Formation and Organisation of Interactive Media Production In Sweden. Doctoral Thesis. Working Life in Transition 2005: 16*. Stockholm: Arbetslivsinstitutet.

Augustsson, F. and Sandberg, Å. (2003a) 'IT i omvandlingen av arbetsorganisationer', pp. 175–201 in *Ute och inne i svenskt arbetsliv. Forskare analyserar och spekulerar om trender i framtidens arbete. Arbetsliv i omvandling 2003: 8*, edited by Casten von Otter. Stockholm: Arbetslivsinstitutet.

——. (2003b) 'Teknik, organisation och ledning – vad nytt inom interaktiva medier?' pp. 433–62 in *Ledning för Alla? Om perspektivbrytningar i arbetsliv och företagsledning*, edited by Åke Sandberg. Stockholm: SNS förlag.

——. (2004a) *Interactive Media in Swedish Organisations. In-house Production and Purchase of Internet and Multimedia Solutions in Swedish Firms and Government Agencies. Arbetsliv i Omvandling 2004: 9*. Stockholm: Arbetslivsinstitutet.

——. (2004b) 'Time for Competence? Competence Development Among Interactive Media Workers', pp. 210–30 in *Learning to be Employable: New Agendas on Work, Responsibility and Learning in a Globalizing World*, edited by Christina Garsten and Kerstin Jacobsson. Hampshire: Palgrave Macmillan.

Babbage, C. (1835/1971) *On the Economy of Machinery and Manufactures*. Fairfield, NJ: Kelley.

Barley, S.R. and Kunda, G. (2004) *Gurus, Hired Guns, and Warm Bodies. Itinerant Experts in a Knowledge Economy*. Princeton, NJ: Princeton University Press.

▶

▶

Batt, R., Christopherson, S., Rightor, N. and van Jaarsveld, D. (2001) *Networking. Work Patterns and Workforce Policies for the New Media Industry*. Washington: Economic Policy Institute.

Benson, R. and Neveu, E. (2005) *Bourdieu and the Journalistic Field*. Cambridge: Cambridge Polity Press.

Blair, H. (2001) '"You're Only as Good as Your Last Job": the Labour Process and Labour Market in the British Film Industry', *Work, Employment & Society*, 15: 149–69.

Bourdieu, P. (1993) *The Field of Cultural Production. Essays on Art and Literature*. New York: Columbia University Press.

——. (1996) *The Rules of Art. Genesis and Structure of the Literary Field*. Cambridge: Polity Press.

——. (2005) 'The Political Field, the Social Science Field, and the Journalistick Field', in *Bourdieu and the Journalistic Field*, edited by Rodney Benson and Erik Neveu. Cambridge: Polity Press.

Braverman, H. (1974) *Labor and Monopoly Capital. The Degradation of Work in the Twentieth Century*. New York: Monthly Review Press.

Burawoy, M. (1979) *Manufacturing Consent*. Chichester: University of Chicago Press.

Burt, R.S. (2004) 'Structural Holes and Good Ideas', *American Journal of Sociology*, 110: 349–99.

Caves, R. (2002) *Creative Industries: Contracts between Art and Commerce*. Cambridge, Mass: Harvard University Press.

Caves, R.E. (1998) 'Industrial Organization and New Findings on the Turnover and Mobility of Firms', *Journal of Economic Literature*, 36: 1947–82.

Champagne, P. (2005) 'The "Double Dependancy": The Journalistic Field Between Politics and Markets', in *Bourdieu and the Journalistic Field*, edited by Rodney Benson and Erik Neveu. Cambridge: Polity Press.

Chef (1999-05-21) 'Mitt gäng ska vara som ett landslag', in *Chef*.

Coase, R.H. (1937) 'The Nature of the Firm', *Economica*, 4: 386–405.

CS (1997-09-02) 'Satsa på konsulternas familjer', in *Computer Sweden*.

Czarniawska-Joerges, B. (1992) *Exploring Complex Organizations: A Cultural Perspective*. London: Sage.

DN (2000-08-17) 'IT-folk tidens hoppjerkor', in *Dagens Nyheter*.

Du&Jobbet (1997-06-09) 'Fria arbetstider-då jobbar många 60 timmar i veckan', in *Du&Jobbet*.

Du Gay, P. (1996) *Consumption and Identity at Work*. London: Sage.

Eckerstein, J., Helm, A. and Kemlin, P. (2002) *Generation.com. En historia om den nya ekonomins entreprenörer och livet i IT-bubblan*. Lund: Studentlitteratur.

Edwards, R. (1979) *Contested Terrain: The Transformation of the Workplace in the Twentieth Century*. New York: Basic Books.

Ehn, P. and Sandberg, Å. (1979) *Företagsstyrning och löntagarmakt. Planering, datorer, organisation och fackligt utredningsarbete*. Stockholm: Prisma (2nd revised edition 1982).

Elsom-Cook, M. (2001) *Principles of Interactive Multimedia*. London: McGraw-Hill.

▶

▶

Ericsson, D. (2001) *Kreativitetsmysteriet. Ledtrådar till arbetslivets kreativisering och skrivandets metafysik.* Stockholm: EFI, Stockholm School of Economics.

Florida, R. (2002) *The Rise of the Creative Class.* New York Basic Books.

Friedman, A. (1977) *Industry and Labour.* London: Macmillan.

Girard, M. and Stark, D. (2002) 'Distributing Intelligence and Organizing Diversity in New Media Projects', *Environment and Planning*, 34: 1927–49.

Hall, P.A. and Soskice, D. (eds) (2001) *Varieties of Capitalism. The Institutional Foundations of Comparative Advantage.* Oxford: Oxford University Press.

Hallsten, L. (2005) 'Burnout and Wornout – Concepts and Data from a National Survey', in *Research Companion to Organizational Health Psychology*, edited by A.-S.G. Antoniou and Cooper, C.L. Cheltenham: Edward Elgar Publishers.

Hallsten, L., Bellagh, K. and Gustafsson, K. (2002) *Utbränning i Sverige – en populationsstudie. Arbete och Hälsa 2002: 6.* Stockholm: Arbetslivsinstitutet.

Hanson, M. (2004) *Det flexibla arbetets villkor – om självförvaltandets kompetens. Dissertation. Arbetsliv i Omvandling 2004: 8.* Stockholm: Arbetslivsinstitutet.

Himanen, P., Thorvalds, L. and Castells, M. (2001) *The Hacker Ethic and the Spirit of the Information Age.* London: Vintage.

Holmberg, I., Salzer-Mörling, M. and Strannegård, L. (eds) (2002) *Stuck in the Future? Tracing 'The New Economy'.* Stockholm: Bookhouse.

Karlsson, J.Ch. (2004) 'The Ontology of Work. Social Relations and Doing in the Sphere of Necessity', pp. 90–112 in *Critical Realist Applications in Organisation and Management Studies*, edited by Steve Fleetwood and Stephen Ackroyd. London: Routledge.

Kelly, K. (1998) *New Rules for the New Economy: 10 Radical Strategies for a Connected World.* New York: Viking.

Kent, S.L. (2001) *The Ultimate History of Video Games. From Pong to Pokémon and Beyond-The Story Behind the Craze That Touched Our Lives and Changed the World.* Roseville, CA: Prima Publishing.

Kidder, T. (1981) *The Soul of a New Machine.* New York: Avon Books.

King, B. and Borland, J. (2003) *Dungeons and Dreamers. The Rise of Computer Game Culture. From Geek to Chic.* New York: McGraw-Hill.

Kunda, G. (1992) *Engineering Culture. Control and Commitment in a High-Tech Corporation.* Philadelphia: Temple University Press.

Law, J. and Hassard, J. (eds) (1999) *Actor Network Theory and After.* Oxford: Blackwell.

Lindstedt, G. (2001) *Boo.com och IT-bubblan som sprack.* Stockholm: Bokförlaget DN.

Manning, S. and Sydow, J. (2007) 'Transforming Creative Potential in Project Networks: How TV Movies are Produced under Network-Based Control', *Critical Sociology*, 33: 19–42.

Manovich, L. (2001) *The Language of New Media.* Cambridge, MA: MIT Press.

Marx, K. (1867/1990) *Capital. A Critique of Political Economy. volume 1.* London: Penguin Books.

Mattsson, N. and Carrwik, C. (1998) *Internetrevolutionen. 1000 dagar som förändrade Sverige.* Stockholm: Bonnier Icon.

▶

▶
Neff, G., Wissinger, E. and Zukin, S. (2005) 'Entrepreneurial Labor among Cultural Producers: "Cool" Jobs in "Hot" Industries', *Social Semiotics* 15: 307–34.

Norman, H. and Sandberg, Å. (2007) 'Journalists' View of Work in the Digital Media: Creativity and Control under Changing Technologies and Markets'. Paper presented at the 25th Labour Process Conference, Amsterdam, April 2007.

von Otter, C. (2004) *Swedish Working Life-Searching for a New Regime*. Stockholm: Arbetslivsinstitutet.

P&L (1997) 'Nu ägnar de våren åt att bota växtvärk', in *Personal & Ledarskap*.

Perkins, A.B. and Perkins, M.C. (2001) *The Internet Bubble. Revised Edition. The Inside Story on Why it Burst – And What You Can Do to Profit Now*. New York: HarperBusiness.

Powell, W.W. and Snellman, K. (2004) 'The Knowledge Economy', *Annual Review of Sociology*, 30: 199–220.

PricewaterhouseCoopers (2000) '3rd New York New Media Industry Survey. Opportunities and Challenges of New York's Emerging Cyber-Industry'. New York: PricewaterhouseCoopers/NYNMA.

Sandberg, Å. and Augustsson, F. (2002) *Interactive Media in Sweden 2001. The Second Interactive Media, Internet and Multimedia Industry Survey. Work Life in Transition 2002: 2*. Stockholm: Arbetslivsinstitutet.

Sandberg, Å., Augustsson, F., Darin, K. and Maguid, G. (2005) *Net Workers. Work, Health and Competence among Interactive Media Workers. Arbetslivsrapport 2005: 31*. Stockholm: Arbetslivsinstitutet.

Sandberg, Å. *et al* (1992) *Technological Change and Co-determination in Sweden*. Philadelphia, PA: Temple University Press.

Sandberg, Å. (ed.) (2003) *Ledning för alla?* Stockholm: SNS förlag (3rd ed.) (under revision and translation into English).

Sandberg, Å. (ed.) (1995) *Enriching Production. Perspectives on Volvo's Uddevalla Plant as an Alternative to Lean Production*. Aldershot: Avebury.

Sayer, A. (1992) *Method in Social Science. A Realist Approach*. London: Routledge.

Sennett, R. (2006) *The Culture of the New Capitalism*. New Haven: Yale University Press.

Smith, V. (2001) *Crossing the Great Divide. Worker Risk and Opportunity in the New Economy*. Ithaca: Cornell University Press.

Staël von Holstein, J. (1999) *Inget kan stoppa oss nu!: en ny generation tar plats*. Stockholm: Ekerlid.

Stinchcombe, A.L. (1990) *Information and Organizations*. Berkeley: University of California Press.

Strannegård, L. (2002) 'Nothing Compares to the New', pp. 221–39 in *Stuck in the Future. Tracing the 'New Economy'*, edited by Ingalill Holmberg, Miriam Salzer-Mörling, and Lars Strannegård. Stockholm: Bookhouse Publishing.

Strannegård, L. and Friberg, M. (2001) *Already Elsewhere – om lek, identitet och hastighet i affärslivet*. Stockholm: Raster förlag AB.

SvD (1997-02-24) 'Bråttom säkra svenskt IT-försprång', in *Svenska Dagbladet*.

——. (1999-05-12) 'Nya recept krävs för framtiden', in *Svenska Dagbladet*.
▶

▶

Swenson, P.A. (2002) *Capitalists against Markets. The Making of Labor Markets and Welfare States in the United States and Sweden*. Oxford: Oxford University Press.

Tapscott, D. (ed.) (1999) *Creating Value in the Network Economy*. Harvard: Harvard Business Review.

Teece, D.J. (2003) 'Expert Talent and the Design of (Professional Services) Firms', *Industrial and Corporate Change*, 12: 895–916.

Tilly, C. (1984) *Big Structures. Large Processes. Huge Comparisons*. New York: Russell Sage Foundation.

Unsworth, K. (2001) 'Unpacking Creativity', *Academy of Management Review* 26: 289–97.

Vision (1997-02-26) 'Vi ska bli störst i världen', in *Vision*.

Warhurst, C. and Thompson, P. (2006) 'Mapping Knowledge in Work: Proxies or Practices?' *Work, Employment & Society*, 20: 787–800.

Williamson, O.E. (1985) *The Economic Institutions of Capitalism: Firms, Markets, Relational Contracting*. New York: The Free Press.

Willim, R. (2002) *Framtid.nu. Flyt och friktion i ett snabbt företag*. Stockholm/ Stehag: Brutus Östlings Bokförlag Symposium.

——. (2003) 'Claiming the Future: Speed, Business Rhetoric and Computer Practice', pp. 119–43 in *New Technologies at Work. People, Screeens and Social Virtuality*, edited by Christina Garsten and Helena Wulff. Oxford: Berg.

Woodman, R.W., Sawyer, J.E. and Griffin, R.W. (1993) 'Toward a Theory of Organizational Creativity', *Academy of Management Review*, 18: 293–321.

Author Index

Subject Index